G000255133

Elizabeth Smart was born in Otta[...] educated at private schools in Ca[...] College, University of London. [...] London bookshop, she chanced up[...] George Barker – and fell passiona[...] the printed word. Eventually they [...] a result of Barker's impecunious circumstances, Elizabeth Smart flew both him and his wife to the United States. Thus began one of the most extraordinary, intense and ultimately tragic love affairs of our time. They never married but Elizabeth bore George Barker four children and their relationship provided the impassioned inspiration for one of the most moving and immediate chronicles of a love affair ever written – *By Grand Central Station I Sat Down and Wept*. Originally published in 1945, this remarkable book is now widely regarded as a classic work of poetic prose.

After the war, Elizabeth Smart supported herself and her family with journalism and advertising work. In 1963 she became literary and associate editor of *Queen* magazine but later dropped out of the literary scene to live quietly in a remote part of Suffolk. She died in 1986.

Alice Van Wart has worked as a journalist and broadcaster, a publisher's assistant and a co-editor of a feminist newspaper. She has taught at the University of Alberta, and has contributed essays and articles to various literary journals, magazines and newspapers. She has written two books of poetry.

By the same author

By Grand Central Station I Sat Down and Wept
The Assumption of the Rogues and Rascals
In the Meantime
A Bonus
The Collected Poems of Elizabeth Smart

Necessary Secrets

The Journals of Elizabeth Smart

Edited by Alice Van Wart

Paladin
An Imprint of HarperCollinsPublishers

Paladin
An Imprint of GraftonBooks
A Division of HarperCollins*Publishers*
77-85 Fulham Palace Road,
Hammersmith, London W6 8JB

Published in Paladin 1992
9 8 7 6 5 4 3 2 1

First published in Great Britain by
GraftonBooks 1991

Copyright © Sebastian Barker 1986

A CIP catalogue record for this book
is available from the British Library

ISBN 0-586-08740-0

Printed in Great Britain by
HarperCollinsManufacturing Glasgow

Set in Baskerville by
Falcon Typographic Art Ltd, Edinburgh & London

To Graham Mason,

Then bless thy secret growth, nor catch
At noise, but thrive unseen and dumb;
Keep clean, bear fruit, earn life and watch,
Till the white winged Reapers come!
                    from Henry Vaughan's
                    'The Seed Growing Secretly'

CONTENTS

Textual Matters   ix

Acknowledgements xi

Introduction 1

PART ONE: 1933–1935

I.   London, 1933 7

II.   Sweden and Germany, 1933 26

III. Ottawa, 1933–1934 51

IV. 'The True Account of a Trip,' 1935 71

V.   London, 1936 81

PART TWO: 1936–1937, 'Around the World with Mrs Watt'

I.   Canada and the United States, 1936 93

II.   New Zealand and Australia, 1936–1937 112

III. Ceylon, Egypt, and Palestine, 1937 134

PART THREE: 1937–1939

I.   London, 1937 163

II.   France, 1938 182

III. Ottawa and New York, 1938–1939 190

IV. For the Little Cassis Book 199

PART FOUR: 1939–1941

I.   Mexico, 1939 209

II.   Mexico and Acapulco, 1939–1940 220

III. Hollywood, 1940 249

IV. Anderson Creek, New York, Ottawa, Vancouver, 264
and Pender Harbour, 1940–1941

Postscript 286

End Notes 289

TEXTUAL MATTERS

All extracts of journal materials have been taken from a transcript of the notebooks typed by Graham Mason and now housed in the Literary Manuscripts Division of The National Library of Canada. I have checked the typed manuscripts against the originals and, though not without some errors in transcription and in chronological ordering, the transcripts, for the most part, are accurate. Smart's handwriting is difficult and the selected extracts may produce errors in transcription though these should not be numerous or significant. Further, although Smart was conscientious about dating her entries, she often wrote in more than one journal at a time and there is sometimes an overlapping of dates within the notebooks. There are thirty-four notebooks of various sizes; the last notebooks, kept between 1939 and 1941, are small and numerous, and they overlap in their dating. I have altered some of the ordering of the transcripts prepared by Mr Mason; my alterations have been based on Smart's dating and on the chronological order of events.

Some notebooks that Elizabeth Smart remembers keeping from this period are lost. At one point in the journals she speaks of showing Graham Spry her 'Red Journal' of a trip she had made to Scotland with her parents. This journal is not in the library's collection. Smart was an inveterate journal writer since childhood and most periods of her life have been documented by her. However, it is not surprising that notebooks may have been lost; she made twenty-two trips across the Atlantic in the thirties as well as trips to Sweden, Norway, Germany, New York, Mexico and California, and a trip around the world.

The selections presented here are less than one third of the transcripts. In cutting and pruning the work, I have tried to stick to a few basic principles: to provide a chronological ordering and to include what seem to me the most important elements relating to her writing and to her inner life. This leaves out a great deal of material: her juvenilia, poems, stories, sketches, lists, drawings, quotations; in short, much of the texture of the notebooks is lost. I have also been ruthless in the cutting; although many of the notebooks contain only poetry, I have omitted most of the poetry, particularly the early poetry. In the context of the journals, the poetry is an appendage of the sentiments and ideas expressed in the prose. I have cut the travel journals substantially and I have also omitted her first fictional and apprentice work, 'My Lover John.' If there is a bias in my selections, it is towards the literary. I have tried, in other words, to reveal the evolution of the romantic sensibility at the root of all Elizabeth Smart's writing.

Because the journals cover a wide span of years and because they are so varied in content and style, I have chosen to divide them into four parts and each part into sections according to where she was at the time of writing. To orient the reader and provide a narrative continuity, I have added brief biographical commentary between sections. I have identified only those people who had substantial importance in Smart's life or the times and I have given dates where it has been possible to find them, yet I have tried to keep such apparatus at a minimum.

Finally, I have tampered as little as possible with Smart's prose: I have, when necessary, broken long passages into paragraphs to make the reading easier; I have corrected spelling, sometimes tightened up a sentence, or shifted a modifier. Any unidentified quotations are from Smart's own poems.

In the course of this work, it was a pleasant surprise to find that, although the writing is of a considerable variety, it is all of a piece. The evolution of Smart's sensibility coincides with that of her writing style.

ACKNOWLEDGEMENTS

I would like to thank Elizabeth Smart for offering me the editorship of her early journals and for her assistance in it.

I would like to acknowledge the assistance of the University of Alberta for its provision of a Social Sciences Humanities Research Council of Canada travel grant to the National Library of Canada in Ottawa, and the Ontario Arts Council for its generous assistance in funding a trip to England.

I would also like to acknowledge my debt to Graham Mason, who transcribed Elizabeth Smart's difficult handwriting into a transcript, without which I could not have proceeded. I would like to thank Claude LeMoine and Linda Hoad in the Literary Manuscripts Division at the National Library for their gracious assistance; the English Department at the University of Alberta for providing me with a research assistant, Sara Harasym; Sebastian Barker for his editorial suggestions; Pamela Russel for her eagle-eyed proof-reading; and Lynne Van Luven and Robert Attridge for their last-minute and invaluable assistance. Finally, I would like to thank Russel Smart and Klaus Pohle in Ottawa and Georgina Barker in London for their hospitality and Denis Deneau for his interest and support.

Alice Van Wart
Edmonton, Alberta

INTRODUCTION

In 1945, a slim work with a long title, By Grand Central Station I Sat Down and Wept, *was published in a run of 2,000 copies by a London publishing firm.[1] Its author, Elizabeth Smart, was an unknown Canadian writer living in England. Six copies of the book trickled into an Ottawa bookstore, but at the request of Smart's mother they were removed and burned. Through the latter's influence Prime Minister Mackenzie King banned its importation into Canada. The book circulated in London and New York, however, and later had a cult following. In 1966, it was republished in paperback and hailed as a masterpiece of poetic prose, thus establishing its literary reputation. However, the author of this work experienced a thirty-two-year hiatus between its original publication and the publication in England in 1977 of a small collection of poems,* A Bonus. *Smart had been busy working and raising a family. In 1978, there appeared a new work,* The Assumption of the Rogues and Rascals. *Although, up to this point, Smart had had a literary following in England and numerous Canadian writers had made the trip to England to meet her, it was not until 1982, after forty years of living in England, that she became known to the Canadian public. That year the University of Alberta invited her back from England as its writer-in-residence. That same year, Deneau Publishers published the first Canadian hardcover edition of* By Grand Central Station I Sat Down and Wept, *thus further acknowledging the novel's importance and bringing Smart into literary prominence in Canada. In the same year a limited edition of* Eleven Poems *appeared and in 1985 a new book,* In the Meantime: A Collection of Poetry and Prose, *followed.*

During her stay at the University of Alberta, I met Elizabeth Smart when she was given an office next to my own. It was a curious twist since I had long admired By Grand Central Station I Sat Down and Wept *and the year before had begun critical work on it as the first work of fiction to break with the English-Canadian tradition of realism. While visiting her in her office one day, I noticed on her desk formidable piles of paper, which she*

*informed me were the transcripts of her journals. I asked to have a look at them
and spent the rest of the afternoon poring over what looked like a wealth of
interesting and important material. I returned them with the casual comment
that they should be published. A few months later, I received a long distance
telephone call from Smart in Toronto asking me if I would like to edit the
journals. I accepted with some trepidation. My interests in Smart's work were
critical, not biographical. However, the journals have proven to be important
literary and historical documents: not only do they provide an intimate portrait
of a fascinating woman, but they also provide glimpses into the lives of some
of Canada's leading political and cultural figures. Furthermore, they provide
valuable insight into the genesis of a major literary work.*

*Elizabeth Smart began keeping journals as a child. They have had the usual
function of such documents in that they chart events in a life. But they are more
than personal diaries because they bring forth from the unconscious the materials
for all of Smart's writing and confirm the evolution of an increasingly artistic
sensibility; they are the repository for the ideas of all her published work.*

*The first indications of Smart's literary interests occur at the age of fifteen
when she gathered all her writing from age eleven to that point – stories, poems,
satires, a play, and illustrations – into 'The Complete Works of Betty Smart.'
From that time her intentions were clear and there have been copious notebooks
out of which came stories, poems, articles, speeches, a novella, and her famous
novel. The journals, then, are both personal diaries and working notebooks that
document a life and constitute an apprenticeship into the art of writing.*

*In addition to their personal and literary appeal, the journals offer new
insight into the lives of a privileged class who travelled between Ottawa and
London in the thirties. The Smarts socialized with diplomats, the bright men
of the Canadian external affairs office, and the rising intelligentsia. They were
close friends with the family of the poet Arthur Bourinot and with the British
lawyer and reformer, Sir Stafford Cripps, and his family. Their summer home,
in Kingsmere, was next door to William Lyon Mackenzie King's summer home.
At a young age Smart was introduced to and became friends with future political
and cultural figures such as Lester B. Pearson, Charles Ritchie, Graham Spry,
and Norman Robertson. She knew the painter Pegi Nichol McLeod, the poet
Frank Scott, and the folklorist Marius Barbeau. As well, the journals provide
glimpses into the lives of other artists: Katharine Goodson, a pianist, with
whom Smart studied; James M. Barrie, a British novelist whom she much
admired; Alice and Wolfgang Paalen and Jean Varda, artists with whom she
became friends. The insight into Smart's extraordinary background reveals the
extremity of her final abandonment of it. Yet, at the same time, the journals show*

that her eventual defiance was not so much rebellion against social conventions as the imperative of a highly romantic sensibility.

From the journals emerge a remarkable personality – passionate, vibrant, extravagant, sensitive, yet subject to lethargy and self-doubt. Her entries, rapidly written, usually at night while propped up in bed, were sometimes daily and sometimes sporadic accounts of events, sights, sensations, and feelings. There are glimpses of her social life, her family, her friends; there are detailed records of her trips and of her relationships; there are lists of people she has met, poems she is reading, books she has bought and read; there are lists of names of flowers, plants, and trees; there are pages of French vocabulary, philosophy notes, articles she is writing, poems she is learning, and poems by Alice Paalen and George Barker; and there are recipes, grocery lists, and accounts of money she has spent. But more important, the journals are the private record of the heart of a woman, a woman who never overtly rejects the standards and expectations placed upon her but quietly begins to construct her own personal values. Rather than accept abstract ideologies or material ambitions, she searches for the vital connections she believes could be found only in love, art, and the natural world.

Because the journals are both a private revelation of the self and an apprenticeship into writing, they vary considerably in content and style. Despite the difficulty of doing so, Smart had a profound urge to express herself and there is a cumulative sense of emotional and artistic development within the journals. They begin with an external focus and an interest in character and event, apparent in the 'Juvenilia,' in the accounts of her early life in London and Ottawa, in the records of her trips, and in her first full-length fictional work, 'My Lover John.' However, the external focus gradually shifts to an internal one, and with the consequent movement away from incident and character, the journals reveal a growing need to articulate the voice of her soul in its search for fulfilment. The changes in voice and style correspond to the growing complexities in Smart's life. As the journals progress, her language also changes: to express emotion it relies on image and metaphor, and it begins to resonate with allusions. The style that characterizes By Grand Central Station I Sat Down and Wept is already apparent in the journal entries that comprise the first draft of Smart's novella, 'Let Us Dig a Grave and Bury Our Mother' (published for the first time in In the Meantime), a seminal work that shows the burgeoning of Smart's distinctive style and voice.

'Let Us Dig a Grave and Bury Our Mother' is important not only as an apprentice work but also as a means of understanding the genesis and evolution of By Grand Central Station I Sat Down and Wept. By the time Smart had written the novella, she knew what she wanted to write and even how it *should be written. In a journal entry of November 26, 1939, she states, 'I want my book to be about love,' and in a later entry, December 6, 1939, she says, 'Poems, notes, diaries, letters, or a prose such as in* The House of Incest *or in* The Black Book *only meet my need . . . But I need a new form . . . each word must rip virgin ground. No past effort must ease the new birth.' Not only is her novella a precursor of* By Grand Central Station I Sat Down and Wept *in style, voice, and form, but also parts of the novel were written before Smart had met the poet George Barker, and before their celebrated love affair. She had already found a voice and a style; the relationship with Barker provided her with the subject she wanted – finally, subject and voice coincided.*

Far too much has been written about the biographical implications of By Grand Central Station I Sat Down and Wept. *Quite simply, it is the book she had been preparing for ten years to write. Art does come out of life, but in the final analysis,* By Grand Central Station I Sat Down and Wept *is not so much about the love affair between two people as it is about Smart's life-long love affair with language. Words are not life; but they are a testament to it.*

PART ONE

1933–1935

I

LONDON
1933

Elizabeth Smart was born in Ottawa, Ontario, on December 27, 1913, the second of three daughters and one son. Her father, Russel Smart, was a successful patent lawyer and her mother, Louie Parr, an accomplished Ottawa hostess. At the age of eleven, while she was attending Ottawa's Elmwood School for Girls in Rockcliffe Park, she became ill with what was thought to be a leaking heart. She spent that year at home and six months in bed, after which point she had to learn to walk again. During her illness she read and wrote in bed and learned the names of plants and trees, pastimes that sustained her and would continue throughout her life. Her journals begin at this point, and thereafter she would never be without a journal; in it would go poems, stories, ideas for stories, lists, and details of her life.

Following her illness, Smart continued at Elmwood School for Girls and went on to Hatfield Hall School for Girls, in Cobourg, Ontario, where she finished her junior and senior matriculation at the age of seventeen. She spent the summer following her graduation at Kingsmere, where her family had a summer home next to the summer home of William Lyon Mackenzie King. Her early summers at Kingsmere strongly influenced her: here her life-long affinity with nature began, and here she would continue to return in the summers for many years, even when she was living in England.

Smart had studied music at school and become seriously interested in it. Following the summer at Kingsmere in 1930, at the age of nineteen, she went to England with her mother to study the piano with Katharine Goodson, a concert pianist.

Smart returned to Canada for the summer and spent it with her family at Kingsmere. The following autumn she returned to England with her sister Jane (two years younger than Elizabeth), a chaperone, Susan Somerset, and her mother, who only stayed long enough to get her daughters settled in the Basil Street Hotel, SW3. She was to continue her studies with Katharine Goodson and Jane was to study art. Although she loved music and it was an important part

*of her life, she was beginning to realize she would never be satisfied with music
alone. A growing desire to write seriously was beginning to assert itself.*

*The 1933 journals present the personal record of her new life in London and
show her efforts at capturing character and event.*

March 6

Woke to sound of Susan saying, 'A letter for Betty and a letter for
Jane' – no expectations so took a last doze deciding whether to get
fully dressed or put on torn blue Marks and Spencer 'Smock.' The
letter was a reminder of the 9/19/6 I owe Freiman for blue dress.
Vurra vurra tactfully put. Jane's from Daddy – asked no questions.
Cold toast as usual – and leathery. Technique. Telephone rang Bill
Aitken[1] inviting me out tonight at 7:15 – dinner – theatre – sausages
and beer and talking afterwards. Felt airier. Brahms. Rushed out
latish to lunch at Mrs Barrington Ward.[2] She lives in Kent Terrace
– a bent-in semi-circle of terrace houses – up past Baker Street, and
funnily her house is behind a scrumpshus (sic) tree area that had
warmed my vitals many times in passing it. She was standing in
front of the fire in a dark reddish dress with fully pleated collar
looking what the word charming means and absolutely devoid of
hat. There was another washed out little woman neat and nice
but not exciting or desirable and I sat in a chair trying to decide
whether to cross my legs and show my underclothes or sit like a
charwoman when I am not a charwoman. Two more women came
in, one a vegetarian with unbalanced permanently-waved hair sticking
out from a half-satin half-hat. She had a coarsish-pored face and a
quite big nose and she was the nicest at heart of the three ladies.
She took history at Oxford and has a baby of four months. The
other was a talkative one – quite amusing – but obviously proud
of her reputation among the girls as amusing – she had a puggish
face and recounted her experiences with a funny little foreign tailor
who had been fitting her – 'Hee could do anythingk.' A very good
lunch but it did not flow freely and the point about whether or not
to go to Oxford got rather stale.[3] It died and again and again was
revived and corpsed between us. After lunch they mainly discussed
their children. The neat lady has two boys (maybe more) one at
school and one of seven. Her problem is this: the youngest is about
to develop whooping cough – he has been playing with some other
children who have it (whose parents are away and who live quite

near) and her husband is coming back from India and she is trying
to move or something. They give them raw carrot and turnip juice,
etc. from six months. One didn't with her elder and he got fat. She
did with her next – David – and he was as hard as a rock.

After lunch Mark who is four and later Simon – pudgy and
trembling – came into the upstairs sitting room (during lunch
downstairs the dumb waiter disappeared with a thump unexpectedly
and scaringly). He had a gun and a pair of glassless spectacles and
a sweater on – very gay in a dull way. Dark and goodlooking. He
laughed at the stories the ladies were telling and pushed his hair
across his forehead, looking at the rug. Sat in the back of car of
gullible lady and other two in front – drove to Oxford St. Sky
blue and spring sun everywhere. The hour was three. My lesson
was completely missed.[4] Went home on a bus with about half of
one side of it on one of those long cushioned seats for at least six
people. There were four or five rather plump elderly ladies all sort
of sitting in abandoned super-relaxed positions with their stockinged
legs dangling apart. They looked so spreading, like cushions. Oliver,[5]
nodding, using his fingers like a shy baby, blinking and smiling and
saying Ah-ha- – took me to a movie – and apologized for not coming
to my party and left for Spitzenberg to discover how to find out how
deep icebergs are.

While winding myself into that awful green dress which cuts into
the back of my neck, and my awful girdle that smells of rubber and
heat and holes, Bill Aitken arrived. He is dark and gangster-looking
but tall and slimmish in a white tie. Susan[6] was shocked at me
keeping him waiting . . . and helped me in with good practical
help when told and demanded exactly and made foolish mental
suggestions – fidgeting and irritating. Went to the Berkeley – Dr
Solomon – an Irish (Jew but unnoticeable) doctor of women's
disorders. Tall with a seductive mouth – small eyes that look as
if he had taken off his glasses and straight hair – getting black
and silver in spots – a bit hangs. Joined by lady with poppy eyes
like Oliver's and said to be shy. Her husband was sick so she went
home after *Dinner at Eight* in his car. Not a bit pretty or flashy but
they both spoke awfully highly of her and seemed to love her. I would
like to know her. She was nice. Went back to 111 Ebury St. Dr Foster
– tall – curly black marcelly-looking hair – rather an amusing mouth
if you got it to work in a smile. Lady with him full – too full and big

lips and smooth and rounded – loose brown hair – easy to get on with – nice but not enviable. Recommended Hydrogen of Peroxide and Eau de Cologne for spots.

Small round man with slight mustache – Irish with Austrian, French etc. descent. Easy to get on with – gets the point. Affable. Had a various life as: driver, farmer, actor, etc. etc. Girl with him popular. Man and wife from Dorset. Round man with reddish eyes and grey-white lady with red lips – both elderly. Invited me to Wessex – house one mile from sea – 700 years old – untouched country – hills – big hill behind house. [Illegible] His sister was there too – she was in the play in rather a small part – nice – skins are coarsened by acting make up. Nice – not exciting. Gertrude Lawrence was at the theatre. Bill brought me home. Said success and etc. (charmingly) it was charming to have you – a nice word [illegible]. The hall porter with the long neat bare face – talked not looking, but friendly and nice – doesn't sleep all night too much work to do. Brain work? Manual labour. Goodnight – goodnight miss (he says miss in the nicest way) – like old [illegible] don't work too hard. Bill said write all the time keep a diary – so here it is.

March 7

At about quarter to five, after nothing but music in its dissected form, I did the only right and inevitable thing to do when the sky is singingly blue and the sun is showing up the nakedness of London and everything is sunshining and smelling of new-forgotten damp earth and crocuses – I went out.

I put on the light blue coat and wobbly blue hat once mine but worn by Jane and made hers and those black Canadian shoes with most of the sole worn away and not even genteel. This was all beautifully comfortable for a walk in the spring – but I had on that prickly red dress with a skirt that won't let you catch buses in a hurry – and it is a horrid brick-rust colour and irritating. But I covered it up with a spotty scarf washed soft.

The streets were full of tulips and narcissus and daffodils and it was spring – really. I passed by that little pool in Hyde Park by the Serpentine, cut off from the bridge by bushes. A heron was standing dark and blue grey by the edge and there were sky and bushes shining in its bottom. The grass was bright green and fresh looking and on all the little hillocks purple and white and yellow crocuses are coming up.

I walked along the Serpentine – not on the bank because there were too many people there. Why do people when they go for a walk look at *each other*? – but up on the other side of the road – and there was a breezy wind enough to blow your hair and make you feel a little like the mascots on motor cars – so I took my loose, loose hat off before the wind did. Before I came to the end, I took a new path across – on my right were two lovers walking away – he bending over and around her with his arm and head. The sparrows were making so much spring noise that I took off my gloves and scarf in spite of the brick red dress showing, and stuffed them in my purse. And then just as I thought I was alone I saw two more lovers on my left who thought they were alone. They were sitting on a seat under a gigantic trunk of a tree.

I had to walk all across that long bare path trying to think of other directions to look in besides theirs. Even painful things pass and that did. It was not that they embarrassed me – I was afraid of embarrassing them and having them send unpleasant thought waves after me. 'Why did *she* have to come along then?' 'Why can't she get a lover of her own?' Very disconcerting.

The path ended at a little dark house or group of them – with a fence around it and another fence between that and the hard path. The space was a hillock covered with unbelievable crocuses, some just suggestions of colour and others splashes. There was an old tree that began down somewhere low and grew up above the hill and it was so old that two of its frail branches – winding branches – rested on the hill. There was a swarm of policemen coming from one of the houses in the group – some on bicycles – some walking – some with coats or macintoshes slung over their backs. I didn't look at them. Everybody flirts with policemen – they're too used to it.

I went down a little hard hill between the groups of houses and heels hit against the stoney petrified gravel with a hard unpleasant civilized sound. The little hill is enchanted – you know you are in England and you think you are in the country and you remember your childhood.

I crossed over to the Bird Sanctuary and there were groups of boys carrying pails coming out of the private gate that leads to the hot houses. I walked around it and the birds were chattering. I looked but I couldn't see any kind but sparrows. I saw a girl in a white hat and dressed to the same effect as my spring costume. She was feeling spring, but I was glad I was looking inconspicuous and therefore independent. I looked at Rima[7] and the still little 'lotus' pool in front of it. It doesn't move me to wrath or tears or raptures – but I think less white slab would have been better. Cut stone in nature doesn't fit especially white bulk.

I crossed the road and looked into Kensington Gardens. It was amazing. There was stretched as far as you could see green grass and hills or wavinesses – with a few trees and blue sky – and a couple of people walking as if they were in the country. There were several cars parked along the road. In London a 'view' of countryness. I wanted to get in and walk in this highest part and look down towards the Serpentine but there was no gate – so I followed the iron fence round to the Lancaster side and got in at last. O it was lovely! The space and lofty feeling and almost sacred feeling that comes with the late afternoon. You are very conscious of trees then, and sky, and little wispy clouds.

You could see bits of water through the bushes by the Serpentine. There was a bird singing a song in a tree and not another soul walking along that high path but me. I remembered what I had forgotten and forgot why I hated. Two little girls about eight, both wearing glasses – and both with long short straight hair were laughing to each other in a glowing sort of way and they got a place where it started sloping down, and one had her arm on the shoulder of the other. They looked at each other with glee and said let's and ran down the hill – rather unbalancedly. The two nurses were walking behind with tight lips – discussing their grievances and the wrongs of others. They were both small and thin and shapeless with the clothes that all people in buses wear. I came to a place that sloped grassily down to the river – without a break or a tree – and continued across the river and seemed to rise higher – grassy and open – and at the top away far beyond I could see that horse statue that I had always only seen from a distance. So I resolved to walk up that free open space and look at it. Besides the wind would blow and it would almost be climbing up a hill. So I came out at a gate and crossed the bridge. There were boats on the water – people lazing – or working hard – and gulls flying and ducks in the water – just like summer. The wind blew my hair the right way. I forgave everybody their trespasses. I got into the gardens again and went down by the river past that mass of bushes that make you so conscious of them and followed the water

– watching the ducks and a child or two – until I came almost to Peter Pan.[8] I had to pass a smug jealous woman sitting on a seat with some male. She tittered. Then I stepped over the low rail and walked on the grass which was quite muddy and hard to walk on in ladies' heels. I walked straight up the middle till I thought perhaps I'd better not and edged in towards the row of trees on the side. The wind was getting blowier – it was a little colder, my hands were clammy. I looked at the statue which turned out to be one by GF Watts called 'Physical Energy' – about twice life size of a huge horse. He was a god with naturally curly hair and a seductive Greek mouth. I saw that the path went in the same unbroken way – a sort of huge green path edged by huge trees on either side right up to the palace – in front of which sits the 'Big Penny' statue of the Good Smug Queen.[9] If you look back from the statue the green rolls on and up across the river. By the time I got to the Round Pond it was quite dark and there were foreboding clouds over the palace[10] – a shadowy purpleness more than an actual cloud – behind there was a pink light – and everywhere there was an expectancy as if something was about to be revealed – something too wonderful or too intangible.

The pond was very still and the ducks were silent – scouring the remains of bread and crust that floated in heaps near the edge in one part. They were still ducks – nature again and not pets – and part of the scene. There was a little white sail boat in the middle of the water dipping to one side in the wet breeze. A small boy came along walking very close to the edge, full of purpose and thought – making, by the sound of his footfalls, the silence more obvious. There was a strange light everywhere and everything was beautiful and rich and wonderful. There was a fat old man sitting on a bench by the pond watching the last lights and colours of the sky. I felt ashamed of my clanking heels and tried to tiptoe. The edge of the water was still, still and glassy but just then the middle of the pond rumpled and crinkled, a faint swell came over the water and two small drops fell into it. The light was so lovely and the queer colours reflected in the water and the pregnant mysterious feeling so intense that I sat on a seat and watched. There was a real sense of water – water – the real and intimate thing. It was alive and had a deep deep meaning – all the things but sky and water were covered in a glowing. The wind came up a little more and it got darker and more drops fell. I

got up and walked over to look at the 'Big Penny.' It was getting dark
so quickly now that I couldn't read the inscription – and by that time
it was raining. I looked towards the pond – people with umbrellas –
their heads bowed and their skirts wet were running towards the gate
and the Broad Walk. The ones without umbrellas were holding onto
their hats. I put on my hat and pulled it down over both ears very
unfashionably so that my hair wouldn't be curly in a cute way. It was
dark now and big sploshy drops were falling in earnest. A small boy
and his father took refuge in a summer house. I had wanted to walk
to the Lancaster end of the Broad Walk and the Cecco Hewlitte tree
and other Barrie spots[11] with tradition, but it was too dark to see and
the rain was splashing uncomfortably onto my legs. I walked back
along the Broad Walk towards Kensington but turned off to the right
because it looked as if it went downhill. There was a woman on the
path talking to a dog. (Everywhere people airing dogs – or putting
them on leashes when they want to run with their ears flapping in
the breeze. Back in Hyde Park there was a woman with two dogs,
one a little thing and the other a big police dog. He ran off looking
terribly guilty with his ears lying back very self-consciously at right
angles – or backwards diagonally from her. He had a secret mission
with a far-off tree and when that was completed – though he never
thought it would be all the time thinking he would be called back –
he joined the others.)

I passed them feeling superior – I was storm proof. That exit led
to a point I had never seen before. Another green plot and it had
the look of a church's grounds. I walked along with my legs soaking
in the water – my shoes wet too – rather cold – with my gloves icy
and one of my hands full of pins and needles in the thumb. O but
that didn't matter. I came out into the lights of South Kensington
by the Empress Room where John Bowker[12] used to take me and
where one day the little French Canadian Leon Maynard[13] came by
mistake too, thinking he was joining a party, and then so tactfully and
diplomatically insistent left us. He asked where he was I remember.
John told him South Kensington and he laughed a hollow bitter
laugh! I walked up by the rails of the gardens and entered them
again for a bit to walk down a lovely bushy path. I passed the Albert
Hall and Albert himself.[14] I got home eventually in a drowned rat
condition and had to share the elevator with a fattish man and his
wife. I heard them exclaiming as I left it – probably remarking with

restrained surprise that it was raining. On my way home one flash
had flashed and thunder thundered and a man in workman's clothes
shouted again and again for a taxi.

I changed and got into the blue fluffy negligee. I found my noble
note on the bed to Mrs Barrington Ward still not posted and being
undressed myself I asked Jane to do it. She immediately with wrinkled argumentative brow thought of millions of reasons why it didn't
need to be posted then and there. So Susan posted it. Just as we were
opening the door to go down to dinner – with my hat and coat on
ready to go to the concert, Mike[15] called up – planned to meet him
after it at Quaglinos – dress first – good – cure irritability.

Dinner rather strained – Jane under a cloud – Susan in a
fog – me charitable on account of being able to look forward
to the immediate future. Made a few valiant sallies – O noble
womankind!

Went to Wigmore Hall but found the concert was at the Grotian –
walked there – feeling light and airy. Jane and I occasionally walked
so fast that S. got left behind.

Seats in the very back row – but it is a small cosy hall. Not
terribly full. Watched the critics. At the back, at the left which
goes farther back than the middle where we were, there was the
one who had had a headache and taken aspirins at Gieseking's
concert and another who puckered his mouth in a true judgement
manner, a weighing-both-sides-of-the-case expression. Both seemed
to think hard and smiled. Laurence Travers has a nice loving
clear pure soft tone – perhaps mysterious and poetical but no
zip, or power or mastery. He doesn't seem to have the piano
in his grasp. He can't get out of himself enough. He was a
funny shape at the piano – his head almost bent at right angles
to his body, and his back going in. I was rather bored. We
saw him after – he was in a cold sweat. He blushed violently
when, after he had finished playing a first performance of a piece
of Norman Foster's, the composer arose and shook hands with
him. Miss Turnbull was sick. Too bad. Went home and put on
red dress and black velvet puff-sleeve little coat and rushed to
Quaglinos feeling like a devil. Cute little Mike waiting – don't
feel 'humble' in society places anymore. Anyway – a pastey-
corsety-badly-cut-satin lot of them with men I wouldn't take up
a mountain.

March 8

Slept much too late. Had no breakfast. Tummy demanded something gave it an apple. Did Brahms. Ballade in G tried to memorize it with great perseverance and willpower – only half succeeded. Also worked on Capriccio.

Jane came in with an orange sweater on and pair of minute baby shoes – blue and red with a little holeless smooth pearl button on the top of each. She had lunch alone surreptitiously. I had it with Susan and watched her tongue wait expectantly for her food and heard her crunch toast in a way personal to herself.

Went to music at Mr Hinton's – had it way upstairs in a little room filled with pictures of Mrs Hinton as a little wistful ugly girl with long hair and high cheeks, and as a young woman with a waist and long velvet and old lace dresses. Thirty years since she was the ugly little imaginative girl and she wants me to go through it and she thinks it worth it. O! Played *To a Wild Rose* on the upright piano with a tone too loud in the base – it relieved my feelings. There is a dumb Claviar there too against the other wall. Had a not too bad lesson reading – terrible. Katharine Goodson came up to say they would be late. Kissed me. Asked after me and everybody. She doesn't love me like she did. She doesn't believe in me. She misinterprets everything I say. She misinterprets when I don't say anything. She disapproves of something. O I wish I knew. I wish I could get back.

I loved her too much. I am all dumb and embarrassed. I left but forgot my purse – went back to get it. Bright and sunny but O – what is it between her and me?

Man – gigolo in a bright green Ford tried to pick me up – even got out of car – raised his hat and said good afternoon – the sperm!

Had a lesson with Miss Mayne – she told me so many times the thing I knew in the beginning that I forgot it. Too garrulous she is, and I don't want to play like her. She is hard. Besides she spits. O but I like *her*. But I hate her as a teacher. She's hysterical and set her going on any subject and she never stops. I adore sanity.

March 9

On the bus on the way back from my English at Bendixon's, the bus was very crowded. There was only one seat on top which a nondescript man was trying to camouflage. However, I was resolute and made him move over – sitting uncomfortably and precariously on the edge. Soon, the seat in front was completely empty and I moved into it – it was the very front seat. In a couple of moments a lady who had been sitting beside someone else came and sat beside me. She was not startling, but if you looked into her face it was queer and uncanny – you could see she lived in a very different world from most people. She had faded reddish hair and an embittered aggrieved mouth – but not hard. Her eyes were the part that gave her away – they were aggrieved too and not level – and they seemed to see rather their design than any concrete thing. She was muttering all the time and at first I thought she was talking to a lady behind and across the aisle – but no – she was talking to herself – evidently for my benefit. I couldn't make out the first things she said – they were said in a lifeless dull suppressed but smouldering voice, a little like a person talking in her sleep. Then when we got to Marble Arch she said in a loud impersonal voice, 'You don't mean to say we're here at last. We went so terribly fast.' The way she said 'terribly,' she spoke like a person – not in an impatient irritation – but as if she had been nursing a secret grievance in sarcasm for years and years and years – not a human voice.

Then when the conductor came up to collect the tickets she said to him in a very loud voice, 'Why don't you stop there and get some petrol. We might get on a bit quicker.' I smiled at her when she seemed to be muttering her hates to me – but I didn't speak for fear of bringing down on my head the accusations of an insane person – though I wished I had later when she left. Then she said something and all I could catch of the mutterings was 'You'd think we were going for a constitutional – we stop and pick up every person we meet. I just want to get an extra 6d.' I almost told her the story I saw in a paper of how if each bus didn't stop for one person each day how many 1000 pounds it would cost the company. But I refrained. She obviously spoke from a deep-seated hate or grievance – yet she seemed to be trying to be funny at the same time – I think she was sort of expecting applause from me – sort of glorifying in her audaciousness – but hoping her sarcasm would amuse other people. I didn't like to turn my head to look at her too much – but when she left, a respectable dowdy dull everyday little woman in black with a pleasant dull face sat down beside me. I felt most friendly towards her sane eyes and placid countenance.

My English lesson was my last one. We started reading *Samson Agonistes*. It was the first of Milton I have really liked – I love the burstingness of it – the broken rhythms to fit the emotion and the great despair and sorrow. Real. 'L'Allegro' and 'Il Penseroso,' I felt he wrote because he wanted to write poetry and that seemed a suitable subject – not because he had a yearning or an agony at his heart. We only read three pages as we got what Mrs Paynter calls 'chatting.' She is very curious sometimes when I make remarks of things about which she knows practically nothing. She knows her English Literature through and through as a scholar and she loves too, I think, history and all her school room subjects – she is Oxford and she has also taught in a school. But she thought Vancouver was near Ottawa and makes often naive remarks. She is more human than most teachers of her age are likely to be, perhaps partly because she is (happily, I presume) married. She has mentioned her husband a couple of times – how he does like his *Daily Mail* and he told her of some of the horrors of the war. She has, I think, children too – a very softening influence. Children make people flow – it loosens them, and expands them. Take the case of Granny's family. She married with nine children – and she is gracious and flowering. Great Aunt Pyra married, discontented with no children. Great Aunt Harma – spinster – hating the world and everyone – tight, always ill – liver and kidneys, sharp – unhappy – screwed up in herself – edgy – I love her – she is alive and an individual – but not a person to live with.

Mrs Paynter said she thought cruelty about the worst crime. She was delighted when I suggested smugness – and added hypocrisy and destruction – having been thinking on the subject lately – and arguing and agreeing with Jane. We could not understand that. Mrs Paynter asked me if I would mind being seen in a snooty place with a disreputable friend. I said NO. I had lots of them. She was pleased – but she always seems surprised when I speak of having had experience. She told me – 'You want me to speak frankly don't you' – 'O *yes* I like you to' – 'Well I think you have a very good brain – you have an interesting mind – but you haven't had a good background – you've had a very poor background' (after I had reassured her that I was all for frankness). 'If you went to Oxford you would have to work very hard and steadily – if, on the other hand, you just want to go on improving your mind then we will just go on in a leisurely way the way we have been.'

She is quite fat and has a very round head – Round round round. A pleasant face, but her mouth can get very hard and stern. She is not a person of *great* perception – but she has arrived at several truths and conclusions – through years of learning. She really feels them – but so do I. She has wispy darkish hair – I think it has a bit of grey. She wears it parted on the side and brushed across on one side with – I think a clasp or something; but her head is so round and her hair so thin and short that you don't get a hairy impression.

I went to the Tate Gallery on a 2 bus and was inspired and thrilled and imagitated (sic) by William Blake's illustrations – especially the one of Dante and Virgil approaching the angel who guards the gates of Purgatory – there are mystical yellow and red lights and rays upon the water – and you can look into it and into it – and you feel a sacred feeling like the light of twilights and dreams when you were little. Strange, lost beautiful things and imaginings and forgotten inspirations.

There were two girls talking very sotto voce. When I came in they were leaning against the wall – saying nothing just then but I knew by the sound of the silence that they were telling secrets of import and gravity.

I looked at the bright green colourful Millais period – Rossetti – Burne-Jones – Wilson, etc. I like the women they painted and sometimes I like a story, but too many of them.

I studied the French – Pisarro and Monet – born 1830 and 1840. I didn't realize they were as old as that. They had painted their shimmering landscapes when Millais was painting his illustrations. I liked the Degas and Manet – I only saw one Gauguin – it didn't touch me.

There are three lovely bright scintillating Van Goghs in the next room – a yellow straw chair with a greenish pipe on it – sunflowers and a treeish one. In this room I didn't take so much in, partly because my eyes were getting tired and my shoulders – and mostly because of an intriguing conversation between two of the uniformed men. They were discussing books, both glorifying in their profound knowledge and *wide reading*.

'Have you read *Dombey and Son*' – 'Yes' – 'That's Dickens isn't it?' – 'Have you read *Tale of Two Cities* – that's Dickens too isn't it. No – Yes. No – Yes.'

One of them, who appeared to have the vaster knowledge of

literature, seemed rather piqued when the other said he had read
all these books. He would have loved to have stumped him. 'Yes
– I haven't read it for a long time, but it all comes back to me.'
'Yes, it all comes back.' 'There's Ainsworth – Old St Paul's.' 'Yes,
Yes.' 'I know a good book for you to read – you try and get hold
of it ------- by -------.'

I think the enlightened one finally recommended a Conan Doyle.
They got down to very exciting novels – of the sea I think – anyway
beyond me. I stole a glance at them from the Van Goghs – one
was writing with a pencil in his notebook the other was dictating
with a satisfied and helping air. They were both hard – with long
noses and long chins – with slightly Cockney accents and joyless
voices – not the real Cockney – ones who know they are upright
and have grievances and no sense of humour – they were lovely. I
saw Rodin's 'The Thinker,' and had to go out. Walked away – too
uncomfortable and I was carrying all my English books including
the big Shakespeare that Mrs Paynter had borrowed.

We decided to go to the Old Vic to see *Romeo and Juliet* and I
felt my conscience urging me so I urged Susan to come too. She,
nothing loth, accepted. We had a sketchy dinner and Susan, feeling
benevolent, acquiesced to a taxi. It always upsets Jane when we go
three – and I hate three too – but it's nearly over and all humanity
is humanity. Three shillings altogether for the taxi – but we got in
for 9d each. Susan doesn't belong in that lovely smoky, relishing, real
audience who know things and love things and are themselves. The
play didn't move me and it wasn't quite as perfectly satisfying as the
Old Vic. The *Daily Telegraph* said it contributed nothing new – and
it didn't.

We came by bus 33 and saw through the window Diana Cripps[16]
in a car with a girl and a boy on the little seat – a car with a chauffeur
and glass between. I attracted her attention and she waved and
smiled her little pale wan puzzled rather wistful amused smile. I
don't think she could quite see who it was.

March 10

Marjorie Borden[17] and Mike Pearson came to dinner. Both rang
up separately and invited themselves. Ached with wanting to laugh
all through dinner while Susan told Mike about politics and Marjorie
about art. Marj put forth all her tackle and I'm afraid Mike nibbled

– he will bite too – I suppose. Men – always fooled – I didn't think
he would be – perhaps he isn't – O well.

March 31

I woke up so late that there was not much point in making an
effort to get up. At last under the instigations of Mummy I did –
and exercised in my wide pink pyjamas with little rather prickly
blue flowers in them. Washed away the horrible dull dry lotion with
Pond's C and Allenbury's Basil soap. Then Mummy was finishing
dressing and she insisted that I have some breakfast. She got quite
heated about it so to avoid unpleasantness I went downstairs. But
I couldn't go into the dining room – it was 10:30 and breakfast is
usually over before 10. It was too late – it wasn't fair. Besides they
snicker or they hate – or something – anyway that embarrasses me
so I wrote a letter to Sue[18] and went upstairs and Mummy called
me a 'good little girl' and I did *not* feel guilty. We took a bus from
Sloane St to the Ritz and our white gloves began to look faintly grey
at the tips. We walked along to Givans and tried on the blue checked
blouse which was wrong and didn't fit. We made an exit there – and
London was making an awful noise. Men drilling and buses roaring
and things falling – you couldn't hear or think. Mummy insisted that
I go up and look at a blouse in some shop before Walpoles – I knew
I would never find it and it was a waste of steps. But it seemed better
to acquiesce so I waddled along and came to an awful, dark blouse
in a window and hated it at sight and returned. And the noise and
confusion was worse and worse – and then what should have been
spring sunny air was filled with gas smells and dust and tired heat
and hard dirty pavement – horrible dusty gas coming out of the
bowels of dirty motors and buses.

O the clashing and jarring. It never seemed so bad. We went to
Lilley and Skinners and sat in a fairly comfortable seat and Mummy
tried on shoes that looked awful and cost pounds. But soon the
irritability began to pass in me and Mummy told me stories of
Daddy as a young courter of her, and we took a taxi and came
home and then Mummy and I had a sherry in the lounge and I
was a little tight but I camouflaged it and she went out to lunch.
Then I reeled into the dining room and had lunch. Then I took a bus
to the Ritz and walked or rather strutted in a clipped sort of way up
Dover St – and my hair was unspeakable and looked untouchable in

fact – I wore a hanky under my new silk hat. The girl gave me a
wash and wanted to pluck my eyebrows which made me mad – why
should they always want to standardize even me? I am sick of this
Mayfair fashionable smart – socialness – *Tatler-Spectator* – jealousy
– boredom – toeing the mark. Went home in taxi. Both at home.
A few complications and complexes about who should go down to
dinner. Jane was feeling lazy and didn't want to and finally she said
something rather guttery to me like 'O you're so smart and smug' (!).
Mummy was mad at her and harassed and large-skewgeed eyed. I
went and changed and Jane came and screwed up in a ball on her
bed and Mummy screwed up or rather lay in a limp mass on *her* bed
and both declined to have any dinner. Mummy said the usual things
about not knowing what to do with Jane – not knowing what was the
matter with her – being disappointed. Jane said in a polite studied
strange voice that she was not hungry. Finally, however, I persuaded
Mummy out of her desire to go on strike because everything doesn't
always turn out perfectly and we two went down to dinner. Mummy
turned soft and kind just before and told Jane to put on her kimono
and curl up by the fire and she would send her up some supper.
We had ours in personal discussions of the present and less present
situations and quite pleasantly. We came upstairs and all sat around
the fire – each in a big armchair – reading. I was reading Rose
Macaulay's *Keeping up Appearances* – a dumb immature book – but
I want to give the lady a chance so I'll try and finish it. Mummy
and Jane both went to bed – I did too finally at 11. But I couldn't
get to sleep – London was still making an awful noise there seemed
so much worry over my head – I was hemmed in. I want to work
more – I must practise well again tomorrow and write – and not go
listlessly apathetically.

April 5

I had nightmares all night that it would be after 12:30 when I woke
up. Too late to go to Barrie![19] So I was up what I would call betimes
though the sun was pouring in my window. I took a bath and put
on my best clothes. I felt scared and elated by turns and inadequate
and unspeakable. Too late and too sudden – all unbeknownst and
unprepared.

Jane went off to her sculpting with a little rare smile and a
shy generous 'Goodluck' and Mummy and Daddy went off to Mr

Blundstones – wishing me good luck too and looking loving and joyously parental and soft and proud – O very proud.

I practised Brahms – because really technique on *this* morning would be asking too much – and as it got nearer and nearer to 12 – the hour I said I would allow myself to start putting on my things – even Brahms got impossibler and impossibler so I took the cutting of the music of 'The Oldest Canadian Christmas Song' of 'D'ou Viens tu Bergère' and read it through and through and through until it was exactly 12 – I didn't cheat – it *was* exactly 12 – not a minute before – not a *minute*.

Then I got dressed – I didn't look very nice – still sleepy and pale and hair too undisciplined – but O well – and I put on my new Worth coat and my hat – and left the flat in fear and elation – I thought I would walk a bit towards Hyde Park corner to kill the time and wake me up.

The sun was glorious. I hailed a taxi and gave the address. The cabman was nice – middle-aged and quite clean with reddy curly hair – he looked rather like an explorer but he had no eight-days beard. We got to Adelphi Terrace and drove along it – but no Adelphi Terrace House – we drove around the block – asked several people – and finally found it – just before you come to the Terrace – on the corner going down.

I gave the man his fare and 3d. He looked disappointed so when a 6d fell out of my hand under the taxi I said, 'Well you'd better keep it.' He did. I asked a policeman who was strolling along the Terrace if it were 12:30 – so did my taximan. The bobby said no 12:25. So I said O and in fear and trembling entered into No. 3 Adelphi Terrace House.

It looked a deserted place – a big bare stone or marble cold hall with firms' names written up on the glass doors. I saw no flat names anywhere so I rang a bell that was labelled Housekeeper and asked which was Sir James Barrie. She said 'fourth floor' in a very hardened voice – what was a mere great man to the likes of her? And as there was no one to run the lift – which seemed automatic or self-lift – I avoided it and chose the stone stairs – up – up. And I was out of breath from fear and anticipation at the bottom so I didn't think I could bear the way my heart was dropping about to my tummy inside me – at the top. I saw a sturdy small figure pass across inside – just a shadow through the translucent glass. I lay my music case down against the wall, took three breaths and with a trembling hand rang the bell.

A shortish-sturdy secretary middle-aged but younger with an ordinary face opened the door – and it opened right into a small square room with windows. I said nothing but raised my eyebrows in query and he said 'Miss Smart?' and I said 'Yes' – feeling thankful towards him for helping me out. Then I didn't feel scared just apprehensive. The time had arrived but I was unprepared.

I followed the man into a big low room (on the right) whose windows look out over the Thames. It was beautifully used-looking and warm with a big tall thing of used-looking and warm books on the left wall and a small old-fashioned piano of a yellowish colour in front of it – and it had all an air of books and papers and tobacco. Then the secretary announced me and I shook hands with Barrie. He seemed to have small stumpy hands and for a minute I thought he was deformed – But No No. He had a big patch of iodine on his left cheek and he didn't look as fragile as I expected him to. He was more the build of Ralph Strauss,[20] but not so robust or cruel. He had those distinctive eyes small with pouches under them and they are sort of triangular because the flesh above them falls in a sort of tent. I think he had on a smoking coat.

On the right as I came in were books and nondescript things and a screen and behind the screen was his big desk – and behind that an alcove – quite big with seats in it and a fireplace and a lower ceiling than anywhere else. It was all brown wood – oak? Something of that kind. It was all sunny and an open *Times* was lying across a stool. He walked up and down – sometimes with his back to me. He said he had forgotten who Mr Herridge was but he was sure he must have liked him extremely from the tone of his (Barrie's) letter. (I had sent it with my note.) He asked me who he was – he couldn't remember him – couldn't place him. I said, 'I think you met him down at Lord Byngs – he was a lawyer and is now a diplomat. He gets on very well with people etc.' He said, 'O yes I remember in the garden. Lady Byng was very fond of gardening.'

We looked out of his windows from where you can see the Thames actually bend and wind into the distance – and seven bridges crossing it. There is a big patch of green grass in front of Adelphi Terrace too. He said to me, 'Do you mind if I smoke?' and I said 'No' emphatically. I sat on a little sofa under a window at the end of the room and he sat on the arm of the sofa and walked about the room smoking his pipe. He showed me Bedlam in the distance and said *I* was 'obviously about sixteen.' He said, 'Tell me something about yourself – what are you doing over here?' I just said I was studying music. He then showed me his piano and said he was not musical in fact. I asked him – he couldn't even play God Save the King. I said 'Neither am I they tell me.'

He *made* conversation – about skiing – about the heat of London bringing out the trees and flowers sooner – about a girls' school in the USA where they had asked him to give an address to nine hundred girls and he said he couldn't possibly give an address to nine hundred girls at once but if he could be in a room and see each girl separately he would give nine hundred speeches. 'Unfortunately,' he said, 'they took me seriously and were actually starting to carry it out. However I escaped from that place in time.' He said Edinburgh was the most beautiful city in the world. He said he admired anyone who wanted an education and didn't think it spoilt anyone. He thought girls that went were better to talk to. He said, 'But a clever woman never lets on she is clever. Whenever you hear anyone say "That woman is clever" you know that she is stupid. A clever woman doesn't let you know.' He said he had sent his sons. 'They aren't really my sons but I educated them and brought them up' to Eton and Oxford. He said, 'I never had a daughter but if I had I should like to keep her at home to pour out my tea for me and I wouldn't have this iodine all over my face if I had a woman around (except my housekeeper)(?) to do it for me. But if she wanted to go I would send her.' Oxford – Cambridge – Edinburgh – he didn't seem to mind which. He said you couldn't get a better man than his friend Sir Arthur Quiller-Couch,[21] and at Cambridge now they had a lot of swells.[22]

He said university didn't make any difference to writing – that just came out of yourself. Perhaps you wrote all wrong according to the rules – but that was your way and right for you.

I went and he called me back just as I got to the bottom in the elevator and gave me *Farewell Miss Julie*[23] and wrote in it then I left and waved but just as I got to the bottom again I remembered my music case and had to go up again.

II

SWEDEN AND GERMANY
June–July, 1933

In June and July of 1933, Smart made a trip to Sweden and Germany with Mrs Alfred Watt. Mrs Watt, a Canadian from British Columbia, had been asked by the British Government to organize the Women's Institute in England to help with food conservation, and to have it on the extant Country Women's Organizations in Canada. She was successful in this endeavour and travelled to Sweden to attend a conference of Country Women's Organizations from around the world. Mrs Watt was a friend of Mrs Smart; Elizabeth Smart was to travel with Mrs Watt as her personal secretary and companion.

Smart kept this journal as 'a book of discipline'; it provides a day-to-day account of her trip and it captures the excitement and the ennui of travel. During this time she is reading Katherine Mansfield's journals and the novels of Virginia Woolf; their influence is apparent.

Preface: The reason I don't like this diary is because it is so conscientious. It thinks it has to describe any and everything with a wealth of words – (wealth? well, abundance) and yet it is too lazy to do the thing with art. Yet it must do it, it must detail everything, with a horrid adherence to the truth, and adolescent affection for emotion. It is not me, and yet neither is it a trip to Sweden and Germany. It is a bit of both. But not either, really. It seems to me that the only fair title to give it is 'Discipline; A Book of Words,' for discipline towards words is and was the only reason for its birth and existence. Still, even as such, it's rather dumb, isn't it?

BS

June 17

I was awakened by Bell and given breakfast in bed as usual. I asked if I couldn't sleep longer but said no. So I got up, feeling as though I should never see enough of my bed or finish my dreams.

Spent the morning packing, in a nice casual way. About twelve or so I took a taxi at the corner with Ethel Jane,[1] my dumb piano, music, little books and personal pronouns. I was all dressed in rather hot grey blue tweeds – a jumper with holes – a little too tight, and a hat that gave me a headache. Left Ethel Jane at Peter Jones, where she is very kindly, really, buying Jane's vests and things I need. She gave me one of her warm but impersonal kisses. I rather like the feel of her clean fat but well-groomed cool dry cheek. We are miles apart – probably my fault, but she does nice things for me though always insisting on a thank you before I give it. Then I went and changed the blue sweater at 27 Duke St for a white thread one. The wind blew and all my little things that had a string around them in a top heavy bundle burst forth all over the taxi. I collected them – all but 'The Lady of the Lake' – she is doomed to a dark dusty death – though she may make some good conversations. I went to Mrs Watt's and left the music and oddments. Doreen and Robin were there and Mrs Watt[2] looking drowned in packing but not too harassed. I put the things in one of their suitcases – mine being already bulging. I joined my taxi again and hastened to Katharine Goodson's to lunch. My taxi fare was immense of course – but I felt that way. The driver, after I had paid him, said, 'If you don't mind me asking, Miss, who was the author of that book *Melody and Harmony?*'

I looked puzzled.

'That book you were carrying into the house – *Melody and Harmony*, I think was its name.'

'Oh – Stewart MacLaren. Are you a musician?'

He looked pleased and shy and said he was. He played the clarinet and piano. 'A man has to have some relaxation, you know,' he said. He was fair and quite young in his thirties – and thin and sparsely haired. He was the oily kind of man and had a rather suffered kind of face. I said 'that's a good book.' He said 'it looked it.' He had never heard of Katharine Goodson. I said 'Good luck' to him and went inside. I had been so surprised and startled by him that I never even thought to ask him if he would like to borrow it – as well as my music for the summer – no one is using it – why not let it be enjoyed? – just what I should have loved to have done. Oh why do I always think too late? I looked out KG's little square sunny back garden, and then I thought – perhaps he's not gone yet.

I rushed to the front door but it was too late. O – what a fool! What a lost opportunity!

I felt guilty and remorseful as I went back to the room and out into the sun in the yard. There is a high fence all round it and a big green elm tree. There were some rustic chairs with their backs to the house. I sat down in one and waited. I felt ugly and the hat was hurting. The sun and the grass and the shining sky made one think of places that are all that – where you can wallow in them. I cannot enjoy anything unless I can be part of it. Harmonize. Sense it itself. The whole beauty, the whole life – the whole point of a place is lost if I have to walk through it in high-heeled clob-hob shoes, stockings – or miserable dresses and coats and girdles or garters of any kind. No use. No use at all.

I heard the door being opened and jumped to meet KG. She was dressed in a big straw hat – a yellowy pale straw with a blue flowered scarf around it. She had on a deeper flowered blue Liberty smock – the very pattern I had as a child. It had long sleeves and smocking around the waist and a beige low V-shaped collar. She looked particularly slim-waisted. She seemed very pleased to see me. There were no doubts or inhibitions. I felt free but not completely unreserved. She asked with her usual enthusiasm and passion for giving to others about the rest of the family. She spoke of Greenlands – her little cottage at Rottingdean; the garden; how beautiful the flowers were; how she and Mr Hinton would stand and gaze at the delphiniums from every angle or vantage point possible; it was unbelievable, she said. She told me of the butcher's young daughter who is a fearless dauntless horse-rider and rides the most dashing steeds and practises jumping out in front of their place, sitting up straight and beautifully – and the buttercups and the lambs – Oh! the field of buttercups – there was never anything so beautiful – she compared it to the cowslips in *Precious Bane*[3] where Prue says it seemed as though angel's feet were not good enough to walk there. She was really in raptures – the tears welled up in her eyes – so that she quickly spoke of something funny. She spoke of the White girls and how one (the married one) recites poems and verses about children. It was so beautiful that she simply couldn't stand it she said and had to leave the room for a minute. When KG is talking about something that seems really beautiful to her she does feel tearful. Mr Hinton is always examining. They had a little joke that she was going to join him by airplane. She can't play for a fortnight. Her middle finger is hurt. It is all swollen at the top joint and crooked. We had a good lunch, very good, waited on by Violet the gentle sweet maid with a quite pretty – in a maid's way – square face. We talked about Jane and how hard the winter was on her. We spoke of intolerance. She said she could sympathize with J because she was intolerant herself. I suggested divine indignation. She said she was intolerant of stupidity – gave an example of how the little maid had put the hot water bags on the chair under the cushion just because one bit of the handle was broken – she said she said to her, 'What was the idea of putting the hot water bottles on the chair – they would be sure to get broken the first time anyone sits there etc. Now that isn't using your imagination.' A picture of Mr Hinton with a far away look in his eye hangs over the mantel piece. I tried to get her to let Frampton[4] paint her and she seemed to know a lot about him though I never told her anything. We went down to her drawing-music-living room and waited for Graham[5] who finally arrived. Then we had strawberries, coffee, liqueur, and KG made polite conversation and showed a keen polite interest in GS. I was very full of delectable chestnut whipped cream biscuit cakes and felt ugly and unwell. My eyes were small with sags beneath – my nose was blue and greasy and my cheeks were blotchy and suggestive of spots. I thought it would be best to let them get down to a mutual ground so I went to get a handkerchief. On the way through the hall, I noticed *Mary Webb's Life* and two Royal Academy books – I seized them at once. Graham had said he would get them. How nice of him! How thoughtful! I rushed to see Frampton's work – one in each. An exciting one of Newbolt with skwirly-jigs and skrolls of paper. It is this – it is this that makes me exalt in unspeakable satisfaction. He gets the supreme greatness out of skwirly-jigs, leather sofa dented buttons and scrolls. He appreciates them – fully! But it is only a thing that can be told in paint. Why *describe* it. I went downstairs and powdered my nose – but it didn't seem to notice and got worse and worse – I took my time – so that they could get started and then went slowly back – I opened the door and was embarrassed, because by the sheepish look on both their faces I could tell they had been talking about me. So that when KG suggested perhaps I would like to wash my hands, I said yes – and went upstairs and took as long

as I could – in fact she was on her way up when I started down. I
got my too tight heavy felt hat and departed with GS. KG kissed me
twice or thrice and waved and waved again and again. (She said, 'of
course I always like to get your letters.') She stood in the doorway
smiling and waving till just as we closed the gate through the hedge
above the wall I saw her turn and go in.

Graham and I walked along in the heat. We decided against
going to the Allwards.[6] We went to Hyde Park – almost ate at the
Restaurant, but weren't hungry so walked to a shady spot beneath a
chestnut tree and sat in those comfortable deck chairs that [illegible]
when you want them to. Graham gave me back my red journal of the
Scotland trip,[7] and I looked at it and then decided that he might as
well see it so returned it. Then I felt no – he shouldn't see it, it's too
personal, so tried to get it back but he took my wrist and twisted it
till I thought I should faint. My innards were all gloopy too, OO, I
felt like tears. So I walked away slowly, straight away ruminating
on this occasional sadist characteristic of GS. I felt sad and poutish
but soon I remembered I had to tell G something – he was just
getting up picking up the things and we met and walked towards
the road. Neither of us mentioned the wrist incident. We took a taxi
home. Had a pleasant few minutes of conclusions and reviews. An
enormous box of red, pink and yellow roses – at least five dozen
arrived, 'Wishing the Stockholm correspondent of *The Weekly Sun* a
pleasant voyage – Alan Plaunt[8] and Graham Spry.' O lovely fresh
roses in rooms with damp tissue paper between. Kenneth Lindsay[9]
arrived to say goodbye. 'Don't they look as though they were in bed
– all tucked in,' he said. He was pally and he was impressed by the
luggage – but as usual seemingly with other thought working in his
mind. He has some silly fascinating quality – I don't know what.

We were too early at the station so went to some dirty little aerated
bread shop and had two treacle tarts, two milk 'and two hairs.' ('Now
I know what a jugged hair is' said Graham). The little girl with a
young old-fashioned face and big teeth laughed in spite of herself. We
were very foolish and witty. It was a lovely end. Fun and joy and no
loose perplexing unfinished questions. Just a complete feeling. After 6
the Watts arrived – the Robins (Watt), Sholto and Mrs Watt. As they
were walking up the platform little John Williams[10] arrived looking
sweet. I wanted to be nice to him – so nice. I didn't want to hurt him.
Sholto's attitude – I could sense it made me mad. Simple goodness –

real stuff – that's great – a snickering intellectual superiority – that's nothing. I hated Sholto – then I saw him let his mother pay for her own magazines which he had suggested she buy. He made a feeble effort to pay but she said, 'It's all right, Sholto, I have some money' and he let her! I despised him. Then he said I had better go and talk to my young man. I said, 'don't worry Sholto, I'm going,' and went. I said goodbye to dear little John then and there because I hated him to be scoffed at inwardly and oh so subtly superiorly – for my sake – he went. We dashed – Graham and I – for the whistles were blowing – and caught. G decided at the last second to come too, as Mrs Watt and her cortège were in a different carriage. We sat opposite each other on little single seats with a table between. It was lovely. We talked and we laughed as we sped through the chimney pots and through some flat queer marshes with cows, and finest houses in the distance. We talked about ourselves – Oh! what a satisfaction really; we thought ourselves supremely luminous. Graham even showed off for the benefit of a dumpy fairly waistless woman across the way. I had a red rose in my blue tweed coat. It was good. To my surprise Sholto appeared – sat casually on the arm of one of the seats on the opposite side, and was quite funny for a few minutes. Then departed. I liked him again. G and I had been talking about him and how we disliked him. G liked him better. In fact, he liked him. The fact is, they both laughed at each other's jokes. I liked them both. We got to Tilbury and all felt benevolent. Graham thought he had got the whole ride for 1 shilling but had to pay 4 shillings. We went through several gates and things, showed our passports (I had to go through the wrong gate and was humiliated). The boat was fairly big. Full of men – heaps of young men with fair hair. How could I ever find Jack Breckeridge with only the description fair hair and blue eyes? The stairs were narrow and hard to descend. Our cabin was minute. Two berths only. The Robins, Sholto, and Graham just got across the gangway in time – they had to jump over a large space into the arms of a sailor. I didn't feel that I was parting from anything or anybody. I never do.

June 19

Gotenburg (Göteburg). Left the boat early. Had a late breakfast of two fried eggs, sausage, bacon, toast. Paid the waitress and stewardess. Smiling and kind faces. Nice Swedes. No worries at all in summer in Göteburg. Rain. Double streetcars with one car open. Art Museum shut on Monday – cleaning day. Horrid shrewd-eyed, cunning leering man proprietor at desk.

We each had separate rooms. Sofa and table – and view from big windows of the rest of the hotel – back windows and views of glass and tin below. Read Selma Lagerloft till dinner. Put on dirty yellow sweater.

Very good orchestra playing at dinner. Real rhythm – Oh almost intoxicating. But no service – no conversation. Mrs Oliver looks like Susan – never says anything. Mrs Watt complained of poor service and looked peeved. Mrs Greese with a big big rose – very intriguing face – joined us at lunch too. Better, as a woman, with a little more realism. Mrs Oliver waits for her food with her mouth and tongue the way Susan did – as most ugly old ladies do. Mrs Greese lives in Wales; though English she is Welsh in sympathies. I liked her. Business men or others at the tables. The dining room was a long narrow room like a veranda – all windows on one side and on a level with the street. People walked by and looked in. They carried umbrellas. The boy and girl students both usually wear a peak cap with a white top (like the handsome sturdy Swedish boy on the boat, who had field glasses and camera and wanted to watch the sunset with me till he found that neither could understand the other). To bed – OO a lovely bed. Early.

June 21

Raining. By now the country was getting lovelier. Fir forests and reeds by the water. We went through locks. Small boys in bright blue overalls and cheery blouses watched us, as they stood with one hip out. They are all so handsome. Sometimes the canal was so narrow you could almost touch the banks.

In the afternoon we had to stop for one and one half hours while the boat climbed seven locks. Mrs Watt stayed on the ship, but most of the people went in a taxi to see the watermen work. I walked along the road a little way and then climbed right up into the woods, up the rocks, through the wet moss and small blueberry plants. I usurped the crows' kingdom. They screamed at me and cawed and were very unpleasant. They circled above me above the pines. The country was lovely – I understood it in a jiffy. Through the trees the water was branching off in two directions – and forests as far as the eye could see. Real forests. Birch and evergreen and underbrush. I went through the wet woods and the drops fell on my hair. The scent of those woods was divine: little yellow scutellarias, wild false lily of the valley and real lily of the valley. The hill I was on hung over the locks. I could see the boat being raised. There was cliff between it and me and another cliff on the other side with fir trees on its top.

I took off my shoes and tried to bunch up my tweed skirt. It was tight and bulky. Fat black slugs like walruses lay about on the ground. They had two little removable horns and creased leather backs. They lay about with a careless nonchalant air. Oh! that was a heavenly hour. My woods, my rocks, my smells.

I found a quiet pine place where wild lily of the valley grew. I found a steep rocky place which would have been a lovely cave if it had had a roof. It was steep rock on three sides. Fearsome to look straight down. I found a little red house connected with the locks and an iron ring in the rock. I kept my eye on red tower with a clock on it, on the other side of the canal. The boat was to sail at 5. It was only 4:30.

Going beneath a boulder I heard faint strains of music. A lonely air. I heard it twice. I hurried in the direction I thought right. I wasn't scared like I usually am. But it stopped. No more. I went back to the place I heard it first and listened. But no sound. It had vanished. I found a little blue flower. Hills over there, covered with deep pine woods, and one big white house – yes, but only one. My stocking feet had holes so I took them off.

I'll never forget this. I will never forget these things. They are always here. At 10 to 5 I put on my wet things on the shaded side of a sloping hill and went down to where the boat had been with my specimens in my hand. The boat wasn't there. It must have gone up the locks. I hurried on up the continuous stairs – then I ran – then I raced – it was getting late the boat was not in sight. I looked at the clock – 2 minutes to 5 – my heart sank so that I couldn't run. My cheeks burned, I ran like a deer. I stumbled along. I knocked on a window (my hair was all wet and hung in dishevelled curls. My trench coat was sopping and dirty). A man in a cap pointed in several directions. In vain I would say no. I ran across the canal by a high bridge again and on and on and on (you can't run in heels). I came to a wide place like a lake. I saw a yard and across that I met men on bicycles. They just looked amused. I was let through a locked gate. He didn't know what I wanted, that fat man. I ran up along a road – then back along it. I was burning. I wanted to cry. So silly. I've missed the boat. I laughed. A car passed – Oh! couldn't it catch it for me. It passed. Mrs Watt – Stockholm. Lost in Sweden – Oh! how futile. I was running in circles. I had ten krona in my skirt. They have gone on without me. Then that fat man with the benevolent face came up and we made signs. He took me up a path to a cottage and shouted at the window. I could see a fairly young fair man and his wife and perhaps others sitting at a table. The fair man came out. He was nice. I talked and he talked and the fat man talked. In vain.

At last I drew a picture of a motor car catching a boat and he seemed to understand and went inside. Then he made me understand that I was to go down to the road with him. I took the left hand of the fat man in both mine and thanked him from my heart. He smiled with pleasure. The other young man and I waited on the road at the bottom of the path. I waited pawing the ground, I felt entirely unreal. I wanted to get a specimen of a little bedstraw, but I thought, no, I really ought to give my whole self to this. I can't be too distracted. Mummy would insist. Several cars passed. 'No. Nudder automobile.' At last it arrived. A taxi of course! Why hadn't I said taxi to begin with. I thanked him and we drove off. We drove along gentle hills and turned corners.

At last, O My! There was the boat with a large crowd around it and the English couple away from it on the road towards me, waving. I got out. Gave him five krona because he had no change. I went on board. Normal again. All over. But shaky. Went up to Mrs Watt. The boat had been kept waiting about three-quarters of an hour. They were all standing around. Everyone looked at me in questioning curiosity. Mrs Watt said, 'O there you are darling' (or words to that effect) 'I knew you'd do that (get a taxi) I wasn't worried.' Mrs White told me she said she wasn't going to worry it was bad for her heart. She knew I'd be all right and anyway I could have caught it later on even if they had had to go on without me. Felt tired and shaken. Watched the scenery. This was yesterday.

Today the boy spoke to me and in the evening we had a nice long talk about himself etc. His name is Geoffrey P. Meggs Davis – he is a partner in a timber business. He left school at sixteen – is experienced and 'bittered about women,' almost snapped several

times on a cargo boat to Egypt. Lovely sunset. The glasses boy sat
on the other side of the deck and watched it. I felt guilty. I enjoyed
Geoffrey. He is clever in that worldly way and stimulating. We 'got
on.' I went down to see if Mrs Watt wanted anything. She wanted me
to come to bed so that if she was sick in the night I would be there.
She was ill all day with terrible pains. She thought she was going to
die. I didn't. She looked cross and discontented and sorry for herself.
I was sorry too, but not worried. She was like a hurt and hungry bear
– she was in pain and had to sit in uncomfortable positions all day.
It was only gas. She thought it might be her heart. She was cross
that other people weren't more concerned. I did everything I could.
I went to bed even though the sun was still streaking the sky, even
though we were stopping to see a candlelit abbey.

But a still small voice of honesty asked if perhaps I had also
thought it good policy to disappear. Ah! Who can tell![11]

June 24: Stockholm

'Life with other people becomes a blur: it does with J, but it's
enormously valuable and marvellous when I'm alone, the detail of
life, the *life* of life.' (Katherine Mansfield)[12]

It was a blur all day. I tried to write – then in desperation I turned
to KM. She says the truth – I know the truth. Work. Work. She was
sick. I'm not. Why can't I work? This blur, this apathy, haze – I
don't know. She gave me some new life suddenly, at last a gleam of
life. When I read that I knew. It is *not* only my vacant soul – it is
that, what she says. I *will* do it and I *can*. I will go for a walk and see
things and *note* things. I will write those things on Sweden. I *can*.

What *is* writing? Isn't it just getting things on paper? What things?
Just putting them down? But there is an art. Yes. But doesn't that
make artifice. Can that be truth too? The truth, the truth – but there's
too much of it. Self-consciousness. Self-analysis. Even writing this. I
am saying – am I pretending? Trying to be truthful and soul-sighing!
Copying KM. Because she did. No it isn't that. Honestly. I hate this
spirit of self-analysis. Selma Lagerloft says something about it. It
kills something. GS gave it to me. He knows it. He doesn't think it's
a poison. It is. Oh! Why can't I write the truth – and if I do, why
isn't it right? What bores?' – surely long windy artifices signifying
nothing? Oh! I *need* something, but I don't know what it is. I wish
I knew. I wish I knew. This morning I slept and lay there because

I was blurred. Then I got up with my nose all oozy and wrote to Graham – a horrid note with nothing. I hadn't the energy to go over things past. It didn't seem worthwhile wielding the pen.

I think I will write a book. But what on? Really, it is awfully hard to decide. I think I will go to bed and sleep, then perhaps I shall have some ideas. Go to bed. Yes. At once. Go without anything for today? No action? No word? That is hideous destruction of youth and waste of life. Yes it is waste of life. I shall sleep and forget.

June 25

Last night after I had written that I looked out. It can't have been much more than midnight but the sky was a deep deep blue. It wasn't really dark. It was a feeling moment. Almost like up on the hill though not so intense. It frightened me. I felt those things – on the edge of something too great – so I wrote it down as far as I could and then I was happy – I was alive again at last. Oh! It was joy after the other long fit. And I was afraid of the spirit.

So I went to bed feeling apprehensive (washed my gloves – all gray and slimy) and mended all my stockings till the light appeared. But of course, there is no night in Stockholm. Only about one silent hour of deep skies and then light again. I never know how late it is. It may be eleven and the last of the sunset or it may be two and the first of the dawn. The two meet with a moment of quivering expectancy. I dreamt all night of people getting married – Joan – Rachel – Helen[13] – and I dreamt of people dying and lying in coffins – Mrs Kirkhoffer – Emily Brontë – she was wax – and Graham wanted me to kiss her dead lips. I wanted to but not while he was there. It was very intense this marriage and death – but not troubled.

O! I was happy when I woke. All the heavy dreary veil was lifted and I was really awake again – after days and days of semi-consciousness. The sun was lovely – it didn't weigh you down. I felt benevolent and powerful to be kind to Mrs Oliver. The bath fixtures shone silver and 'the detail of life' was joy-inspiring again. I dressed with all vanity. Vanity is a vital aid to nature: completely and absolutely necessary to life. It is one of nature's ways to bind you to the earth. That perhaps is why a dead person's little personal things are the saddest. I took infinite pains before the mirror. Oh! It was fun. I like being vain. I ate two bananas. They were good. O

how heavenly to be free again! You don't know. You can't imagine.
I went for walk.

June 29

Miss Zimmerman took me to Ministry to tea. Ate too much. Bored
by so many unsatisfied women. Just think – nearly every one of these
women have been loved – violently – in their day! Went to Mrs
Wrightson's. Waited. Read the poem on Town Hall – went with
her, Miss McK and other in a motor boat up and around the town
by water – waves and depression – water like a negative. Houses
and buildings and nondescript things. Back to Exelcior Hotel with
Mrs Sykes, friend, Mrs W, Miss McK and me. Too much dinner.
Man like Radberg across the way. Cold lobster. Nice Mrs Sykes.
White-haired dark-eyed and alive and teasing. Played piano. Oh
what forgotten yearnings all came back. Sad. Sad. Sad. Oh why
can't I do or be. This eternal inertia. This stagnation. That is what
must be settled first. *There must be abuses. There will be.*

July 4

Left Stockholm at 10:50 PM.

Small stuffy berth. No room. Dirt smells, no air, cinders. Didn't
wash. Red oily nose. Read *Without my Cloak*[14] till late in the
morning.

July 5: Stockholm to Hamburg

Through rather dull lowland Swedish country but then, as we
neared the sea it got warmer. The train was put on a ferry and we
sat on deck in the sun and looked at romantic island of Rugen. It had
white chalky cliffs and fluffy beautiful green dipping forests – where
there seemed to be no underbrush. The wind was very warm and
the sky a happy happy blue. At a little village – red roofs climbing
up to a red church we got onto the island and crossed it. Many little
lakes, sloping luxurious fields of crops, and sun everywhere. Women
with white scarves on their heads and big farmers working in the
fields. (Finished *Without my Cloak*. Very good indeed. Surprising.
But she *didn't solve* her problem). The change from Sweden was
distinct. Everything was more beautiful, more luxurious, richer,
and bigger. The crops were tall and thick. This island is not flat
but it is not hilly. It is wavy – with whispering fields reaching a long

way and climbing a slope – a little reedy lake here – far over there a lush forest. (I don't like the word lush – do you?) Blue skies. Tall, well-developed trees in the forests, substantial – not meagre – even when the floor is bare. Another ferry to the mainland. A long train journey through blue green wheat and things where tanned people worked in the hot sun with 'big substantial sit-upons,' through big powerful forests to Hamburg.

Mrs Watt phoned up a boy – Carl Warburg. He showed us the city in his car. All lit up. Water everywhere. A moon. A whole building outlined in lights by the water. A warm fragrant evening. Mrs Watt boasted and was snobbish. Carl had a twinkle and he was very polite in a nice way and very intelligent. Fireworks that made terrific noises like guns and bombs and shells. The German people adored them and clapped and cheered for the loudest bangs. It was not thinking – just noise and confusion – a coloured firework 'Rotary' and an elephant that waggled his legs. They all enjoyed it hugely and laughed and were an agreeable and appreciative audience. Hamburg seemed gay after Stockholm. It is the people. They are more enthusi-astic and excitable and emotional and unselfconscious.

After the fireworks the band played some Viennese waltzes and some other music. Then Carl and I dropped Mrs Watt at the Reichstad (?) Hotel and went to a place and danced. It was not a fashionable place – not, as Carl explained 'one that I should like to tell my friends I had been to' – but more a sailor's haunt. There were no sailors, however. In fact, there were not many people – and several girls were dancing alone with no success. A funny little man with a camera on a pedestal tried to get people to have their pictures taken. I felt too substantial in my tweed suit and thin white sweater. There were two orchestras. The first not so good. The second very good. A cabaret. First two girls in tight – I mean small – blue cotton bathing suits trimmed with silver. They had lovely figures – muscular but not unbalanced. They caught heavy balls on their necks – juggled – and balanced precariously upside down on a chair swinging hoops on their arms and legs. They failed several times and had to repeat their trick. They were too coy altogether – and cursed each other under their breath when they failed. But they gave idiotic suggestive grins to the audience who sat all around the round dance floor which was in the middle. The second cabaret was a dumb combo who threw a limp girl around ingeniously. It was too long. They appeared again, one of them doubled up with a false head and a white dumb face.

We had Rhine wine. I was too sleepy to walk. We left. We had soup in a quiet shop. We looked at some silly photographs of girls dressed as sailors and then went home. I thanked Carl humbly but I had been dull. How could he have enjoyed it? I ate some nuts and compressed fruit. Washed my face sketchily in cold water – got into bed. Ate some more nuts and did not brush my teeth. HOW WICKED!

July 7: Bad Nauheim

Had a nice roll and cocoa breakfast in a feather pillowed bed about 9:30. The little thin-faced sallow – dark-eyed – tall maid brought it. She has no resentment but she has rings under her eyes. After that Mrs Watt and I made a tour of the town; she very anxious that I should like it. 'If you see anything that you like or that you think is specially nice for goodness sake say so.' I admired ardently a yellow tin sign. She smiled a bit. *She* admired anxiously and continuously as she went along. The flowers everywhere – red geraniums, roses, delphiniums, petunias, red and purple window boxes overflowing. Brightly-painted hotels with a maximum of flora, mature trees. The whole town is pervaded with an airy, sunny, contented atmosphere – it is impossible not to feel it – an air of untroubled well-being – or at least contented lazy convalescence – yes – not unlike the atmosphere in an almost-well-sick-person's room with the sun shining on the bedspread and flowers and smiling kind people everywhere, not the smile of mirth, joy or extreme happiness, but a smile of yes-everything-is-all-right and as it should be. Oh I don't know. I expect this is a bit too involved anyway.

The people taking the cure, who stroll along the streets, parks, or sit idly on the benches which are placed every few yards are, strangely, masculine in the majority. There is a good proportion of middle-aged women and quite a few odd young boys. But by far the average are middle-aged. We strolled down – 'don't go too fast I can't you know,' and looked at the parks and a slimy green river with a whole red rose bank on its edge and two smooth stone bridges almost side by side and the very small shops which are all the size of a drug store and about as exciting. On one side of the wide street, there is a sort of Boulevard place where the better luxury shops are though of course they are only one-storied and one-roomed – and there is a roof that shades all of this side of the street and there is an open-air café and music there. We went and made an appointment with Dr Noest. At first we had no results but an amazed tolerance that we should come and expect to see the mighty man without an appointment – but when Mrs W mentioned Dr Shott, the man showed more signs of action, went in and came out saying he would telephone what time to come.

We went back to lunch. Not many people. Individual tables of quite a good size. A few middle-aged men and women all of the same appearance some alone – others together. The proprietor during the meal comes round to each table with a little joke or kind enquiry. He is stout with a twirly mustache.

After lunch I had a glorious sun-bath on my little semi-circular iron balcony. To the right at the end of the street is the lake – through some green foliage. I wrote in my blue bathing suit. Very hot. Very satisfactory. Just on verge of being dizzy when I went in and lay down for a minute. Then Mrs Watt said we might go if I were ready – 'not if you don't want to darling.'

We walked to the end of the street – across the shallow stream by a wooden bridge from where you could just catch a glimpse of the swimming pool where children were making a tremendous row – there, almost at once, in front of you is the lake. A small one with a flattish island and large open air restaurant with a wooden getting on place for boats. There are gravel walks all along the edge of the lake and benches very often and a fairly substantial border of trees. Sometimes when the ground is higher there is a little lookout with a bench and wooden railings. If you walk along to the right you come to some small duck ponds with a water spout and walks between and around.

We sat on a bench and ate cherries and spat out the stones and a little female chaffinch hopped daringly near us, not for the stones just for the excitement. I noticed everything, not with richness or amusement – just as you look at a magazine. I was not bored – yet not full.

We went to the doctor's at five. We waited in a room. I looked at unintelligible German magazines searching for pictures of mountains or beautiful bodies. Waited till the chair grew the wrong shape. At last, 'Would you go in?' I had at last found something I was interested in – something about a USA chemist in the *Mercury*. Mrs Watt said something to me. I hurried to finish the paragraph, then I put it down and went jumping after her – I got through the door. 'No. You wait there till I've finished.' But of course, how silly of me. Now I'd lost my place. I waited and waited and waited. I looked at magazines and magazines. They were mostly stacks of the same ones. Thin cheap paper. No beautiful women and unintelligible jokes in German. A book on the dullest part of Germany in English. An odd book with shiny pictures of buildings – dull. Who cares? Photographs of buildings – I mean old or middle-aged buildings leave me cold.

At last I came upon a book about Japanese Art by Lawrence Bing. A big flat book. It was in German translation but some of the pictures were lovely. I should like some postcards of them. Right trees. Flowers and little birds. I don't like the people ones so much. I got interested in this when I heard Mrs Watt and the doctor. I tried to finish looking at them hurriedly. They came in – I took a rapid glance at the last one. I went in with the doctor. He asked me a few questions then put me in the next room. I took off my dress. He came in. I lay on the couch and let down my straps. He tested my heart. He's Dutch, has grey eyes, very black hair, and is about forty and affable. He took my blood pressure and felt my legs and looked at my tongue. Then he said he could see that there was some trouble not bad or anything but slight, but a cure might be worthwhile seeing I was here.

He made me rush to the top of the house and then took my pulse. Then he made me go into the other room while he talked to Mrs Watt. I thought this was unnecessary. I sat down and waited despondently. They came back. Then they retired again about prices. I had followed them to the door and was waiting leaning against the wall with my arm above my head. The doctor saw me and closed the door. He thought he must have been rude so he opened it, half stuck his head out and apologized slightly. I didn't care. I went into the waiting room and began to cry. I cried until I thought I should like them to see me crying. Then I couldn't make the tears come. They trickled down right to under my chin. I left them there.

Mrs Watt and the Dr came back. He was quite concerned. Mrs Watt told him I was sad to be so far away from my own land. I said I wasn't. We left. She didn't refer to it. We talked cheerfully. We

walked on. As we were coming to a road a car stopped – its door was
opened and the little round man was offering us a drive. We accepted
with more alacrity than graciousness. Mrs Watt apologized for me
saying, 'Miss Smart is feeling badly because the doctor thinks she
should take the baths and she doesn't want to.' He said 'Oh?' I said,
'I *do* want to take baths. It isn't that.' He is a throat doctor.

The car was a small five-seater with a slight chauffeur in grey.
The front seats were all one. We drove up the mountain. It was
rather nice. You can see another higher hill in the distance. I shall
go there soon. There is a footpath along the road all the way up with
a bench every few yards. A big restaurant near the top overlooking
Bad Nauheim, another castled town and the wide plain. Woods and
trees not wild but quite acceptable with dappled shadows and foliage
smells. Fir woods, dark and regular with no underbrush. He drove us
home. We rested and had dinner. We sat on our respective verandas.
I sat inside and wrote to Katharine Goodson, Daddy, Gilbert, and
Frampton. I didn't post the one to F. I was rash to post the one to
Gilbert.[15]

July 12

Reading Virginia Woolf[16] makes me remember all the things that
have made me blush. My 'breaks.' I praised Frampton, artificially –
it would have been bad enough sincerely. I pried into him. I poked
him. I said things with capital letters – like 'friendship.' I wrote to
Gilbert, stupidly, adolescently.

At tea with Mrs Watt and Helena Wirtz the lake was thick green
and shone like a wet olive. Two swans with snakey necks were being
fed by middle-aged people with relaxed and silly expressions. The
lake was good, but it was a disgusting day, I thought a lot of evil
thoughts. I mustn't think. A good description – 'a cross old woman'
it might jump out in a rage by mistake and I don't care I don't
care. And snobbery and overbearing and insistent pride in personal
distinction. And pettiness and sulkiness and aggrievedness. But no
hate I felt. No hate at all. No bitterness. No resentment. Glory be.
Then in *Wood Magic*,[17] I came across a passage where the squirrel
moralized about the little things that get in and grow and reproduce
and rot, finally a whole beam, etc. and I took it to heart. But that's
all the good it did you O Queen. I was cross and prudish and I
hated and glared at the children because they were titteringly and

confederately amused at my blue canvas shoes. And I had stockings on too and I trailed along and felt like whimpering and letting go of my knees. And there was no mail and my face is showing signs of spots and my hair needs washing rather but not enough.

The wind blew my short raincoat and showed my bare legs because I only had a bathing suit on. I wanted to sun up alone on the mountain. Fat men stared. The sun went in. I gathered a little flower trimmed oak leaf basket of strawberries for Mrs Watt. They were few and far between. It was fun. It gets you – Russel[18] and his butterflies – stamps – anything. Exciting.

Hung by my hands on a tree. Lay in a swamp. Itchy.

I looked at the queer lake and thought it is like something. What is it like? Oh! It's like a wet olive. That's good I said. It will go well in my diary. It is like a wet olive. It will be impressive. Then thought: I am copying Virginia Woolf. I am being influenced and 'making phrases.' I am cheating. I am not being myself – but taking her construction putting on a light meaning and saying O how original I am – and how apt. Then – isn't all this truth-speaking and self-analysis, isn't it all her influence or someone's – not your own? All this pretending to get at the core. It's not true, really. But then I thought as I scrubbed my back with a lint cloth and French Fern soap (brown and oval) isn't it permissible to be stimulated by people honourably, to be made more alert and alive and noting of things by others? To be shown and *taught*. Cannot I be stimulated by Virginia Woolf and Katherine Mansfield (who is sometimes reflected in VW) and Mary Webb and Barrie and the others? Yes, why not? To be only my own original nature self – to be the thing that is the strongest urge at my depths – that is to lay all that down and laugh at it and walk on a mountain alone – really alone in a wild place. And not want to meet a soul. And that is really true and it is the urge and the flame and it needs no fanning. Things seem false if they are conscious. Conscious fun – nothing – revolting. Spontaneous they must be – bursting and self-forgetful.

July 13

I read today some Marcus Aurelius Golden Thoughts to make me snap out of it. Everywhere I looked, even in *The Daily Telegraph* were sayings – 'How long have you been putting off – there is no tomorrow – live today.' O I know, I know. I am wallowing in sin, yet I should not abuse myself they say. I should remedy, not condemn O! I know that too. Bath in special water at place. Doctor who always, ridiculously makes me weep. Why on earth I don't know. As soon as he leaves the room I wash my face and go on reading cheerfully. It's terribly silly.

Read *To the Lighthouse*. Finished it. First half specially good. Mrs Ramsay not unlike Mummy in some ways. Helena Wirtz came – went to tea at Kurhaus. Ices. Proprietor teaching me German and laughing and genial. Helena's motherly ways with me – her little caresses – in voice and arm. I shall hurt her I fear. She would be easily hurt. I left them and had my hair washed and read *Finch's Fortune* because I think it my duty to read Mazo de la Roche. I didn't like it. It annoyed me intensely and after V. Woolf, it is like a resort advertisement. Went to bed right after dinner. Mrs Watt brought me some fruit and asked me if anything was the matter, I 'looked blue.' She kissed me, and told me a story of how someone had said it was depressing here. 'That's probably what it is,' she said.

I had an immoral dream of Gilbert last night. He kissed me hard hard and painfully and his hair was all untidy. And it was infinitely comforting because he did it because he couldn't help it. And Tink was there and I was trying to excuse myself for neglect of her – and she was accusing me and talking vaguely about her lovers. And Graham took me home and intimated that he knew of my relations with Gilbert and was resentful and bitter, but resigned. I was sorry but too elated to care. In enormous exuberance and health you can't help stepping over – I was going to say the dead – I don't mean that – . If you are happy and in health and the sun is shining and you see what you want it is impossible to really get down and be part of an aggrieved person's point of view. There isn't sense or time. But this is vague and involved. I mean something else.

I shall wash my face in cold water and put out the light. I have spent a perfectly good evening in writing self-sick trash. Why not work? Why not will?

Oh. Wash your face and put out the light by your bed.

I will be strong tomorrow.

But that seems false too. I am all false. It is even false to say I am all false. I know it. False. False. False.

July 19

The beginning of James Joyce's *Ulysses*. Hot hot sun and another excursion with Herr Wirtz. Cherries laden on the trees – all over the ground – wild, dark purple, red and yellow, red, flimsy, firm, pure amber, pale moon yellow, staining my hands and lips purple – and the stains are blue now like ink after many washings.

A still profound evening sky – striking. A deep quiet pure intense grey, with firm scalloped fine pink clouds. Something rare and strong. Like a precious great man without conceit – who understands and yet digs his potatoes with the other labourers without explanations to them on a lonely island. That sky had something of Pegi McLeod.[19] She comes sometimes into books too. VW, almost anything psychological. And she was quiet. I can remember her amused grown-up eyes with the light of older knowledge looking at the lot of us – and seeing it as a picture – and yet she did not think she was superior or greater or farther on because she analysed while we only lived. It is dangerous though, psychology, that's what it gives you – false superiority. I can feel it too. Norman Robertson and Harry Hodson[20] – yes they have intellects, and brains and wit – and they have read and been told. So they think they know. Well it all slithers into nothing on a mountain, almost shame. But there is the greatness. I am vague – no, not vague, uneloquent, unexplicit; well, it is unexpressible. And don't you think that what we will reach eventually, I don't mean in the end, just after this long while, will be a universal and complete *silent* understanding. We shall talk like horses. That's not going back? No! It's true that the greater the person and the feeling the greater the silence – and how adolescent – words!

Some tramping and bugling and drums went by outside and rhythmic marching songs. A thunder storm is coming up and the lightning is flashing now and then. Apprehensive. That quiet deep sunset!

July 21

Ten letters, four from GS good – raising, exciting, and elating. Oh ain't it nice to know that someone has great great faith in you.

July 25

Excursion with Herr Wirtz. At 7:20 AM he came and I had on my 'worst' dark green sun-forest dress and blue finnigan shoes. We hurried to the station – oh! it is good to get up in the morning –

really early – with that renewed – fresh – infinite possibility look of a new day. Nine is much too late – a day – a whole lost before you but not the blessing or the enthusiasm – it stands out then – drabbly or even overpoweringly. But in the early early hours stimulation and other beauty everywhere. We got out at Butzbach. HW said he had been awake since 4. He was thrilled. He even bought second class tickets and produced a little white bag of sticky fruit drops – the hard kind – round and coloured. 'We have joy?' he said. 'Yes?' Ya Ya. We walked up across the railway tracks; across the street people were already going about their business. We climbed to the top, sat on a bench and studied the map. At least he did and I rather wished he wouldn't. Then we started through much wilder forests with tiny sunbeams slanting through them – no benches or gravel. We saw a weird figure and called to him. He was a fairly young man, thin and rather frail with a slight stubble all over his hungry looking face. He had a shirt open at the front and loosely tucked half into his trousers. He had almost a hairless chest. On his arm was a basket full of mushrooms – pifferlings – and in his other hand a knife. He looked tired but keen-eyed and alive. Mushrooms are scarce this year. He looked wistful and asked some questions which I didn't understand. '*We* wouldn't like any?' 'Oh no,' HW laughed. 'We were going to the forest to look for them!' he said *auf-wiedersehen* and his sad haunting face turned away. We walked on and heard him give a loud strange call to someone through the woods, two of them gathering mushrooms.

Then as we walked along in the dim light and to the left there was a slight noise. We looked through the tall tree trunks and shadows and saw two deer, one following the other running parallel with us. They soon were far ahead. We watched them disappear. The beautiful thin legs and the rhythm of their bounds. Their ruddy coats. Their lightness. Their divine life and secret places. The sense of silence and noise made the woods theirs.

The plums, which I had thrown with everything else, skew-gee into the soft basket broke and squidged all over the bottom and dripped gooily through the soft straw, and daubed everything up. So we scooped them out and ate them bending over, dripping, making succulent noises, and licked each finger separately afterwards. I sorted out the basket and wiped the things on old newspapers lying about.

We emerged from the wood and climbed over a sloping ripened field in the hot sun. At the top were two or three farms and an old bent woman bent way over and very small and wrinkled and brown, with a child with blue eyes and soft wet red lips, inside a fence in a yard. A middle-aged lady with ruddy complexion and cloth over her head and pleasant friendly ways leaned out a little window under the roof and answered our questions. The child put its soft face and hands against the fence bars. The old lady looked uncomprehensive and bent. We went in. Children in a little school yard were shouting and playing. There were a few – poor and small and scraggly. HW watched them. He used to be a Director of Education for Hessen.

We walked this whole day thirty kilometres. On Hausberg, 486 feet up we had our lunch. I sat on top of a seat on top of a ladder for hunters looking over the sunny tree-planted field. There were forests a bit below beyond – dark green – through grassy forests and a place through the tree trunks down a slope ablaze with firewood. New growths of pine and fir. Sun at the meeting of the ways. Still sun-baked silent forests. I had not much on. We came out of a deep wood to a view of rolling green and mature blond fields – ripe and abundant and developed – rolling up and down and up to meet the woods again. Down in the middle of the rolling fields a cluster of red roofs huddled. We walked down the road to it. It was a tiny village that smelt like a barnyard, where the hens strolled down the road and cats sat in the sun.

Right by here was the pub where we went in and had buttermilk. I asked to wash my hands and an old doubled up woman with leathery skin and wispy hair done tightly up from the sides of her hair took me to the kitchen and poured some water into a tiny basin. I washed my hands and tried to tell her that I wanted something else. I didn't know any word that could express it – I said, 'Ladies room bane zimmer.' I said 'bathroom' but then she thought I wanted a bath – she *wouldn't* understand – I said *you* know – *you* know. But she just looked amused. I hadn't the courage to demonstrate literally – How could I anyway? She stuck a spoon into a yellow looking pan of buttermilk and tasted it. A little white and reddish kitten jumped about. An old very creased man with knobbly hands and a stick quite immovable sat in the room where we drank it. It had several large-sized black spots in it but I drank it. There was a couple from Hamburg there having lunch, a definite-minded man

fair, strong but thinnish with glasses (I think), who reminded me a
bit of Gilbert Ryle, and his wife who was large with a green dress
with flowery trimming, rather a peasant dress and pleasant, with
mind in her eyes and alive. They both talked to us – very friendly
and we had fun. I had cider wine and said I was going 'crok crok';
we had jokes and things. He was nice. It was reviving. Oh for *definite*
people to talk to! and to be wallowing in mind – I mean to have to use
your wits to answer – to be exultant in the fray – KM says 'the high
luxury of not having to explain.' You can leave all the unnecessary
things out – and take for granted the unsaid. Oh joy! and no matter
how tired or washed out apathetic you are, you forget it and your
cheeks glow and you are enthusiastic and alive and *alert*. And it's
fun. Well it was good after six weeks of the other, if only for five
minutes in a pub in an incomprehensible language. They got up,
shook hands with the two old people, said 'Heil Hitler!' and left.

The last four kilometres to Ober-Mörlen were along an asphalt
pavement, a curving highway with an avenue of huge trees – to the
right a woody bank, to the left a view of fields, down, and going up a
hill. Fields on the side of a hill, vast expense, and hay stacks – small
ones – and people bending and working in them, and a late afternoon
sun. Blue and white figures in the distance in the sun, in the blond
pure rich field. But then the road went flat across a plain – Oh! it
was a long long walk – my feet hurt – I could not bear to speak. I
knew the meaning of 'footsore and weary' but I felt endurance and
willed myself on. I could go on and on for ever – by will to endure –
(women's) – but it was awful. As long as HW didn't ask me if I was
tired or try to talk or teach me I could go on. I said I wouldn't speak
till we got to Ober-Mörlen. He understood. He is seventy years old.
I could hardly believe it.

Herr Wirtz accompanied me to the door of *Englischerhof*. He was
joyous at the door. I thanked him ('Oh! No!' he said, shocked and
chiding, you must not say 'Heil Hitler' to a 'hund!') A letter from
GS. His first one – it had been to England. Stimulating. He told me
to write write write. 'There is no other way to write.' Fearing for me,
what I fear myself. How good. How good to feel he is to the rescue.
I thought of a plot about sinking into the bag of the White Orchid[21]
– which, ironically, I am – I am. I wrote to him, incoherently and at
length – and I wrote a bit about the bog. But I can't think which way
to do it – allegory and really the bog, or symbolically and details –

sex, and blades of grass, and scum on mouth. Which would be more
powerful? I was dead tired physically, but he set the light of love of
work alight and I was stimulated. Good. Even to write a tiny page
about a bog is to feel fire such as I have not for ages. I *must will*. I
must. I will. There was also a letter from John Williams, but nothing,
nothing. There is no point in our correspondence – we are not that
keen. I shall not write again. I shall see him in London and have
fun, but never write. Anyway, I know, of course, he is not powerful
enough for me. In fact, though he is sweet, there is no *point* in him
for me – I mean to be my friend.

July 26

   Diaries – I am getting sick of this one – I am too lazy. Paid for bus
trip to Winterstein with HW and Mrs Watt. Nothing. Futile. Always
to be polite. Read six and a half hours of *Lady Chatterley's Lover*. Read
till 1 o'clock. Good. Very good. The last letter from Oliver Mellors,
the gamekeeper, is *great*. And pure. And, strangely, it was infinitely
comforting.

At lunch:

   'What's that you're reading?'
   '*Lady Chatterley's Lover* by DH Lawrence.'
   'Isn't that book banned in England?'
   'Yes. I think it *is*.' I read her extracts from Frieda Lawrence's
letters.
   'Is it on moral grounds?'
   'Yes. I think it's because he goes into detail so much.'
   'It must be pretty disgusting if England won't allow it. They're
really awfully lenient about literature.' Pause.
   'I certainly don't want to read it.'
   Pause.
   'I think it's perfectly disgusting to want to read a book my country
won't allow.'[22]
   Well! I did not reply. I could not. Why tell her I did not even know
it was banned. That several 'Oxford people' had been a bit scornful
because I had not read it. That I bought it because I thought it
was something I should read? That anyway I didn't care one way
or any other what my country read? That it was good. Great. I did
say, before her last remark, that 'Oxford people' had asked me if I
had read it. And also, I said, 'Goodness! Can't you form your own

opinion?' She looked glum and aggrieved. I hurried back to read it after lunch.

How people can contaminate things! She almost made it unclean for me. But no. There it was and I was swept on its great tide. She had made me feel as though I should read it in a dark corner secretly and then hide it. But when I finished that great declaration of DHL's faith in the last letter, I was conquered, and not ashamed of the book and not influenced by small minds. For in that direction many minds are small. But there's no good explaining or arguing with them. The book is good and essentially *clean*. Why on earth are sensual joys supposed to be so low? Flowers and pretty things! But flowers are unself-conscious and sensual and joyful.

'If the men wore scarlet trousers, as I said, they wouldn't think so much of money: if they could dance and hop and skip, and sing and swagger and be handsome, they could do with very little cash. And amuse the women themselves and be amused by the women. They ought to learn to be naked and handsome, and to sing in a mass and dance the old group dances, and carve the stools they sit on and embroider their own emblems. Then they wouldn't need money. And that's the only way to solve the industrial problem: train the people to be able to live and live in handsomeness, without needing to spend. But you can't do it. They're all one-track minds nowadays. Whereas the mass of people oughtn't even to try to think, because they *can't*. They should be alive and frisky, and acknowledge the great god Pan. He's the only god for the masses, forever. The few can go in for higher cults if they like. But let the masses be forever pagan.'[23]

This is *true*.

Well, now this great bulky waste of paper is finished and it is not anything but a wind that bloweth nowhere. Oh! It should be better. And it could. Do you think it is just an awful example of:

'He who looks both ways in the stream of life, sinks into the bogs of the white orchids, before the end of a long day.'[24]

III

OTTAWA
December, 1933–September, 1934

*There are no journal entries from the end of July, 1933, until December, 1933;
it is possible that a journal for this period has been lost. Following her trip with
Mrs Watt through Sweden and Germany, Smart returned to Canada. She spent
the remainder of the summer months at Kingsmere and in the fall moved with
her family to their home in Ottawa. During December and January, 1934,
she was in bed with water on the knee. Despite a full social life and the initial
excitement of being back in Canada, she soon found herself fighting lethargy
and her enthusiasm waned. She returned to Kingsmere for the summer.*

*There are two notebooks for this period; the journal entries from April until
November, 1934, are poems that reflect her despondency during the summer.*

December 18

This is going to be a disciplinary diary. *Something* must be written
every day. For certainly it is better to make vows and be conscious
of striving than to go vaguely, morbidly, unhappily, subconsciously
thinking I *CAN'T*. Oh! Oh! Oh! And with a power of despair and
resignation. No more of that. No. Nevermore. I am in bed now with
water on the knee, and a tight factory cotton bandage over it with
frayed edges – and my leg bulging over the top, and a hot-water
bottle balancing over all. This diary is going to end the desperate and
futile period of coma that followed the days after Kingsmere. There
was no more joy. No more enthusiasm. No more work. No more
appreciation. No more desire. Not even any more fear. All hopeless
and tired spirit. Especially after Daddy left for England – hardly a
moment – except perhaps those walks around the rifle-range before
breakfast – in the early, early morning – and the pine tree – but even
then the vows were not whole-hearted – and half of me was fighting
against the resolution of the other half and saying, Oh well – I want

it to get worse, really – worse to the very depths. But it was not depths
it was vacuum of apathy and uninspiration – the worst I ever had.
The only day – perhaps the turning point was last weekend when I
went down to Montreal to write a play with Jane – and we fought
against uninspiration and we worked and we really accomplished
something. But the exuberance only lasted a day after – and then it
was worse than ever. But there was that skip in the windy twilight
and the darkness fallen – and the sound of Ottawa from the point
– and the river glistening deeply deeply below, and the bridges in
the dark – and round about the great pine trees hugely laden with
snow. That was the peak – and very high – but then – nothing. So
luckily the water-on-the-knee – which I almost expected.

And I am not going to mind the cryptic criticisms of self-analysis
and introspection – it is childish and dishonest to deny it. I shall say
what I feel and I shall talk about myself unto the last page, and I
shall make no apologies. You can't squash everything.

Besides, points must be cleared up, discussed, sifted, concluded.
And I shall not be ashamed of being adolescent or even childish –
provided it is always honest.

Because anything and everything can be made into a joke or
super civilized over, of course. Nothing matters here but producing
the child – deformed, premature, blind or legless – but produced.
I think it is death to keep it all in.

I have a week till Christmas – eight days – well, say seven. Are
three written things too much to ask? No. I must write three things
a week – a week – and no excuses. Stories, articles on travel, or
opinions, poems and impressions or plays. This must happen. Yes.
It can. It will.

Bed is the most auspicious place – the only place to get your
bearings. Then the great things come out clearly and nature is
nearer, because you have more vitality to give to infinite details. The
'entrancing life' – the infinite delight in taking pains – comes back.

It is beautiful on the hill alone. The pine trees are whispering and
moaning the long lost song, and the air is biting, and there are wild
and secret things abroad. But there it is all through a veil – through
a thick mist – no – heavier than a mist – it is all flesh – that is almost
excluding the view – the beauty I know – I know it to be there – to be
about me – but it can not come and permeate slowly into each little
cell, with a slow, complete and satisfying beauty. It is not all over

me and in me. It is not an experience. And all beauty, all greatness
should be an experience. Like a mother too tired to enjoy her baby
– almost so tired that she resents its intrusions – the spirit is tired
with so much clothing on – so much that it cannot see, it cannot
sense, and when greatness comes, because it has not enough vitality
to respond fully, it looks the other way – and is lost in a hopeless,
futile, unhappiness, whose very self, even, is tired and apathetic (not
sharp sorrow or quickening pain) because it knows it is killing itself,
and denying food.

But here, from the bed, the mists melt away, and soon there is
clearness, and the pores begin to breathe. And what made it sloppy
on the hill, because it was unable to receive it, comes back and melts
into the consciousness and greatest of joys! Oh! *There* is the joy to
create, the love of pains and the striving, without which there is no
life here.

It becomes so easy – Yes. Though it is not light, and comes
from deep within, with a pull and a heavy strain – it is easy –
the concentration is easy, not like the poor hard ill-shaped thing
that is forced out at the other blurred time.

These mutterings, *then*, would have seemed ignominious, stupid,
futile, and shame-worthy. But the first step must be taken *first*. Why
be ashamed? Surely it is more adolescent to be ashamed if you look
at it largely . . . like Sholto and the ice-cream and milk in the Savoy.
But he was young. I thought to myself: 'I want milk and ice-cream.
It's the conventional thing to take tea and sandwiches. Sholto would
think it unsophisticated to ask for milk and ice-cream. But surely
when you have passed the young sophistication and generally *grown
up* it would be childish to take what I did not want because I thought
it was the thing to do. The really mature thing then would be to
take what I want.' And I did – three stages – but if you are in
the second how can you know that the first and third are alike, and
which is which?

Goodnight – it is half-past eleven, and there is no sound anywhere
– but only the silence singing.

December 20
Another day too full for accomplishment, but not so fuddled –
there was a clear low stream flowing underneath all the time, with
a drawl, a slow movement, but continuous.

More salt and boiling water for my face and the end of my nose burnt and fiery red. Then I betook me to the bath and had a very shallow awkward one, with my bandaged leg up in the air, and laid upon the various fixtures. However, as a triumph of mind over matter, I did not wet the bandage.

Three parcels came for me. They contained a beautifully done, quaint very old English song – all in red and black with each word large and hand-done originally. It was from the Allwards and it and the thought that sent it made me feel airy. There was 'just a little Xmas card' from Toby Weaver,[1] which was in fact *The Adventures of (Dr. Gabriel Mathews) in his search for Mrs. Shaw*, and which I forthwith read. It was quite amusing, but each line did not compel you to the next. I do wish someone could write a reply to show as wittily as Shaw could himself – with a few nuts and spice. And sometimes I remembered (to Dr Mathews) – 'that is not it. That is not what he meant at all.'[2] But I liked getting it. It will be useful if I ever have to write University essays, etc on George Bernard Shaw. The third parcel contained a music manuscript from Delacour Beamish[3] with original and personal words as well; I chuckled over it for half the morning – it is almost too good to be true – but even so I do feel traitorous when I cast him to the mob to be guffawed at and jeered at too. Can he really take himself seriously? Sometimes I wonder if *I* am not the one being fooled.

Russel came in from a heavy morning's shopping and did some more typing. Helen and Helen Grant at tea – Helen's[4] sociability and marvellous companionableness. She was describing her size before Johnsy arrived. Mrs Carter early and Clifford later and invitations all day. Mummy was in Montreal today. Russel invited Helen 'to the theatre' – it was 'to be his party' – on the telephone.

The two little red-nosed faces of Esme and Sue[5] in the doorway. Esme's little elf-face and her big brown eyes which she drops in shyness like her father. Sue telephoning Jim to ask for an address and saying, 'It's Betty Smart's sekrity speaking.'

Daddy arriving and being happy and approving the list – and a bit of mutual satisfaction. Daddy and Russel had dinner alone together. Russel eager with plans for a motor trip through Southern USA next summer.

Then later at 10:30 the arrival of Jane and Mummy from Montreal – merry voices in the hall – satisfied and showing of presents by

Mummy and Jane's photographs by Jane. All well, including M's approval of carrying out of invitation plans. From time to time an unwarranted snap from J.

We were all gathered together around my bed drinking ginger ale and soft but pliable date cakes – and suddenly J irritably referred to the fact that Helen Bradly had to be invited. It wasn't a minute before the storm broke. The prop that holds up the sense of humour flopped – the sanity – I mean saneness – snapped. All of a sudden the irrevocable depths. Too late to be retrieved but to run its course. Jane lying across my bed at the bottom – 'Well what of it?' Daddy smiling because he was upset and yet optimistic. M going deeper in and no hope for a word to avert the already arrived – how can it descend like a curtain all in a second? Hysterics. Then a walk outside by M and a return to astriding up and down below 'Oh! Where can I go?' – and loud wailing void talk – like a person in sleep stumbling on along one path in an energetic way – but unaware.

Another walk – an interlude in my room – another walk – and then I played with a piece of string. Jane came in to wash in my bathroom, finished and said goodnight. Soon she returned with a nosebleed. Then she stood at the foot of my bed and said she was anaemic – 'Something the matter with her inside' – she was a bit hysterical too – a little bit theatrical – but of course dead, dead tired. She had not slept for forty-eight hours. She talked about Barny, drunkenness, sneaking out once till 4, and various parties. She was rather sweet. Quite a while after she had at last gone to bed, after saying how red with sleep her eyes felt, M came in – dead tired, exhausted, and lined, but herself. She asked in a low tired voice if Russel were in yet and went to her room. I heard the bath water running. Later I heard her conversing with R from her window in Motherly sane, heart-restoring tones and R came in and said *SOS Iceberg* was good.

December 25

Awakened late and later by Bourinots Merry Christmasing in hall below. Johnny[6] staying here. Presents later after Russel was retrieved from the skiing hill. No lunch – no tea – Jane and I in the car with Donat driving. Delivered belated Xmas presents and called on the Bowles – surprising Eugene[7] in his dressing-gown and not finding ourselves particularly welcome. We were shown the puppy and

finally (I feared it would not come to pass) were offered candies.
Hazel Hope said how jolly the dance must be going to be and we
beat an untriumphant retreat.

Our next stop was Aunt Harma's[8] where we disturbed gentle Mrs
Gough and saw Aunt Harma asleep with a little wizened up face, the
lines running to a point like a beak and her clawlike hands resting
near it. We said 'Merry Christmas!' and she said, 'It isn't so Merry!'
Then soon her bad humour passed off and she was fond of us and
we were fond of her, and she told us of her arthritis, her new-made
poverty, her dislike of where she was going for Xmas dinner, and
her dislike of books about people who were not nice and whom she
wouldn't know or want to know.

Jane and I sang carols and idiotic songs on the way home.

We had a sleepy dinner *almost* on the edge of an eruption – but
happily too sleepy even for that.

Later Jane's guests started arriving and Graham came. Later
Daddy, Helen, Graham and I went out to the Country Club where
there was a 'Dutch Treat Dance' – about two hundred there. There
I spent one of the gayest and pleasantest evenings dancing I ever
danced. I was completely on top and terribly happy. D'Arcy[9] and I
developed. He talked of 'pedestals' and 'unattainable' and his success
last year, and his dislike of 'scenes.' He calls me Bettina. I like that.
Denis Cooligan I resaw after four years. Jack Wilson asked me to
dance – and danced two with me. But he dances Englishly.

There were Paul Joneses. I got old Mr David McKean twice. We
got on. The Mike Pearsons were there. I had on a red dress.

As we were leaving, I went with my white fur coat on to look for
Malcolm Grant to tell him I could not have the next dance with
him and as I was looking I met Mr McKean and stopped to talk
to him. Then I asked him if he would mind giving Malcolm the
message. He said he would give it and a kiss to him. I said he
needn't bother about that. He said Oh – and looked up and saw the
mistletoe almost above me. At which point, Graham came up. Then
Mr McKean drew me directly under the mistletoe and kissed me, at
which point Graham's hand shot out and grabbed Mr McKean's tie.
Then G and I crossed the room and G threw the tie into the fire. I
saw Mr McKean retrieving it. I didn't realize at the time what had
happened. We drove home – then Daddy, after we had dropped G
laughed and laughed at the absolute insanity of G and we went home,

I feeling completely satisfied and rich with the evening particularly on account of D'Arcy.

December 29

Now, in this first lull in the middle of this holiday time, is the moment to write my birthday résumé, which should have been written Wednesday December 27th. I have finished my twenty years a-growing. I have passed out of my teens. I am no longer visibly adolescent. I may now start a-blossoming. So, though I hate to be growing older, I shall say hurray! hurray! Those painful red-nosed years of 'girlhood's hopes and fears' may no longer be pointed at with allowances when I speak.

On Wednesday night after the Drama League *Romeo and Juliet*, I asked Daddy for some advice on my twentieth birthday. He said, 'Never do anything that is not up to your best idea of yourself.' And he enlarged on that and said that he, even 'at his great age,' was 'still on the side of the angels.'

After I came up stairs I bent over and looked at myself in the glass. And I seem to be on the side of the angels too.

That was yesterday. I was urged to play anagrams with Russel and I did, with a great effort of will. And we played, he very keen, and joyous to win, but not so merry if he didn't. Kathleen and John Stevenson[10] were here to dinner and played bridge below. Russel and I anagrammed for ages, till my eyes grew blurry and my hands all dry and hot. He was very cute when he was particularly witty – 'I wouldn't eggsackly say that Betty' – and quite convinced that certain words were spelt the way they were not spelt. He brought me an apple and a glass of water. Each time he comes up to the typewriter lying on my desk he thumps it violently, very concentrating and incessant, and says – 'Is there anything you'd like typed?'

December 30

Today is not so bitterly cold, but still the hinges of the windows are white inside and all the window panes are befrosted. More snow fell today. The doctor came this morning and said I was to stay in bed till Monday, and after Tuesday's dance for a week or two, or even three. He made some rude remarks on my Pepper picture – which I have not a full satisfied love for yet myself. I had to go up town for a fitting and hair appointment. Everywhere lovely pure dazzling

banks of white snow, shoulder-high, and only distinguished by the
pale blue shadows from the shovelled paths and roads. Oh it is
beautiful winter, and the fresh cold smell is more wonderful than
anything I ever imagined in England. Afterwards I came back to
bed. All day I steeped myself in the Pre-Raphaelites – Ruskin – and
his mother problem (Frampton and his) and Rossetti and spirit and
flesh, and Holman Hunt and Brown (again I was often reminded
of Frampton). My head is bulging with the facts I am trying to
take in as I go along, and yet it is all stimulating, and egging-on.
A new *Studio*[11] arrived, with a review of the British Art Exhibition
at Burlington House and I was very pleased to see a Holman Hunt
and Madox Brown.

Jane is in a letting-go state where she wants sympathy. I don't
know how to give it to her. When I do I feel so detestably school-
teacherish and moral, like the 'explanations' in Aesop's fables. I
don't know why but I only need to see other people feeling weak
and discouraged to feel strong and controlled and progressing myself.
This diary is sort of petering out. It is fear, I think, as well as lack of
inspiration. I am afraid to talk too much about the family and their
mistakes and triumphs, and I am afraid of being too egotistical.
It is fear that it shall be seen and the final, damning, judgement
pronounced. I hate anything to be known or judged before I have
finished it complete and satisfactory.

How many I's on this page?

Stupid!

I read the beautiful *Translations* of Maurice Baring and 'The Fairy
Tale,'[12] and it was the old magical longing back again. Cat-tails
and dragon-flies, and mossy places and blue grass and wild apple
blossom, for which there is no answer other than the old childish
one: 'Oh Oh Oh beautiful beautiful Oh Oh – home! Oh' – and then,
because that, being inadequate and inartistic, receives the answer:
'Goose!' it is silent.

Perhaps when it is satisfactorily expressed it will no longer be
magic. I hope, Oh I hope that they will haunt me until they are.
For when they are, if they really are, it will be great and breathlessly
beautiful. Is this book really a discipline? For I shirk even as I write.
I don't attack the initial problems that lie at the bottom, that *are* this
period. I put down a few facts about the day, with a few superficial
remarks. It is just like great oblivion and stagnation. Would it be

a better plan to write it in the daytime and so avoid letting myself persuade me that I am tired? Yes. But I must write. The vows are unfulfilled. More definite strife. I could climb the mountain if only I could persuade myself that I know the mountain is there.

Oh give me more willpower and less self-consciousness – no that's misleading – less shirking – and less distrust of adolescence, which, after all, may not be so shame-worthy.

January 3

It is late at night. I have been tossing and turning vainly trying to sleep, but all the ideas and excitements come crowding through my mind and inspirations, and will to work, and vows, and plans for writing, in a vivid conglomeration. Writing and eagerness to begin at once; then Frampton, and imaginings, and then Patrick, and then D'Arcy and his disturbingness. It comes down over me with an awful swoop, and inside as if the waters were all tossing about and mixing madly. Then the desire to accomplish something written swoops down, with an even worse churning, and different yearnings all straining to begin, and remorse at beginning twenty and having done nothing. Then more vows and desires, and then jazz with its thrumb and disturbing D'Arcy. Today was a grumpy frumpy one full of the hellish discontent, not the divine. No. I don't want to read. No. The jazz is thumping its continual dropping. I won't write my diary. I can't be bothered. Oh! I wish someone would come to talk to me. It's D'Arcy – he's trying new ways to get me seduced. Well he's succeeding. He jumbles me all up for twenty-four hours after I see him. Then *he* subsides and is nothing but a bit of fun and a testing of my power and strength. At last, I started to make a little blue satin romper for Esme's Teddy Bear for her birthday, and I got absorbed in that. I love the feeling of something forming under my hands, every little detail fingered and perfect. It has a little white real lace Peter Pan collar and cuffs and white smocking, and it buttons with an enormous button between the legs. Mummy and Mr Bourinot came in for a minute and Mr Bourinot read Sue's play *Christmas Eve at the Palace*. That was good and we all laughed.

But it's when the final crisis comes at the end of a sluggish day that the mind is too up-jumbled and excited to sleep. The blue snow: I can see it if I lean away over and I can smell it.

Graham was simply dreadful last night. He was drunk a bit too.

'You don't drink. No – You ought to. It's better to drink than to think.' I told him not to be silly. He said he wanted to be silly. I said that wasn't the kind of silly I meant. It was disgusting. He broke icicles off and threw them willfully at us. He said in a loud voice with Duncannon near: 'Oh shall I go up and ask your friend Lord Duncannon[13] to dance with you? You're very fond of Lords aren't you?' And other unspeakable things. So I broke free from him and wouldn't dance any more the whole evening. He was wild-eyed, and browny greasy; I was almost afraid he was so desperate and insane. He pulled Jane downstairs by one leg and broke her heel off. I was too furious then to feel sorry. He was so completely dumb, not funny, not a bit, though I knew it was all for love and jealousy of me. It is a cruel love and a crueller jealousy – all on account of repressions and suppressions and things he can't express, and has left too long, too long.

Today he called (I am in bed again with my knee) and I sent down word that I was sorry I was not receiving. I felt the first softening when I heard the front door closing on his departure. But the pathos, the sadness, the music, the might-have been, have all long ago died out; they have been played to their uttermost, they are dead – unrevivable – there is nothing left of them. No faint, almost forgotten air, not all used up, to bring back the sympathy with it. When he says words like, 'There's such a rare understanding between us. We have so much in common,' it almost sickens me. Actually there was never never any weakness on my part – I always knew there was no hope for him. As soon as we got to the stage where we discussed our emotions and relations I told him frankly. I never tried to fool him after the first child flattered year. Only for a minute on a hill near Oxford did I ever in the least desire him – and then he missed the minute and it died. A very feeble effort of nature when tried to her very uttermost.

I like Doug Watt. Suddenly, it was lovely to find myself in the other world, where the other person knows what you are talking about. Bill and his 'Expose without being exposed,' and other psychological and absorbing things, but Doug said, 'I should have to take you out at least once before I could be rational with you.' He looks a bit like Noel Coward, of whom he spoke, and of whom he obviously thinks a lot. So did Bill Aitken. But Noel Coward evaporates as soon as you've read him – well at least a couple of hours afterwards. He's all gone by the next week. Clever, of course. Terribly. Witty. Yes. True observation, and right psychology. But still, not deeply great. Not yet, anyway. I have read most of his things, yet I can't remember which, or why, or what about them, unless I saw them several times as well. But perhaps I didn't study them properly. Anyway they are more like Bill than like John Pentland,[14] and John is the greater of the two, though perhaps Bill is the more brilliant. Today when I was feeling sad Russel was adoringly comforting and solicitous.

'What could I get you Betty? I'll do anything you want or get you anything you want if it will make you happy.' He brought me up a big silver candy dish full of those little hard sticky candies and he plunged up onto my bed, and leaning with his elbow digging into my middle and lower quarters, fed me, and tried to cheer me up. He was all rosy from skiing, and boyish.

Last night I sat and stared at myself for ages, and stared all over the place, after I got home, still with my white fur coat on. Everywhere I looked I saw Doug's face and head – back, side, looking grim, laughing. It's so annoying. He disturbs me like jazz. Just the same. And he goes as quickly when I get into the other world. But he is certainly succeeding if he is trying to make me desiring. Tomorrow he will have subsided. Unless he comes to see me, which I doubt.

Anna Wilson has grown big and fat and her breasts are large and plump; in fact, she owns a 'bosom'. She was rather shy and had on a flowered dress, the kind I used to be so ashamed of, and Mummy used to think so suitable. Bob Inch's big dark eyes, looking at me fondly, as if he were about to say something, and thought it didn't need saying because it was understood.

Yes. This diary does sound vain. But that is what it is for. To get it out of my system. I can not even pray without the little jeering thoughts saying 'Ha! Ha! Ha! Being melodramatic. Lying prone. Seeming urgent.' It's devilish to keep them down. That is one of the biggest reasons for this blabber-book. To write here and thus away all the little jibbers.

January 19

These are the sensuous days with the bang, now pushed back on high curls. Nothing but sensuousness seducing me, cajoling me, muffling me up in lazy luxury. That will to work is a faint idea,

not an urgent immediate one. It is pleasant – no, it would be
pleasant, but for the feeling underneath of time flying, of waste,
of unaccomplishment, and the story of The Talents. This is the
fight against the powerful, the irresistible, the compelling monster
Sex. So now, though I have just been writing I *WILL* on sheets of
paper, it is not wholehearted, and at the bottom I know it is only
an excuse to postpone my work, and sit dreaming idly, of sensuous,
earthy, vain things, that sap vitality, and are nothing, and leave
nothing the next day, but more desires for the same, and a power
of discontent without.

I had a letter from Frampton a week ago Monday – and that was
when I was just finishing my Mary Webb articles[15] – my last day in
bed – as Daddy came into the room and said, 'Ah! Here's a letter I
almost forgot to give you.' I was reading the book on the Rossettis,
and it kept reminding me of him, and I kept blushing for that letter
I sent him from the boat. I wrote on my Xmas card to him to tear
it up, and so instead, he enclosed it with his letter. Oh then it was
too exciting. Out of the night – the same sky – the English night –
remember that dark hill – I got up and went down in that dark
blue velvet dressing gown – I wrote to him first and gave the letter
to Henry Blouse to post that very night. Then it was well for a while
– the night life – and well for the proper values – but it is so long to
England. I shall not hear for at least a month.

Now it is sensuousness again, sensuousness with jazz, and flattery,
with Doug as its centre – Oh! It is very pleasant, but look what it
leaves – discontent and *NO* desire to work – to accomplish, to have
my cheeks glowing and forget what country I am in. It should be
greater joy with good results, and ambition, and *POWER*.

Lots and lots of snow fell in the night – after *The Skin Game* of John
Galsworthy, with Sally Biggar and Jane Smart playing very very well
indeed. Produced by Rupert Harvey, and a real experience; the first,
and only Drama League I enjoyed every minute of.

It is not so cold. My frozen ears are recovering.

Purer, nearer heaven, nearer real nature.

Oh direct the sensual force into some more creating channel.

January 30
Not even sensuous. A coma. And a tiredness after the long ski
on the blizzard-blown hills on Sunday. What a waste. This is sin.

And no effort. And no will-power. It is dreadful. It is hell. It is the greatest crime against heaven. What remedy? An uncaring unhappy yielding to every minor temptation such as eating candy, macaroni, reading the newspaper instead of studying, staring into space or the mirror, not being interested in anyone, and hating poetry.

All but the moon! It is a most exhilarating globe in the freezing night sky: a deep mellow yellow – full and substantial. But the moon-responsive days are not now. And even the will and the joy to face the blast and wild open places are gone – absolutely dead.

Up there under the moon on the side of some frozen hill, they have laid Mrs Bronson in a new grave and covered her over, and left her. The cold white snow – the bare trees.

Yes. Oh the moon. I still want to live. It is still valuable and precious.

Perhaps I need sleep. But there is always some excuse the drudgery of looking up continual Latin words. My neck is still.

D'Arcy has presented me with himself. Therefore, in me, he has subsided. And he does not trouble me any more. Now I am free again but oh, how dull. He is pleasant in me now, but he cannot disturb me – the truth of:

> Never pain to tell thy love
> Love that never told can be
> For the gentle wind does move
> Silently invisibly
> I told my love I told my love
> I told her all my heart
> Trembling cold in ghastly fears
> Ah she doth depart.
>
> Soon as she was gone from me
> A traveller came by
> Silently, invisibly
> O was no deny
> William Blake

I was presented at the Drawing Room on Friday night[16] – and I quite liked the 'subservient' curtsey in the end, because I felt very lofty as I did it. D'Arcy said, 'It wasn't fair for me to look

as beautiful as I did.' 'Honestly, Darling.' I walked up and down
that long hard hall a couple of times looking for Desmond who I
thought was to meet me there. Finally I went in and eventually he
and the McDougalls and Peggy and John Rome arrived. It was a
dreadful party – the Blacks – a rubber floor, glaring lights, a small
uncompromising room, and a lady in yellow with an intense face all
screwed up and concentrating with a *cello*, and a man with a violin,
and a soulful fellow at an upright piano, playing long-forgotten airs
with no rhythm, not even a waltz time.

I had a long time with Doug Watt and then D'Arcy arrived on the
scene and we went upstairs by way of the little elevator and walked
down the long bare corridors to the door of a little room where we
stood and talked – he presenting himself. As soon as they get to the
point I lose interest; honestly I don't want to be kissed at all (because
it is so incomplete to start what is meant to go on) but I should hate
it if they didn't want to. So then I go serious and start thinking of
something else – quite involuntarily – and he is perplexed. But when
he asks me my attitude how can I explain it to him. How can I expect
him to understand how much I desire him until we are alone and he
is wanting me to do? and then I go cold and passionless. He thinks
it is queer that I look 'pouty' and different then – 'he has seen me
in all kinds of lights. I don't think many people know that' – you
shouldn't look pretty when you're having emotions that aren't worth
anything, should you? And when you find yourself suddenly in the
centre of a problem – do you *want* to remain serene? Not I – even to
please my smooth and sophisticate loving D'Arcy.

Saturday I was at Dome Hill skiing with Daddy and Arthur
Bourinot. The snow was silken and the pure hills white against a
soft grey sky.

Sunday I went to pictures with Arthur, Hugh Hughson, and Graham whom I hated. The night before there was Anne Sedgewick's
paralysing sleigh drive with all the jolly throwing-off of one another
and high jinks and wise-cracks and halitosis – then we left it (Graham
and I) and he took me to what I thought was to be a party with the
McDermotts and the Mike Pearsons, but instead of the latter there
turned out to be the old Cowans – Charlie and Mina – it was a
dreadful evening of course – Graham always lets one down. But
Mrs McDermott, who is a sister of Anne Savage the artist, and
also of Mrs Brook Claxton, was adorable and beautiful in a real

and shining natural way. She has three little children – and she had a 'Puritan upbringing' – Mr Terry McDermott is also darling – but I wonder if he is vital enough.[17]

Yesterday I saw Eddie Carter with Helen, and it was a rich entertainment. I adore women without clothes on if they are beautiful – sometimes even if they are not. I want to go to Paris and see them absolutely nude. I love love love them.

But even so, though that may sound full and eventful – it is all a waste because there is no effort on my side, just a drifting, drifting, drifting with soporific senses.

Last Thursday I had tea alone with the Duncan Campbell Scotts[18] at their house on Elgin St. The nice big room and the contented atmosphere and the sane language. I felt at home, though they were both polite to me – she especially asking about my foreign travels and other things which make me suspicious lest she be trying to make conversation and thaw me out or something else incompatible with mutual friendship. Left loving them both and walked all the way home in the cold. He lent me a book on the Rossettis, Morrises, etc.

February 28

Perhaps it is rather unfortunate that it is only when I am in a certain soul-searching-self mood – the egoist to the extreme that the need for this diary is so urgent. For success doesn't need a confessor, and neither does a dull contentment. What a lot of autobiographical writing there has been lately! Tonight I picked up *The Atlantic Monthly* and it was all diaries and records and autobiography – perhaps in the wake of *Testament of Youth*[19] – or perhaps just a sign of the adolescent emergings of the age. If it isn't frightfully good it's boring – at least to one who so lately has been in its throes.

I have been successful lately, and my problems have all changed – I had got so very far away from that eternal hill – so there was a sort of resurrection at Wakefield in the deep snow grey day – and those words of Enrico Belcredi's[20] – 'that is the soul of this country – so vast – somehow – I don't know – so desolate' – words something like that but said in his broken accent with sincerity and unself-conscïousness – casual but serious – they did something vital and I am eternally grateful. Nothing seems so bumpy now. Easier. But is it because I am slipping? Leaving real stimulation and joy and achievement for something more feminine and humourous?

Edward Ford,[21] Chichester, Belcredi, D'Arcy – they are now in my consciousness, with the French Revolution and Nell Gwyn. Edward is there a lot, because he gave me something rich and real. The others might.

Aunt Harma is dying. 'You go way and send Nebuchadnezzar,' she said, slapping Aunt Georgie. She calls everyone 'dirty papists' and is otherwise funny.

Ottawa – the Sparks Street life – it is really impossible. It gets you down. Ambition gets suffocated. People are so pretentious – if they are not sweet but unconscious. That's silly. So is this. I haven't even written a letter for so long, that I am out of practice. Anyway – I have nothing to say.

Last night little tingles ran up and down my back because I remembered spring, and frogs in the swamp singing, and fresh young breezes and young trees.

Why doesn't Frampton's letter come? If he didn't intend to send it why did he cable?

'The Spring's in you.' Dark and fresh.

March 27

Music is the only thing that will save me. It is the only thing that will give me back the meaning.

April 7

The Stafford Cripps are here and they are infinitely stimulating and love-inspiring.

Work is the only only only remedy for life: for happiness, for interest, for stability, for security. Hard, *willed* work. Oh *work*!

I have just been for a walk, by myself, part way round the rifle range in a pair of tightish rubber boots. The red-winged blackbirds are crying and calling by the lake and the crows are cawing. The sky has clouded over. It was sunny and blue this morning right till we came home from the Chateau after the Car Club luncheon where Sir Stafford Cripps spoke and Mummy and Lady Cripps and Mrs Spry and I were shunted into back seats by Graham – whom I saw today for the first time in ages.

The hills of Kingsmere were a fragile blue – clear cut and soft and rich.

The poplar trees were vital today for the first time in many a day. That is Stafford Cripps' stimulant.

I think I shall refuse all invitations to go dancing at the senseless Chateau or to the movies when they are sickening extravagances. And I think I shall not go out at night, but go to bed early and work hard. Some music? Some writing? Some intense motivation?

Have I always had something or someone to lean on? Except when I had undiluted nature or undisturbed self. They left me alone then. No one ever tried to poke or pry into my soul then. And I loved much more.

April 19

And now it is spring. Birds are singing. Wistful notes and jubilant. And bare streets and no need for coats, and skipping ropes and bicycles and a thin new moon.

I was determined to practise and I cut off my nails and I went down the stairs with a million pounds of death and blackness off my mind – and the sun was shining in the windows and all the doors were open. But Mummy and Nora were in the living room – and so it was impossible. Lunch came soon – and afterwards time taken. Lighter is the burden because it is at last a whole-hearted return to IT – which having once served – as no one else can know who has not known.

Do I want to go back (to London) now that Spring and Canada are here – the Canadian Pictures collection – the twilight robins – the moon? Is over there now something else – inevitable and irrevocably part of London and not to be transplanted? Not for here? Doubts. I doubt – But essential for an *English* spring. I cried and I was ashamed. But worst crime – I told, I told. Faithless and full of self. Even to him. How could I have told when I felt so secret? Pink red glowing sky behind a mass of hazy grey-bark tree trunks and limbs and branches. And birds – meadow-larks whistles – wrens low trilling – calls and mating cries. Significance everywhere. How can he bear it if he loves? 'What he?' *Any* he that loves. Last night I heard the real frogs singing in the swamp beyond a cool warm night – a still fresh and very young spring. A whole year since the ghost-frogs sang in London – a year of unravelling what was knit?

A year of sinking beyond recall? What? and Where? and Why? I
used to know all these things. How can you fight if you are not sure
which is the thing you should fight? It is just me. No use to blame
it on any but myself. Perhaps Graham worked for three years to
make me dependent and though he didn't gain his end – yet broke
down my reserves – my reserves of fighting strength and knowing
integratedness. Oh! If I could only show you what I mean – it can't
be *said* – you would know. Now *I* don't know. But surely if I were ever
strong I was strong enough to resist Graham for three years – but I
was young and the skin was tender. But if I was wise, I was wise –
Oh make no more excuses – it is I and only I. Oh! to be at Kingsmere
these birdsong mornings and these breathing pregnant evenings full
of meditation, music and silhouettes – and smell of earth and very
tender flowers – and swamps of frogs!

I don't think I want anything but nature.

Later: Jane and I have both been miserable this winter – no use
to deny it. Absolutely and utterly without the spark of life that
comes with living. A great black heaviness was over us both. She
at McGill and I here. So it was not any petty immediate irritation it
was something more fundamental. Last year we were both working
hard at something we respected and loved and thought worthwhile,
something that required nearly all we had and discipline worth
giving. This year – what? But you say it was possible to continue
your music and your sculpting if you really loved it so – if you were
just babbling and 'posing.'

How I hate that word 'posing.' It rouses all my hate against
the whole civilized world. But – see, we are both in different
surroundings, we are both ambitious – neither of us was influenced
by the depression or apathy of the other because we did not even
correspond. Yet we both felt full of tears and listlessness and lethargy
and *could* not write or work, no matter what we willed or how we sat
in front of our study books. Last year we were not always happy –
there was the eternal and unchangeable irritation of Susan – but she
was a definite thing to be overcome, surmounted. We consciously
strengthened our characters. Now it is no stimulating sadness where
you see all things like a drama dripping with tears, and full of
meaning, but is a mist, a veil of hopelessness and uselessness. Well,
what is it? What is it? We both have wills and an ordinary amount
of discipline – sometimes more. We must find our paths and then

we will follow them running and laughing instead of stumbling and unhappy.

'Coleridge was one of those unhappy persons – Donne, I suspect, was such another – of whom one might say, that if they had not been poets, they might have made something of their lives, might even have had a career; or, conversely, that if they had not been interested in so many things, crossed by such diverse passions, they might have been great poets. It was better for Coleridge, as poet, to read books of travel and exploration than to read books of metaphysics and political economy. He did genuinely want to read books of metaphysics and political economy, for he had a certain talent for such subjects. But for a few years he had been visited by the Muse . . . and thenceforth was a haunted man; for anyone who has ever been visited by the Muse is thenceforth haunted. He had no vocation for the religious life, for there again somebody like a Muse, or a much higher being, is to be invoked; he was condemned to know that the little poetry he had written was worth more than all he could do with the rest of his life. The author of *Biographia Literaria* was already a ruined man.' (TS Eliot)[22]

September 18: Monologue in the Chateau Cafeteria
I don't see anything clearly. It is all so unimportant. The clinking of cutlery as it is washed and the sliding of it away into drawers. I don't feel distinctly, minutely. It is so easy to sink into a lazy kind of laissez-faire – even these words are bunkum and fit for nothing but the gutter. It is so easy just to sit and let the cat lick your feet, and the mind mess about idly. Nothing has significance. *That* is the neurosis that comes upon you as the result of living with other people and not caring to fight them as they, in the throes of what Virginia Woolf calls 'Sister Conversion,' swoop down upon you with their stamping blocks and downright positive assertions of errors. O spirits of departed souls who have felt *urgently*! Send some help or at least the knowledge that what I have lost is not the most important thing in the world.

Oh it is awful. I have nothing to write about. There is nothing. I care for nothing, but the glorification of myself – and not even my whole self, as of yore – I am content to have my body extolled and eulogized in meaningless hackneyed words out of the mouths of 'smoothies' with 'lines' who speak for effect or result and care not about the recipient.

Ah me! and yet the clatter of dishes keeps up – and the clinking of the plated heavy forks and spoons – and silver covers big and substantial. Chairs scraping along the red tiled floor. And the chefs serving behind the cafeteria counter sweating under their ridiculous white hats as they dish out the steaming food.

Yes. And what is the point of all this? What indeed you may well ask. And those intellectuals Virginia Woolf, Edith Sitwell – oh what would they all think – would they be willing to accept one who knew and yet willed not? What would Graham say? And even if he did I wouldn't blush as I would have then.

Why all this continual talk and thought about yourself? *Do* something. Work. Occupy your mind with anything – and your time. Naturally you will be bored if left with an empty purposeless day – and being lazy what could be more natural than having thoughts drift back to that easiest of all topics – yourself?

Get busy – build up something!

But I have lost the heart for building. I no longer care to be thought wonderful. I have no pride in labour or myself. Poof to a reputation! But don't you think it might be built up with so little as even a few hours concentration?

Yes. I do. Honestly.

But where is the little hand to set the machine in motion?

November 18

    I'm going to be a poet, I said
    But even as I said it I felt the round softness of my breasts
    And my mind wandered and wavered
    Back to the earthly things
    And the swooning warmth of being loved.
    Bright and hard and meticulously observant
    My brain was to be
    A mirror reflecting things cut in eternal rightness
    But before I could chisel the first word of a concrete poem
    My breast fell voluptuously into my hand
    And I remembered I was a woman.

IV

'THE TRUE ACCOUNT OF A TRIP'
July, 1935

There is a gap in the journal entries between November, 1934, and February, 1935, and a journal from this period may be missing. There are two extant journals for 1935; one contains poems written between February, 1935, and March, 1936; the other contains an incomplete account of a boat trip Elizabeth made with her father in July, 1935, when she accompanied him to Sweden and Norway. They left from Montreal on July 3. The account provides a glimpse into the social life and the intrigues aboard ship; and it shows Smart's burgeoning awareness of her sexuality and the power of her attractiveness.

July 3
A hot morning battling with condescending French and pseudo English salesladies who pitied me because I wanted a navy blue blouse under, five dollars. A traffic-jammed drive to the boat. Honking. Shouting. Men selling stiff bundles of cornflowers and other hard red flowers. A boat brimming over with agitated and excited people saying goodbye, kissing, shouting addresses, throwing streamers. Three middle-aged ladies talking to each other in artificial tones, each trying to impress the other – each bored to death – each unwilling to give in. The hard playing as we pulled out – the gradual disappearance of the people. Lunch at a table for four with the other occupant a big fleshy man who rose and bowed slightly when we finished and left before he did. I slept all afternoon, thinking it was the next day. Had a salt bath and dressed in semi-dinner dress. The man turned out to be a rather affable American of thirty-five. Daddy appeared at my cabin door and said, 'Well! *I've* got *one* life story already – you'd better hurry up.'

The other man at the table is a worried little German from Springfield USA who is in the hotel business. He does not add much either to the gaiety or conversation. He seemed preoccupied with his troubles.

In the evening the three of us – American, Daddy, and I – sat around for a while drinking coffee. Harris told us how wonderful he was. *He* wouldn't make the effort though *he'd* always be pleasant if anybody talked to him. The night before we sailed he and his mother went out dancing all over New York. He and his two brothers had always found their mother more fascinating than anybody else. The women in their families had always been the matriarchs. He had written two unsuccessful unpublished novels. He had had three years at the Sorbonne, and six years teaching English Literature at Yale. He waxed and waned. He waned considerably when he told us how wonderful he was. When he waltzed he waxed. We walked around the deck and saw Daddy with a beautiful Scandinavian in his toils. He was leering at her. She was giggling. He had only left us for a minute. They looked old pals already. We went in and met her. I went to bed. Harris brought me down and said at the top of the passage, 'I guess this is the proper place to say goodnight.'

'Goodnight,' I said with my too wide smile.

'I'm so glad you're sitting at my table,' he said.

I undressed. In the bathroom I met the Finn washing her stockings. I washed mine and my underwear. She was friendly, smiling and affable – a generous woman with the proper attitude of woman to woman – friends not enemies or rivals.

D'Arcy had sent me some flowers – gladioli and cornflowers.

'I didn't say anything,' Daddy said.

'I didn't say anything and I didn't imagine anything,' I said. 'I think you're mean to even think such things.'

'So do I,' said he, 'I said nothing.' We both laughed.

July 4

I rose after ten and went up to the writing room. I couldn't write well. I tried to write to D'Arcy, but though I have been wanting him so much it is not the sort of thing I want to put on paper – I wish he were here – that's all. We are so single without a mate. So pointless. I had a Swedish massage – pummeled and pounded – my toes and fingers – and a sunbath under the lounge with a pair of paper-padded sunglasses – Oh! I felt a new and tingling woman.

I made more effort towards Harris and smiled sympathetically at the worried little man. After lunch we sat – the atmosphere was not vital so I left and went down to my cabin. I rearranged my papers and altered some poems. Then I had my hair done. Then I sat in the sun and read the *Oxford Book of English Prose*. The sun bewildered my eyes. I sat in the shade. It was coolish. I sat in the sun and read bits of 'The Song of Solomon.' I thought about D'Arcy. I thought what lovers they could be and aren't these men who think they are lovers. They have no overpowering passions. He didn't adore my whole body.

I had a salt bath and dressed in my black taffeta. Tonight a fourth of July dinner and dance had been posted up. I look well and feel potent. I swished up to the cocktail room in search of Daddy. We were all to meet there as a tactful way of switching the Finnish girl with the worried wee German. Daddy negotiated this very smoothly and satisfactorily. She (Lydia Mattson) was late and finally arrived in a black taffeta dress with frills. Her hair is light and brown and curly. She has lovely eyes – with something of Helen's expression in them and a conscious rather pretty mouth quite wide – too wide when she laughs loudly and shows too much tooth and gum.

We had a gay dinner. She reasserted fun with paper hats and with white wine. The Harris boy (he is a Momma's boy not quite a man – with occasional peevish look of Mrs Watt) became more worthy pleasing because he became more pleased, and the whole of dinner ran off smoothly. After dinner we adjourned to the back sun deck which had been covered over with canvas for the occasion with only a bar between tourist and first class and the orchestra between. Little tables were ranged around – full of people drinking in their evening gowns. We waited and waited for Harris. I went below again and powdered my nose. Daddy danced with the Finn. Finally, blithely, he appeared.

'Your coffee's cold,' I said, and felt the injured wife – that terrible hard lipped feeling crept over me; I shook it off. We danced. The rest of the evening was good, occasionally having its moments. We did Swedish jigs. He was rather good – I felt an intimacy, an understood friendliness between us. Daddy joined his friends, the Norwegian story writer, and three Cuban professors. We did too finally. The Charlie Chase law professor came over, was introduced by a self-conscious Daddy; he bowed slightly and said:

'May I congratulate you on your excellent dancing just now. Is this the first time you have done the Swedish dances?'

'Yes,' said I girlish, blushing.

'May I?' he said.

I smiled at Harris who didn't appear annoyed and left. We had a rather sweaty dance. Our conversation was clipped.

'What do you teach?' I said.

'Law,' said he.

'Too bad,' said I, etc. etc.

We went back to their table. I liked the Norwegian lady – real character – real sympathy – a real grasp of everything including people – she flattered you by making you think she appreciated you at once. She could say things like, 'She's a sweet child your daughter' in the right way. The dancing grew wilder and sweatier. The Havanan Cubans (de Soto (two brothers) and Dehigo) gave us Cuban drinks and we danced and were generally pleasant. The Finn was in a gay eye-rolling mood. The drinks were bad for me. My eyes grew small and hard. I lost interest. The Norwegian lady went to bed.

'Oh do stay,' I said.

'You have all these nice boys,' she said. She left. Soon I saw no point so I left too. I tucked in the corners and slipped into the warm bunk. Harris had accompanied me to the same place and said goodnight even more affably. I had swished down the corridors.

July 8

Daddy came to wake me at 11. The night faded into the day. I did not want to get up. My limbs were tired of the bed. The boat is slightly rocking. The rafters are creaking. Yesterday the Norwegian lady held her breasts with both hands and kicked her legs in the air in the massage room. She is sixty. Nearly every morning she comes down and says, 'That young girl does not need a massage.' She wants my time. She plays the violin. She is worth watching. I do like her. But she is headstrong.

'When you are fifty then perhaps you will need a massage. Not a young girl like you. You are just lazy.' She wrapped her towel around her slightly drooping breasts. My masseuse pummeled away at my legs. I lay under the sunlamp on the hard couch. Then I went into the pool in my skin. Lydia was there too in her skin with little breasts with big thick points. The sea was tossing the water in the pool from side to side. She looked like an elf with her big eyes and her bathing cap. I tried to ride the waterhose. I had corn on the cob for lunch because I saw the personality lady having some. Harris did not come down for lunch. Daddy is very brown. The other night as I left my cabin in my kimono to go to the bathroom I saw Lydia and he entwined staggering down the passageway. As I came out I saw his back returning to his own cabin his hand to his jaw.

July 10

One day the Personality Woman came down to the pool and I hated to go in naked while she watched. The day is better. In the evening I wore a blue dress with the moonstone. I had my hair done yesterday and spent all the rest of the day reading. I did nothing else.

This night I spent with the Marcosons and some people who have been in Japan and then the purser asked me to dance. He is lean and brown with a stern face and very blond hair. He looks hard and clean – he looks as if he had to and knew how to deal with innumerable women. There is undoubtedly a fairly substantial 'chemical reaction' between us. We went out onto the deck to see the first signs of land – two distant lights. He took my arm and gently stroked the inside of it. He did it well with good technique. Masterfully. We walked around to the other side and leaned out of a window. The light of the north was in the sky. There was a gentle wind. There was a large torpedo-like cloud to the left.

'That's imposing,' he said. 'Is that all right – imposing?' he said.

He told me I would have many interesting experiences and how nice it would be to be starting out with so much to be experienced and learnt. I asked what particularly.

'To make love,' he said. 'I think these things are mutual,' he said.

'Sing me a Swedish song,' I said.

'What kind?' he said.

'Something suitable to the occasion,' I said.

'What might that be?' he said.

'Something exciting but subdued,' I said.

'You are clever,' he said. 'You must have inherited your father's legal brain.'

He said he would like to kiss me all over . . .

Then he made the great mistake – 'Will you let me kiss you goodnight?' he said.

That should never be asked. I said no.

He said 'I am sorry. I was looking forward to that pleasure.'

It was getting lighter.

While we had been sitting in the smoking-room, Harris had wandered in rather listlessly and sat in a chair and looked around the room – and studiously avoided looking my way. He had talked across the room to Daddy at another table – but his eye never came near us.

The purser and I sat on the sofa near the stairs. Daddy and Lydia came by on their way to get coats to go up on the top deck to see the light. 'I will too,' I said, 'I'll get my coat.' We all went down. I got my coat feeling exhilarated. I came back to the foot of the stairs with Lydia. Daddy was waiting. The purser was there talking to another man. He made no move to come. Daddy and Lydia moved towards the stairs. I moved with them. 'You're going to get some sleep?' I nodded. He nodded. I went upstairs proud and falsely cheerful. We went up to the deck. The wind blew our skirts and whom should we meet coming towards us but Harris and Erikson. I had thought him in bed. I was glad. I took his arm. I felt affectionate. Just when I wanted him. The purser did all the work – but I would rather have bestowed the benefits on Harris. He said he was cold and he was going down. I tried to make him stay. He seemed resolute. I turned my back coldly. He tried to appease me.

'Oh why do women always get moods just when you're cold,' he said. He stayed on – so I relented and said I would go to bed too. As we got down to B deck whom should we meet but the purser pacing the floor. He shrugged his shoulders with a French gesture at Harris. I laughed. Harris showed me to my cabin passageway – then he said he wasn't sleepy.

'You wouldn't like to get your coat?' I said again – unwisely.

'No. Betty – I really don't think I will,' he said.

I walked down the passageway. 'Goodnight,' I said haughtily.

'Goodnight,' he said pleadingly.

I hung my porthole window open and looked out at the light-growing night. I felt too stirred up and alive to go to bed. I half-hoped half-expected at least the purser. The door opened. I turned round with almost a start. It was Daddy with Lydia not far behind.

'We just wanted to see if you were down yet. We thought you were still on deck.'

'Is Harris in there?' said Lydia.

I kissed them both goodnight and stared a long time out of the porthole.

Then I got undressed and went into the bathroom in my dressing gown. When I came out I looked up the passage and saw Lydia's back in her fur coat half ermine, half black near the door of Daddy's passageway. She hesitated a minute and then disappeared down it. I felt a revolution. I went back to my cabin. Then I came out again and looked down the hall. I saw nothing. I went back and waited. I looked again. Then I got into bed. But I couldn't sleep. I tossed and turned. I felt sort of sick. Why should I mind? When I myself? I thought you were on the side of the angels. I thought Mr Coe was so annoyed because – I thought, I thought – I thought why should I mind? It seemed as if I didn't sleep at all until the bright day.

July 11

Daddy woke me. He was disgustingly cheerful and friendly. I was cross. At lunch I wasn't hungry. I looked at them but saw nothing significant. I played tennis all afternoon – being reinstated in the tournament as partner of Frank the handsome Howard. But today – he and the blonde baby seem to have reached a better understanding. I sat with Mrs Humal while the two little boys played Mr Hazell and partner. She wanted them to win as 'the fat man' had been unsporting and besides he played a mean game. She and I tire each other in fear and excitement. They won. We played. We won. It was a beautiful day. Sunny and deep blue sky – a day for sailing.

I ran for my bath revived. I dressed carefully in my yellow chiffon and I looked alright. Harris knocked on the door and said, 'Mr De Soto was waiting.' That he didn't want to give his party without the champion tennis player present. I finished. I went up and joined them. Almost eight all sitting around two tables. The three Cubans, Dr Gustav Munthe, Harris, the 'cute' small fluffy lady with the bang and the cat, and an elderly pompous lady who leaned over to me and said, 'I had the honour of taking Miss Kjeld in to dinner.' I was baffled. It turned out to be Winifred Kjeld and the connection was the fact that we were both Canadians.

We had champagne and a good dinner. The lights were put out – the music stopped. A waiter appeared in the doorway with a huge dish of ice carved in a curious way and lit up inside. The music started.

July 12

There was land when I got up and much movement checking, arrangements, etc. – running over the whole ship. After lunch I went up on the top deck with Harris. 'You don't want to pack yet do you? Come up on the top for a while.'

There we met the little Swedish aviator who has the pretty dimpled wife with the common sense. Harris took pictures of us in turn and the boy took him against a blue air funnel. We joked and were jolly and I felt warm and friendly to Harris on account of impending departure. We watched distant Denmark through the field glasses. It had some white sand shore and cliffs. The smell of land began to move over the sea and the water and the ship took on more colour. There were fishing boats and boats with white sails and tall masts. Then Denmark was left behind and the open waters once more. I went below and packed and packed. I thought all the things would never fit in. Especially shoes.

When I looked up from my labours, there was real land, not distant specks, real land with colours and houses and people, pink rocks and grey rocks. I rushed up on deck all excited, way up to the top, there was a gentle sailing breeze and the divine smell of earth. There were groups of people up on top watching strangers suddenly growing friendly towards each other. The purser was among them so I didn't join them. I stopped short and looked out happily at the rocky island with the white lighthouse. By this time the water was teeming with life, people in motor boats, land on all sides. I was running to go down again when Harris jumped out from a funnel and caught me so I went arm in arm with him and watched the blue and purple land come nearer. A tug came along and let some people on board. Three of them were reporters. I saw Mr Marcoson sitting with his elbow on his knee talking to them while they bent about him with their notebooks and one on tip toe took a flashlight photograph. I met Daddy merry-faced. 'Oh yes! I was photographed too!'

'As a friend?'

'Yes. I'm afraid only as a friend. We were standing there talking.'

We drove to Liseberg and had coffee on top of a veranda.

After Liseberg we tried to get an open air motor to drive us but we couldn't. There is a regatta on and the ship in. We went to the Stadgarten and had ice cream, beer, etc. and listened to another band and watched the blondes doing their stuff. Then we went inside and danced to a jazzy band with one violin woman of mature build in a long white long-sleeved dress and dark bobbed hair. Genberg was a good dancer and held me properly. I danced with Daddy too. The Cubans arrived. Mr Hazell with Dr Munthe with the fluffy woman – the sleek one and the others – and Mary Howell and her mother and the blond boy who had been with the blonde were there together. There were balloons and he was a good dancer. I felt independent of the world again – not compelled to be what they thought me on the boat. The childishness evaporated. I was happy. There was a very attractive dark girl in a satin dress of steel blue and black with a cherry coat. 'Yes. That girl really is unusually attractive.'

I got jealous.

Harris came in looking for us but wouldn't stay. He had missed connections in all directions and was now neck high in stewards. He made a few pleasantries and jokes, asked for my address. He shook hands with a let's be serious attitude and left us. My bath steward was dancing. We left about one or so. Genberg taught me some more Swedish. The sad de Soto was in the hall. So were Hazell and Munthe. My door was locked so I sat with de Soto my eyes sinking with sleep. The other Cubans came in with the fluffy little lady hugging her black and white cat and holding lopsidedly one of the pom-poms on sticks. A few rather eugenic gallantries. Then Daddy and bed.

'Call us at 7:30.'

The cabin seemed a different place so still and deserted, so bare. I slid into the bunk which seemed whiter and stranger than usual and slept in the unaccustomed quiet without the motion of the ship to lullaby. The silence of a sleeping town breathed about the light night, with an occasional sound to emphasize it.

I had met the other horrid Mr Erikson (whom we had seen being firmly kept from entering the Stadgarten dance place) as

I was going to the bathroom in my kimono. He looked so evil
that I stared right through him. Actually I was scared. He looked
malignant but not surprised. I tried to lock my door but it
wouldn't work. The stillness of the harbour was soothing yet now
exciting.

V

LONDON
February–April, 1936

There is another gap in the journal entries between August, 1935, and February, 1936. In August, Smart visited Eric McKenzie at Braichlie, Ballater, Scotland. The journal entries between February and April, 1936, are intermittent and the entries from April to July, 1936, are poems. There is possibly another missing journal that documents this period.

Following her trip with her father, Smart returned to London and resumed her classes at the University of London and her social life in London. She had met and was seeing Lord Pentland, the cultivated and cerebral grandson of Lord and Lady Aberdeen. In December, 1935, she had spent ten days with Pentland and friends in Grindelwald, Switzerland. In March, 1936, however, she left England and returned to Canada to put some distance between them. During her stay in Canada, she began working on her first full-length fictional work, 'My Lover John.' In it, and in her journal, emerges an articulation of her belief in the power of love and nature.

February 20

Why should he, why should any man, have the right, have the power, to send me to bed disgruntled? Are the real and steadfast things of life, then, the static inanimate things, like the long shadow of a streetlamp on the deserted pavement?

Is it colour and form and sound that are to supply the great ecstasy, a yearning towards, and intimation of, but never a realization of unity?

I saw the delicate rhythm of trees on the horizon. If he could only reach that! Even that! After all, that is not the huge whole, but only an enviable suggestion. How, *how* can I possess the richness I find on the sky-line? Have I ever desired to possess his personality the way I desire to possess that little curving tree forever and ever? A little is too much, and yet I have already cried into my pillow because he left me, and felt sick in the car and hated the jarring voices of my friends because I was going to meet him.

Unrequited desire is a horrible thing. Obviously. It is a surging up to meet something which isn't there. Dust and ashes in the mouth. It is not the holy desire to possess intangible beauty like spring sunshine and birds in the morning and faint flower smells. Stretching toward the unattainable and reaching for something that is suddenly snatched away are two things utterly unrelated.

Where shall it turn now – this desire, this uncontrollable desire which was towards him? Will it grow, like Blake's apple bright, on a little poison tree till it kills my foe? Will it grow into a hard little censor that will stop any sudden spontaneous love-feelings?

Shoved down, stifled and insulted, it will retire, bitter and rebellious, to plan revenge, and a labyrinth of misunderstanding for the future.

And yet I am almost thankful for this sickening feeling. It is wasteful, and futile and full of rebellious despair. Yet it is an omen of good. For there is no depth but what is balanced with some height; no height but what must pay for its sublimity with depth.

Thwarted, balked desire leaves only a sick foam on the bleak shore. I will not lie awake and long. Longing is over. I do not desire now. My pride is hurt. It could never be the same now.

Oh! The vile revolting of the sensitive body! So much and no more can it bear on its frail strings. Only a monotonous tune can the unhealthy fiddle sustain without trembling and spasms, without the unhappy shuddering. The frame shakes with the unknown joy or sorrow.

And after the exhaustion of the frustrated body, by tears, and writings, and gazing at the deserted streets, the death sigh, the hopeless abandonment to sleep and forgetfulness. The bitter, unendurable, inevitable acquiescence.

Why should we acquiesce? Why?

That, I told him, is the word that began the world. And it is the end too. Only more intense. A more dramatic word, a desperate deathcry: Why? Why? Why?

Sunday was an exquisite day – never once out of control. He and I went to Leigh Hill and walked for miles and met Graham and Archie Haldane[1] and Mitchenson but that was nothing. The great thing was the new feeling of more independence and yet more affinity. At the inn, after tea, I was unaccountably overcome by a longing. Such an overpowering feeling, numbing all else; if it hadn't had some satisfaction it would have eaten me up – it did a bit of chewing anyway. Two beady eyes and a straight mouth with all the rest dissolved. I was afraid at what I saw – cruelty in the eyes, love on the mouth. I was aghast. I have never been so physically compelled to love. We were very late getting back and went to the Pearsons[2] for supper. He was placid now. My eyes were heavy. 'Wednesday, then,' said he, and got out of my car. 'Wednesday,' said I.

February 24

Tonight I danced in my room with the furniture pushed back, in my bathing suit. Jazz, Ravel, Mozart, Jazz. The compelling rhythms. You must dance. Abandon all else.

He has no rhythm.

To dream and dance. A whole evening extravagantly spent! A mild gentle damp night outside. I am looking forward, I am looking back. Isn't the body the most wonderful instrument – the most wonderful plaything!

I hung pictures in various places, hammering nails into concrete walls with high heels, losing the nail, hunting with Job-like patience and a long mouth.

Today Mummy flowed and she loved me, and so she loosened my atmosphere and I was happy. And every minute he is in my thoughts. But oh! To be met in a leap!

March 3

But Wednesday, though it went smoothly, ended in frustration and a repetition of the other night but more tired and hopeless. We had an excellent dinner *Au jardin des gourmets* and he talked about business and Bill.[3] I listened and was interested and tranquil, but slightly shy.

The terrific shyness that breeds gawkiness and a stiff face, immovable, uncomfortable and uncontrollable.

At the inn he said, 'I could make you all smiles in a minute!' Is he God to thus mete out punishment and suitable reward? Or is he trying to breed pride in me? I am too full of pride. But pride shouldn't be mixed up with love. Love is large and permeating and accepting, like nature. It is not a calculated, civilized thing. It is not an art, but religion – or it is nothing.

Since then Mummy has been sick. I get no evenings and spend long hours plumped down in the car, being driven about, wishing the race of chauffeurs were more human and less antagonistic.

He phoned me from Mary's party. But he has got far away again now. I read Grey Owl's *Pilgrims of the Wild* and felt a traitor. How can I take him when he isn't a part of that? The rhythm, the harmony – Oh! has this been weakness in me to get so specialized in man? Is the 'Understanding' a subterfuge? Because that is the greatest thing in the world. It *is* the world. It is God. I want an ecstasy – not a comfort. If I could love him and be faithful to him all my days, I would be made bigger by this compassionate step and understand all women in the world. I would love him more and more and be absorbed by the whole of him. I would be freed by him too and I would forget the small disgruntled ego. But have I like Endymion fallen in love with the Moon – with God? No *man* can be God. Oh why has it turned out to be such a small substituting cruel mate for resignation, not realization, full of weakness and unfulfilment and never the intimated greatness?

All women must be loved. I can't see the beauty of starvation. All women must be loved outside, and are enlarged by this. If he would only love me with his whole soul and not with reservations and control. I would love him forever and forgive him the blackest sins. I could forgive and accept anything no matter how little or mean or unworthy if he had that love and desire.

But what about this? Is *this* unreserved love?

If I fall in the small-eyed gesturing fashion, all women of all time fall with me. Is it only a great ego and the female body 'demanding to be adored, stamping its petulant foot, insisting on homage, tossing its arrogant head'?[1]

But if a man is sick give him medicine and he is well. Sickness may do his soul good – but we must try to make him better. Women are only made whole by physical love. You must not turn me out. It is not coarsening. O why O why O why can't you understand nature and forgive and love and be rhythm with the one true harmony?

I worship worship the wild and my fierce humourless prayers are breathed secretly and intensely. Sentimental? No!! Cowards cowards

cowards to hide behind words, to be afraid of a gust of wind. Oh the wild wind!

And this is no adolescent yearning.

'Nature, then, to me was all in all.'

So many have understood. Have you gone *further*?

O well. The cold night, the moonless shameless Pont Street calm. Canada itself gets nearer and nearer. Can I give myself to a bit of fluff dancing in the dream? You can't compare such things.

March 5

I walked through St James' Park. Still the same desire. I wrote John a letter but when I had finished it I said this is not J's and sat by my fire. I can't give him all with abandon and urgent desire. The moon. Not a joke but a poem.

March 6

Today I have hated Mummy and she has hated me. All day she had the aggrieved martyr's look and called me just when I had settled down, looking for trouble, making a grievance by the tone of voice she called me in. I went with Tom Davis to lunch[5] – it was not important – and to the Gainsborough Exhibition which seemed unimportant too and to the dairy to tea and dance which seemed worse than unimportant – sinful. Home with him on a bus, sagging with tiredness from the long walk to Park Lane from Mill Bank. The sun in Westminster Cloisters, a lady sitting alone on the stone railing.

At lunch there was Tom's sister Peggy who is like a headgirl or prefect or even head mistress and always makes me feel in disgrace or at least like a cheeky new girl, and Pamela the fair girl with business like manner, tight lips and taciturnity, and Leslie Roan, the footballer, disinterested, but aware of his own worth, nice and fair, and Leslie Hill, architect, tall and taciturn, engaged to Pamela ('it doesn't matter to me as long as Pamela can be persuaded to come') and Gilbert Yates,[6] tall large and blond.

When I got home I saw the tight look. I cried in my room but not much. I felt desperate. She cried loudly in her room. I sat and read James Thurber. I sat stolid and hating. I rebelled and revolted and felt like rushing yelling into the streets. Shut up – shut up. 'I've hated you all day,' she said. 'You've been sneaking. You're the meanest little

thing. You haven't done anything with your time. Any child could
write the drivel you've written. Jane's put rings around you. She has
a definite purpose. You've had your chance and you haven't done
anything with it. You think of no one but yourself.'

There was a long black hair in my scrambled egg. When I finished
Thurber I read Herbert Read's poems.

I must marry a poet. It's the only thing. Why don't I know any?
My neck is dirty.

No! I am a fool. A complete egotist brooding on myself because
I haven't enough to occupy me. All I need is hard work, exercise.
'Get into bed.'

'All you do is worry worry worry me. Get into bed at once.'
Damn!

March 18

I bathed with great joy and surrender and tingling and powdered
and perfumed and put on a new soft green sweater and walked across
St James' Park. The moon was one-half visible. I stood on the bridge
and prayed for the evening. The wind blew my hair. I had no hat.
The crocuses were hidden in the dark. I prayed joyfully. I ran with
glee. I took a bus. It was sooty, a bit, but I said nothing shall mar
this evening and I shut my eyes and prayed. I skirted the crescent
close to the houses and went breathless up to his flat. Kitty all smiles
opened the door: 'I thought you weren't coming you're so late. No,
his lordship's not home yet. I'm expecting him shortly.' She laughed
when I said, 'The world would be a terrible place without the Irish.' I
played jazz and sat or stood by the fire with my hands joined. I flowed
all around with a soft untroubled magnanimity. But the music played
on and I reversed the records. My deep flow grew slightly stale. I sat
and sat.

At last he came. All air and bundles. We had dinner. The dinner
was light and easy – politics – general lightness. After coffee he
began writing letters. I sat in the big chair. He sent me way down
stairs to see if there was any mail. I stumbled and he smiled but I
went anyway. He said I could be his secretary. (I told him I'd had
a sudden conviction – 'a vision' – to stay) – after a long while he
finished. We sat on the sofa. Reluctantly I showed him my earlier
and later works. I wished I hadn't. At 'The Woman of Stone' he
said, 'O I can't read any more of this now,' and got up and walked

to the fireplace. Then he turned round and said, 'My lust is upon me.' I said 'Good.' He looked pleased. He came over to me. Soon he helped me to his room. He was tender, but too precipitate. I was warm. He jumped up. 'I don't like being troubled,' he said. Ruefully I rose. He made me have a bath.

I combed my hair. He sat with his legs dangling. 'Did I need satisfying tonight?' he said. 'I won't tell you,' I said, 'I'm mad at you.' I was stubborn. It was a mistake. He was tender and humble. But finally he reversed and got his hat. I weakened. Come in here I said going into the other room. Come and have a conversation with me. He was fierce. I fled. I bumped down all the stairs. He caught me round the corner. We sat in his car. He drove around a corner but said he had said to himself it made no difference whether I stayed or not. He would see me occasionally and give me comfort. I cried. I felt hard and hollowed out. Full of love he returned to me. I was exhausted.

March 25

Mid-Atlantic. The farther I get from England the happier I am I have left it and the more I resent John and the cringing shape into which he was making me. I stand up and blush for my humble acceptance of importances and his too reasonable, joyless unnatural view of life. It's that he *might* so easily have made me happy and *didn't*.

Anyway I am glad victorious Canada is ahead of me. But the influence is deep-rooted. I have become indifferent to the little unkindnesses – like *not* seeing people I don't want to talk to – and *not* feeling it my duty to be bored or unbore the bore; and I am more of a snob, and have less generous love for humanity, and I see sordidness where I don't really think John would. Sex was to him a shame. *That* is a shame, a great shame. I don't, though I pretend I do. I do think he had a sense of humour or God. After all, he *did* call the moon pleasant. Dignity is too important with him. Great people don't need attributes, they *are* everything. They don't have to stick on their amenities.

And yet his bravery – he was a shy little frail boy and fought valiantly against his self-consciousness, and the fact that he wasn't one of the gang, and built up this marvellous defence for himself and held his head high when he felt humble inside. He put on the front for something greater than himself.

But has he fooled himself into thinking that he *is* the person with the high high head? Oh! If he would only be human. I could be fair to him and love him. He can't strategize me, it will only make me unjust to him and hate him and sit in Canada planning strategy for him.

I couldn't bear that hair-splitting life.

How I have come to hate the words 'good taste' and 'fastidiousness.'

And he said that my poems – or whatever other name better fits them – should be written and then destroyed – either destroyed or sent as a letter to a friend – to him! Doesn't he keep a diary? Mayn't I, without too much conceit or death-dealing self-love, arrange in order the heavy moments of my life? Set out my life for myself without shame, without the strategic self-depredation? – unnatural most unnatural idea that I am bowing to I!

Sometimes the colossal task he has taken on his shoulders to be God to be Nature staggers me! *His* small puny reason is to supply the great floods of God – is to order and arrange the world and bend it to his orderly will. And yet, yesterday, when I read George Herbert's poem 'In The Temple,' the second one on advice to young men, nearly every bit of wisdom there John has lived up to. He obeys all the laws of reasonable goodness, and civilized conduct, and social comfortableness. I learn and I learn.

But what's all the great reason of the brain, the arguments. It's the sea and fluff again. 'A dandelion fluff alone in worlds of space.'

The first smell of vital wind full of pine needles – every breath pure and exquisite! The first grey rock! The first blue hills and lakes! The first kind and naturally friendly people, the porter, the train men, the youths standing about.

The plain wooden houses!

The innumerable winding streams! The bricks! The pine! O the sun! The air! The friendliness! The unbreathed-upon beauty!

What's he to this!! If he could only see. Wouldn't he understand too?

April 29

Most of my world's not real. The real bits are rare and brief. I talked to Ansell for a long time and again, like a sudden flooding over of a dried up lake, I was full of London and I came home and I read the unsent letters and played the music – and knew that H. was H.[7] But of course my responsibility to John is great. Then reading the letters I got looking into this book and came upon the lewd rhymes I made up one sleepless night[8] and so trying to improve them I passed on to this everyday this brittle this most unreal life – where all else seems like the unaccountable longing for a dream. It is gone now.

Only the comfort and the pleasure. Oh! How incapable are we of sustained feeling and real life!

PART TWO

1936–1937

'Around the World with Mrs Watt'

I

CANADA AND THE UNITED STATES
August–September, 1936

In the summer of 1936, Smart decided to accompany Mrs Margaret Rose Watt on a trip around the world, again as her personal secretary and companion. She felt the trip would give her time to decide upon her future, and she appropriately called it 'a detour.' Mrs Watt's purpose was to visit and to speak to the Associated Country Women of the World. They travelled through Canada to the United States, Hawaii, Fiji, Samoa, New Zealand, Australia, Ceylon (now Sri Lanka), and what was then Palestine.

The journals kept during this trip are a record of the places they visited and the people they met, and Smart's responses to them. The emphasis is accordingly on character, place, and event, although the emotional vicissitudes she experiences while travelling and a growing sense of urgency to settle her future are apparent.

PREFACE

I call this a detour because it was only an excuse to put off for a little while longer the settling of my future. It is my long-winded excuse for never having done anything. An alibi, in fact.

August 18: Departure from Ottawa

I wish the realization came sooner with me. I never go away on a trip, or say good-bye forever to my best friend, or see history made, with half the proper emotions. They always arrive too late, afterwards, in the bath, on a boat, or lugubriously in the middle of a dance floor. This time my usual apathy was intensified by the after-effects of a second pumping in of typhoid inoculation.

I stayed in bed till 3, but all day my bones and muscles ached and cried out for rest and when I gave it to them they still tugged and strained in all directions. Mummy had cold-pains in her tummy too and a slight fever and halitosis, but she was loving because I was

going away and unharassed because Helen and her two babies left
the day before. Jane was affectionate and her face was happy. Russel
was sweet and gallant, dropping the odd compliment and taking my
arm. He has tact. He disappears without resentment when he realizes
you don't want him.

Esme and Sue helped me pack. I gave them things which delighted
them. 'O but Betty you shouldn't. Doesn't Jane want this? O *thank you
Betty*.' I gave them a case full of red lipsticks. 'Do I look pretty?' says
Esme. 'I put on seven at once.' She had a hard red gash beneath her
spectacles and shy eyes.

Eileen packed dresses for me. Norah and Arthur, Helen and Dick
came to dinner. Helen and Jane went to a party, both looking soignee
and pretty. Sally came up with a large box of candy. They looked at
my Canada photographs. I lost $100 in travellers cheques but found
them again. I wore black with my alphabet black printed dress. The
Bourinots and Russel drove me to the station. Russel wanted to be
efficient by checking all my bags but I was too fearful of my ticket
round the world to be completely tactful. I wished Charlie[1] were
home but was feeling too sick to pine and resigned. I was almost
glad not to see him and be redisturbed. Peter was at the station in
a hat with a newspaper under his arm, alone. The McLaines with
one-armed Barry German arrived. I went in and put my inoculation
on ice and then came out to greet them. Jane came tearing down the
corridor from the Chateau entrance, running and bouncing in her
evening dress, and Helen in her glasses, less abandoned and Dick all
knowledgeable. Jane was obviously having a good time at the party.
'I'm going back,' she said. 'Hamilton's there. It isn't finished.' D'Arcy
was at the party. That made me mad. Why couldn't he have come
with them? Helen was a little disgruntled. Perhaps I should have
given her the suit. Peter, Helen, and Jane, and Russel got permission
and came through with me. They sat in an empty wagon. When the
train started Jane leapt along by its side. Helen sat beside Peter.
Should I have given her the suit? She was not resentful – but she
would have liked it. She's generous that way. But she makes me feel
mean. Mac was touched just because I thanked him for getting me
the photographs.

I undressed and washed in the ladies' room and climbed in my
travelling pyjamas into the upper berth where I spent a hot night
trying not to touch my swollen and very sore arm.

August 19: Toronto to Port McNicholl

I put my head outside the heavy green curtain and said, 'What time is it?' and the chocolate coloured porter said, 'Thirty-five minutes.' I said 'Thirty-five minutes to what?' 'You have thirty-five minutes till we get to Toronto, lady,' said he crossly.

In the washroom was a plumpish blonde with her darling son. I thought him too big for a ladies' room. He stared at me when I brushed my teeth so that I had to spit less than usual.

Graham met me. He was not glad to see me. Not particularly. He was all concerned with forty-two of his men who have been put in jail in Cornwall.[2] We went to Irene's.[3] She opened the door first and came out. I felt shy. I think she did. She was rather staccato. She goes that way when she's shy. I go hesitant. Graham telephoned to a million people. Irene fried the eggs. She has a little wee kitchen and a living room with a fireplace and Graham's Carmichael and Pepper,[4] and a bedroom. Her hair is short and naturally curly. She had low navy sandals on. She gave me addresses in various countries and asked about my trip. She said I hear you know Peggy Sinclair,[5] I was at Cambridge with her. She's very pleasant and very competent. She and Graham talked about the prisoners and Graham's affairs. Graham was all absorbed. I have now become only his sentimental past. He wants me unchanged, ungrown. Always the same tunes on the piano, the same talks, pictures, enthusiasms. Naturally I balked. I am proud that I balked. When I did it was instinct. Now I see I was right. I'm glad. Politics is his whole life. He said so. He revels in the intrigue and the complications. 'All my friends are in jail,' he gloated. I went with Irene to buy her a hat. I persuaded her to buy two. She looks pretty in hats. She is pretty. But she has a sternness about her mouth. She laughs well and often. I went to Kathy's[6] and kissed Uncle Billy's moist face. We phoned the Plaunts and Alan asked us over. We took a car to the Diars' street and began lunch. Irene came, and Terry McDermott,[7] shy and shiny, and Graham distracted, and Alan very late. We ate out in the garden. It was very hot. Your dress stuck to the seat and you felt you had a wet spot behind. I liked the lunch. Terry stimulated me. Kathy's little remarks were not quite understood. When I looked at her and then at Irene I felt sorry. She looks old and her hair is greying and wiry and she has goitre or thyroid glands to swell her neck. She is so sure of what live people think and do, and what comprises a sense of humour and understanding but will she grow? She's suffered and remained respectable under unbearable circumstances and kept her pride. But alas! I don't think her understanding is real. She can give digs that hurt, that are slightly malicious. For example, when Graham said there were about 11,000 communists in Canada I was interested and said, 'Why that many?' and Kathy said, 'Get out your notebook and take notes.' I gathered my dignity. She is very shy and self-conscious yet assured, a perfect example of what even the most broadminded virginity does to a woman. Nature's methods of attack are so subtle and elusive and yet so inescapable. Self-respect used to be such a god – material self-respect and pride. Pooh! What's it worth? Give up living to appear neat and cheery? Better be adolescent like GS. Irene and Graham motored me to the station. Alan presented me with a beautiful leather copy of Shakespeare's sonnets from a 1609 edition published in 1931. I was touched. Graham saw me off at 2:30. I didn't let him wait. He was with his constituents. Irene and politics first now. I must grow, and Irene is wonderful for him. He leans on her and takes her advice and she laughs at his jokes to please him. She will harden him and he will perhaps soften her. Maternity (maternal feelings) is good for women.

All the hot afternoon I travelled through low-lying green country. Woods, and low hills, and fields. It was too dusty to sit out behind. Two nuns were in my carriage. We passed the end of a forest fire. The smell is delicious, you can't smell enough of it. Sweet, sweet and suggestive. We passed woods wild and close to the train. I read EM Forster's *A Passage to India*. The train drew up at the boat at Port McNicholl. The boat is called *Keewatin*. Mrs Watt waved from a top deck and said, 'There she is. There's Betty.' I waved back twice, but had to walk a long way over boards in my sore feet while they watched. I felt independent. Suddenly I turned and saw a grey-haired almost toothless old lady big with child. I was shocked. But she wasn't big with child. She was Mrs Watt's sister who's been sick. She has some of Mrs Watt's little characteristics but none of her fire. It's queer to see similar sisters one of whom has something of the divine fire. One that took and one that didn't. So what is the thing that makes one person unimportant like Mrs Watt's sister, buried like millions, unknown, unenterprising, unambitious, and another important, so like her, yet with something added?

We sailed at 6 (daylight) and went past the low green islands, some very wild and bushy, some all edged with reeds and cat-tails. Gulls poised above us. It grew cooler. The country was flat. Some of the islands had summer cottages on them, small ones, not elaborate. I don't like boats. They don't give me a sense of adventure. Trains do. Water makes me resigned and thoughtful and philosophically inclined. I hate the 'getting to know period.' The sky and the gulls and the water and the wind. Low green islands and soft caressing air.

At night I finished *A Passage to India* and ate three candies which I regretted. I thought the book good, and from my limited knowledge of Indians, true. I was hunting, all the time, for the reason for John's autocratic demand that I see no more of my Indian friend in London. 'I don't want you to,' was all he would say. 'I *know*.' That's not enough for me. That's never enough. *All* Indians taboo? That's crazy. I *loved* the Indian Aziz in the book. It was so good the book – it kept me sane. It would have been easy to lose sympathy by the least overbalancing. Fielding is the sort of man I love for a friend.

August 21: Port Arthur, Fort William, the Kakabeka Falls

Mrs Torenblom and her daughter about to be a school teacher. Hasn't been to Sweden for twenty years. Didn't want to come to Canada. Lost a five year old son and Mother last November, and a beloved twenty-four year old daughter. She cried about her. I cried too. When I said, 'Ya tucka omdeeg,'[8] she hugged me. She was squat with fat strong arms and a sad face. Her daughter was very pretty with naturally curly fair hair and no make-up. 'She was a good girl,' she said about the one who died. Miss Friedberg read the reports from the news chronicle. Young. Check suit and pearls and 'new' hat. Dreadful voice but nice and frank and naive and interested.

Mrs Russell, the President, is a Jew – efficient, kindly, tactful. Thirtyish. Green wool suit. We met Mrs Daly and her daughter-in-law. Went to Kakabeka Falls. One hundred and thirty-five feet high, and to Kaministiquia River and Power Co. All the woman at the meeting were rouged with powder rouge (much too much) on the cheeks.

Mrs Watt's mix-up about port of arrival. Long wait on deserted ship while the crew whistled and sang and polished up the ship and took up the carpets and covered the furniture and the chief steward

threw things at his friends and ducked and hopped on one foot and
swung around pillars.

At last Mrs Russell arrived and we were driven to a hotel where
several scared looking ladies received us. We had a few minutes in our
hotel room where they had put a tight bunch of sweet peas and then
we assembled in the drawing-room and more women came and Mrs
Watt talked to them about raising funds and keeping their money in
the Women's Institute.

Then Mrs Watt and I were driven to the meeting which was in a
big dance hall. I wondered whether 'Prohibited Gentlemen dancing
together' was a joke or really necessary here in such an outpost where
men are supposed to be men. Another reporter sat beside me, a small
town girl with long skirts and cut out shoes. Mrs Watt spoke well
and held my attention throughout. The benches were hard and
backless. She spoke about the hard beginning of The Associated
Country Women of the World and peace. It was quite inspiring
and stimulating. Before she began the 'Acting Mayor' made a few
halting platitudes and then left. Suddenly Mrs Russell got up and
said, 'But there is another person here today who I want you to
meet and whom I wish to know we welcome no less heartily and
am glad to have with us today.' I looked around with glee to watch
someone else's embarrassment when she said, 'Miss Smart, would
you come forward.' I stumped up to the front and said in a weak
voice, 'Thank you very much.' Then I hesitantly sat down on a chair
there and embarrassedly crossed my feet and looked with abnormal
absorption at Mrs Russell and the other performers.

An Irish lady gave two amusing recitations and afterwards all
trooped up to buy the pins, magazines, and books Mrs Watt
had been propaganding, and many of them shook me by the
hand. Then we all motored miles to see the Kakabeka Falls
which hurl themselves brown and white with a great roar to the
rocks way below. This was fearsome and profound and brought
forth thoughts of massed lives and what if *one* is a brighter bit
of foam than another? The flow goes on, each atom crushed.
From the railed cliff we looked down the stream where it sobers
itself somewhat, clasps a well-washed island and goes on through
a pleasant green valley surrounded by hills. Nearly all the trees
around here are birches and aspens. The opposite cliffside was
dripping wet with trickles of water falling out of the rocks and

below there is a great wet green softness continually under the spray.

August 22: The Prairies

All day flat country. Genuine golden west in the afternoon – long, long fields of gold, hay stacks, or cut hay, sometimes a patch of black marshgrass, and an occasional alkaline lake in the morning, small, and puddlish. Long horizons, unthinkably limitless, and hot warm air over all. Only patches of scrubby trees. Everywhere gold cropped fields. No colour but the dry hay and the sky. No change. Regina stop for a leg stretch. No views but slight wariness about it with its hay-coloured expanse. Towards 8 in the evening we stopped for about an hour at Moosejaw, and it was Saturday night and I walked up the wide main street and all the farmers were in from the country and music from a radio was coming out a barber's shop, and the youths, browned, and reeking of ploughs and sun and honest labour, have the only masculine pulchritude that can make me desirously turn round and stare and stare and feast my eyes upon perfection – the voices western and the snatches of conversation jovial and friendly. Some of the men in shirt sleeves and a hat walked the streets with their ladies on their arm. Finished Constance Holme's *The Lonely Plough* and disliked it as much as ever. The story plot obvious, the sentiment sentimental, the delicateness hammered in, hammered and hammered, the moral pointless, the whole thing pointless, the descriptions dull, overdone and not vivid. Altogether rather hysterical, I thought. Lord Elibank raises my spleen by booming on about Canada's need for defence. Bah.

August 23: Rocks and Rocky Mountains

My hair is like my old doll's, straw-coloured, and stiff with dirt. Soon after Mrs Watt insisted that I get up we stopped at Calgary. The E's departed. I strolled on the platform in the early sunshine and went through the station to see what I could see. But I couldn't see. There was only a wide straight street running straight ahead up hill, and one running into it with streetcars. It straggled out quite a way. The country began to roll gently but less gently as we progressed into the heart of the ranch country which gave even a greater idea of space, with hills on the horizon, slight dips in the landscape, clumps of bush, bumpy land, horses with their manes

flying, and colder weather. They have added a glassy observation
car and the day is bright and cloudless. People are unstiffening as
the anticipation of the Rockies ripples over the trainload. Some small
Scottish hills begin to appear, and higher ones in all directions, then
sharply faintly outlined, the Rocky Mountain peaks. For a long time
we climbed toward them over blunt grass hills, and when we came
up to them they had very naked rocky tops, steep and lifeless, with
small fir trees hanging there as high as they could. On the left and on
the right and ahead they were; we did not look behind. It is wrong,
on the verge of mountains, to look back to a valley just left – not till
the mountains are safely gained.

The sun shone on those red and grey tops, so nude and unscalable,
so definitely shaped.

Along the way, the fluffy seeding of the firewood was the only
colour. The pale blue cloudless sky, the dead coloured rock, the very
dark green (a coat of dark green with pinky-flesh-buff coloured fur?).
The mountains in this part were too direct. It was all there. Too
straightforward. Evergreens going straight up, then sharp staccato
rock to a peak. Peaks and peaks. Some of the bare fir trees looked
ashamed of [illegible] and their branches are all turned in as if to
hide their [illegible]. There were flowers, yellow poppies, planted
round the station, and mountains to left and right. Ahead, just seen,
the hotel.

On all day through heights of rocks, so rocky these mountains,
with their tumbled pebbles about their feet, and the sturdy climbing
dwarf firs, some green shallow ones, the others grey.

August 24: Vancouver

After lone lunch at counter in small shop and lonely movie *Trouble
for Two* felt groggier and groggier. But accepted Sam Dickson's[9]
invitation. He called for me and showed me over Vancouver's parks
in his car. There was a coloured fountain and all the flowers in
the parks lit up, lights everywhere, twinkling in rows across the
water, gay flags, and coloured hangings. He took me to where all
the people were dancing in the street to a jazz band. The stone
road was powdered and made a good floor. They were all young,
very young, and gay and *really* enjoying themselves. Hundreds of
them, with people watching from the roped-off sides, and shining
faces, and laughing, and girls dancing together and boys too, and

children dancing and running in between. Jerry McBeen, the Mayor, said a few words and was cheered, but not wildly, and also booed, just for the fun of it. It's Vancouver's Golden Jubilee.

After a few dances we went and had a beer. Lots of the girls wear slacks or trousers, and seem free and independent. In the beer place, there were quite a few groups of girls drinking, seemingly just for the fun of it, enjoying it and themselves, not looking anxiously around. Then we had another dance and then we went to see the Chinese festival, (admission 35¢) and there was a huge pagoda and high elaborate Chinese things, and a woman's get-together voice over the loudspeaker describing the coloured fireworks. And there were little booths selling Chinese cheap things rather expensive: junk, and garden ornaments, and incense, and Chinese books, etc. etc. I had a rather raw hot dog. Sam Dickson is pleasant and easy, rather stout and a little shorter than I am in my heels. Rather Uncle Morrisey but more experienced and 'world weary.' When I got off at my floor at the hotel another man got off too. I could hear him breathing at my back, then he said, 'We seem to have come home at the same time.' I turned around surprised, smile-sneered, and bolted fast my door.

August 25: Vancouver

I wondered, as I walked up the broad walk on the outskirts of Vancouver, in the hot sun, and saw the new Japanese starling with the white wing bars, and the city way below, smoky in the haze, what Aunt Ella[10] must have thought as she made this same trip. A long streetcar ride, a longer bus ride, suddenly stillness on the edge of nowhere. The house was small, on a little hill, covered in ivy and hops. A rooster crowed. The garden was full of gay flowers. My offering of yellow and mauve zinnias was out of place. Kaye answered the door. She was pretty and her cheeks were blooming, but she seemed hidden behind her glasses. Then Aunt Lillian[11] came along and greeted me after wiping her hands on her apron. Dorothy came into the kitchen with her glasses and slightly crossed-eye and dark hair.

Uncle Alan finally got back from the mix-up about my bus-meeting; he is stoutish with blue eyes and snow white hair, a strong reddish face and a bright brilliant blue pullover. He showed me his garden, his hens, small and special, his pear tree and grape vines. I liked the whole family. They motored me to Deep Cove.

August 27: Vancouver

Get to the meeting to hear Mrs Tustin's sister, Mrs MacGregor, give an hysterical oratorical speech on petty patriotism, a Lady Honiton type that should be swept from the face of the earth. ('I stand for BC') and she straightens herself up proudly. It was too too purple and embarrassing and vile and miles too long. She'd been taking elocution lessons. She's a menace to the whole country. She capitalizes the fact that she's small and enthusiastic, and *she* thinks, feminine. Really a fargone case of hysterical self-love.

Mrs Watt's speech was delightful after hers. Human and absorbing. She ends by saying, 'I had a grand ending all ready but I can't remember it,' and sits down. They loved that. I had an uncomfortable lunch with ten ladies at the Georgia Hotel.

The mountains rise around the city in the sun. Sam Dickson calls for me at four and takes me a little way out to what he calls 'new' people's places. Mr and Mrs Jones ('Jonesy' and 'Louise Peewee') and their daughter Bev, and a boor called Erny. The house has lovely grounds and looks out to the mountains, with the odd evergreens rising between. They have peaches and apples and pears and prunes and rowanberry trees in their garden and a minute swimming pool of fresh water where we swam. Peewee is plump and wears very short shorts and high heels and bobby socks and a yellow pullover and a short-sleeved white blouse. She is nice and unpetty and kind. They sweetly understood that I didn't want my drink. Bev is six and has an ugly little old woman's face. Peewee said she had been criticized for letting Bev see her without clothes on. I gave her a lecture on this point and said if she made such a powwow about things that should be taken for granted her child would grow up complexed and not sane. I got too indignant on the subject; I think it would have been more effective if I had been quietly incredulous at her attitude. However, perhaps I reinforced her good instincts. Why should the Leighs' criticism of 'immorality' affect her? Such ridiculous nonsense!

The boor drove back with us and got out just before the hotel. Sam I liked better and better. He's a 'nice fellow' with sense and understanding.

As I was lying here in my petticoat writing this the phone rang and a man's accented voice said Hullo. At first I thought it was Varley,[12] but it turned out to be only the man who spoke to me the other night as I came home late. He was trying to inveigle me to have a cocktail with him. I was polite but firm.

Before dinner Beatrice and Sam phoned me and asked me to drinks tomorrow on the Governor General's train. Michael and John Boyle[13] are in this hotel. Tonight I began a speech on Canadian art. Not good enough, but a start. The man phoned me again. I was cross and curt this time.

September 2: Vancouver to Victoria

At 7 I woke up and thin, gay sunlight was all over my room. I got up and packed and bathed and then hopped back pyjamaed to my bed for breakfast. Afterwards I paid our bill ($47.75 or thereabouts) arranged (as I thought) for my luggage and walked, light as air, down the street, down the hill to the docks. All around the sparkling morning, the surreal, tall modern buildings. Here when the stop lights change a bell rings and then rings again, instead of having a yellow light. The boat is the Princess Marguerite. I found my luggage hadn't arrived in spite of the $2 on my bill, so a Mr Kennedy, under purser or chief steward, phoned and it arrived by taxi. The sweet air blew on the boat and the sun beat gently, and the mountains decorated the horizon, and the gulls with snow breasts, grey wings, and red-spotted lower bills hung against the green water and stood in rows upon the canvas stretched over the lower deck.

The Fraser River opening. Riptides. Islands with round rockiness, wild. A meal ticket of $1.00 for lunch. Mrs Watt congenial.

I found a good wise saying – 'Tis hard for an empty bag to stand upright.' Benjamin Franklin.

Rows of porter boys. Should I tip them? So many. So uncomfortable. Such heavy bags. Clam chowder for lunch and curried shrimps. The lovely skyline of Vancouver with its surreal, tall, modern buildings. The narrows. Then, in the sun, Victoria. Quiet, easy, leisurely. Gardens tumbled with flowers. Smell of petunias, greenswards. I suddenly understood England and was almost momentarily faithless to my wilderness. In the distance the Mountains (Olympics) looking, by being far away, huge and inaccessible.

Mrs Cowan says they say this is a place for the 'tired and the retired.' I distill the jubilee in the garden of Victoria.

The interviewer was a kindly middle-aged person and she and Mrs Watt chatted about this and that. (Next morning her article was good.) I was sent back to get a 'Fund' Book for Mrs Watt and there I encountered Rolly Parkin. He didn't know me but I said, 'Hullo!' He looked. I went up to him. I said, 'Aren't you Rolly Parkin?' 'Yes,' he said, but he was still perplexed. 'Don't you know me? I'm Betty Smart.' The tenseness in his face relaxed and flowed on naturally again.

We had tea in the lounge and crumpets, while a man with real feeling for it played a Mozart fantasia. Rolly said it wasn't Mozart. But it was. We asked. We wandered in the garden over the isolated squares of cement with the chasms between. The garden is good. It has shade. Shade adds mystery and atmosphere to a garden. Archways with thick shiny green leaves crawling over them making a cover edged the smooth green lawns, where a few used deckchairs were sometimes grouped together in a leisurely conversational way. The petunias and phlox were full of smell. We sat beside the fading rose garden. I talked and was excited.

In the lounge I said how can I *make* him interested, so he won't want to leave me? Then I let him talk. For hours and hours. About his trip. I listened sympathetic. In the garden I talked, so it was successful and I saw him more alert. Which was the thing that impressed him? He's only a *little* man. Not like Frank.[14] My lips were blue. We wandered down a path behind a high shiny ledge by the kitchen garden and saw dahlias as big as your head and as bright as the sun, yellow yellow, and mauve, and pink, and orange variegated, and asters, and pompoms neat, and a few mothy delphiniums, and we went into the earthy-smelling conservatory, but no flowers had smell, only the earth, a pungent, heavy, herby smell. Then we walked up and down behind on a shaded path, where horse chestnut trees, and arbutus, and a shady garden shielded us on one side, and on the other thick bushes and trees.

He hasn't read Proust and he didn't recognize George Herbert so of course I felt brilliant. Especially as he's a mental snob. He took my arm. I tactfully withdrew it several times by saying, 'Oh. What's that,' but each time he got it again with an even closer grasp. Finally he put his arm around me and his fingers crushed in my breast a little. Really professor. He got quite excited. All the while I got academic and delivered a harangue against Constance Holme. I felt so old, all passion spent, so undeceived, but patient with the enthusiastic blood of youth. Wise and serene, stimulated

by his youngness and ignorance and even lack of strategy. He walked
up and down more times than he should have and managed to call
me after the meeting to join Frank (for whom I suffered him) and
the Cassidys.

Excited and full I rushed up and had a bath and emerged beautiful
and magnanimous. But to save fifty cents Mrs Watt walked up town
for dinner and I with her, up the once-familiar-to-her but now not
clearly remembered street, to a restaurant she once knew. It was just
closing. Up in the sky was a clear cold gibbous moon. We crossed
the street to an almost empty cafe. There was a strawberry spot
on the table cloth. I ate a few abominable sweetbreads and some
tasteless canned mushrooms and a custard pie. We walked home.
You know our waddle. Mrs Watt bought a detective magazine and
The Weekly Times.

At home I lay covered and read Proust. I got sleepy and my
excitement subsided. My eyes got white and heavy. I lost enthusiasm.
Finally Rolly phoned. He came. In the car which met us at the cold,
moonlit corner, were Frank (adorable Frank) and the Cassidys. We
went to their house and had talk and fun. She is a little too willing
to be amused to be the best audience. Too cooperative. He was nice
but had to work. He retired with brief-case. Frank had an electric
razor which you plug into the wall. I demonstrated by shaving the
hair off Rolly's leg. 'A Modern Delilah,' said Frank. It was rather
awkward when I said I hated the people who took their Communism
like the Oxford Group. Silence. (Was *she* an Oxford Grouper?)[15] Her
social approach was rather adolescent, but she was very nice. He was
chock full of politics, absorbed by, obsessed by it as they all seem to
be who are. We saw the three men off.

Mrs Watt wanted me to go down and change a three cent paper.
I went down but hadn't the courage. 'Give it back to her and ask
her to send you up tomorrow's when it comes.' I *couldn't*. So I said
she wouldn't.

September 4: Victoria and the Butchart Gardens
This garden is so alive, so potential. I feel that if I turn my eyes
away from it to be enclosed in this book I shall miss something. It
is full of smell, and a damp, sharp, early autumn air, stimulating,
but not too cold. One of the trees, a grey one, with thin but definite
branches making a generous motion towards the sky, has dropped

all its yellow leaves in a circle on the grass. All except those on its third part, which are hanging, yellow drops, lit by the setting sun. The flower borders wind around in exciting curves. They have spots of vibrating red dahlias, and yellow flowers in little circular groups, and purple heartsease.

I feel hidden and secluded behind a grown hawthorn tree, loaded with dull red beady cherries, like a gypsy with too much ornament on. The path flowers are all cloud pink, and the grass is very green and short and smooth, and damp. There are roses behind, magnificently ruined, like a wonderful evening dress the morning after the party. The chairs are grouped in twos invitingly in romantic spots. Oh! it is a very potent garden, and yet not disturbing. It doesn't arouse desires it can't fulfill, as The Seigneury Club does. It doesn't cry out for material, for suitable occupants and occupations. It is quiet and generous. It says simply, here is a spot where you can rest and yet be full, quiet and yet rich. To be alone at the Seigneury Club is not right. It offers no help to the humiliated. Only the pretentious can go to it and enjoy its suitable setting, and enact their already-planned incidents. But anything might happen in this garden. It is only waiting for a chance to squander more and more of its wealth on you. It draws forth thoughts and meditations, and keeps them alive by its keen evening air. It has always in reserve something unexpected and colourful. And always it sends out flower scents like will o' the wisps, to ravish and enchant, and make your senses stumble after them in a vain attempt to understand their meaning.

To find utter quiet which is yet alive, I suppose is true happiness. And happiness that does not die. It is hard, in travels, to estimate the potency of a place. When a mind, teeming with half-followed ideas, finding no time to sort and digest, suddenly steps into a tranquil place, it makes that place which might have been only stagnant, seem alive. Would it always have the power to stimulate, even when the ripples caused by the former motion have subsided?

I never used to like gardens; I always saw the dead weeds thrust out of their rightful place. I loved woods and wild places and dead trees. But perhaps Wordsworth was right about the 'still sad music of humanity.' I used to think it was self-deceit on his part, physical laziness growing with the years, because his body could no longer make the physical effort to bound over the mountains like a roe (doe?)

or his mind the mental effort of imagination. Man is, without doubt, the defacer, the destroyer. But spending at least the last three years in trying to understand the enemy has almost seduced me to his side.

September 12: Victoria and to Seattle

Ate two apples in bed. Inefficient packing. Mrs Watt and the roley poley hold, both of us cross and tugging away. One of the cross straps pulled out with a snap. 'That was too careless of you Betty.' In a sprinkling rain I went to the Parliament Buildings with the big book *Middletown* by Robert and So and So Lynd,[16] covering it with my purse on my tummy to keep it dry, till everyone stared. A distinguished man with a stoop helped me find the right room and led me to it. He was one of those who put one finger behind an ear and their head a little on one side before asking a question of the porter. He was pleased at being helpful but would *never* have admitted or shown it. I was about to write Harry a note when he arrived and seemed pleased and amazed for this afternoon. I walked down to the docks. A whole flux of American sailors, swarms of them in their white hats and saucy jeering ways. The 'Streamlined ferry' all incredible like a toy, insubstantially silver and podgy. People all willing to direct and help. Buses and cars waiting to take people sight-seeing to the Butchart Gardens. A good lunch of scrambled egg and bacon sandwich and chocolate ice cream and coffee. Hair. Read and ate apples in the sun in my armchair by the window. But it began to get cold.

Tea with Harry Cassidy in the lounge. He deplored a certain Tory attitude in Victoria – politics, housing; he thinks I should go to a University: truths vs. facts (distinguish between truths, truisms, facts, platitudes, clichés, aphorisms). Suddenly I looked at his watch and it was one minute to 5:40. (I thought the boat left then.) My knees wobbled. I tore upstairs. My bags were gone. I tore vainly around. My room was empty and sunlit and full of wind. Incredibly empty.

Harry drove me to the boat. I forgot my gloves. I was in time. Mrs Watt was still in line. Harry went back for gloves and to look for lost Proust book. We had dinner. We were cross. Beautiful melting sky all in blue tones, soft fluffy blues, with only a few live touches of deep glowing pink. The Olympics and Mrs Watt's point. 'I never go near the house, you know, because that was the scene of all my husband's tragedy. I just couldn't.' Mrs Watt thought the tall boy

who delivered us off the Princess Marguerite was cheating us so I
overtipped him. Fat immigration officers, but helpful and friendly.
Customs man: 'Open your bags, sisters.' 'Got a bit of lunch in there,
sister?' Taxi through Seattle's crazy hilly streets, going up in tiers in
all directions, and hilly sidewalks everywhere you look and some tall
buildings and many bright lights. We gave our tickets and got one
receipt. Mrs Watt said, 'Do we only get one receipt?' 'Yes lady,' said
the benign fellow, 'if you lose her you're done for.'

They take such a human interest. Also the people are more colourful. A girl in a checked brown suit with a white hat, curly red hair,
red lips, well made up, red earrings, bobby socks, not good taste, not
smart, but gay, gay and colourful. The tall languorous negro porter,
when Mrs Watt complained about ordering one upper and one lower
and getting two lowers, said, 'Well Ah reckon yois ah lucky.' Mrs
Watt decided not to wash. We're both eating pears.

September 5: On the train

These night-and-all-day train rides remind me of Peter Fleming's
comment about the Trans-Siberia train – 'About the only thing we
all had in common was constipation.'

Between reading some nineteenth century critical essays and
typing and eating and trying to take an interest in the scenery,
and talking without enthusiasm to one or two old men, and taking compulsory exercise in the cold ten minute stops, there is no
awareness to make the day alive.

Lamb is a great relief after Wordsworth. Coleridge had a much
clearer brain than WW, who ranted. Lamb is so sane. Wordsworth
I had to read – Lamb is modern and human. Yet there was only
five years difference in their ages! The Englishman is reading *Inside
Europe*[17] and is going on the *Marinta*.

September 14: San Francisco

I was awakened in the small hours by the persistent unreasonable
porter and dressed in discomfort in my upper berth. I went to
the Women's place to brush my teeth and it was full of women
unbeautiful and shoulder-strappy.

We got to San Francisco about 7 AM and walked out in the
delicate morning sunlight onto the ferry. The white skyscraper
skyline was before us in the distance, and a great five mile long

orange bridge, in two parts, meeting on an island, and away off to the right, Berkeley, and more and more neat white patches of houses stretched and stretched. We sat at the very front of the ferry. The Englishman was there with a camera. Three of the vilest specimens of scum humanity came slouching to sit directly in front of us. Absolute pimps. One had a red nose with glasses on the end of them, a hat plumb on and a loose, vacant mouth. He yawned from time to time wide open, and fingered his face and genital organs. His finger nails were dirty and made any thoughts obscene. Beside him was another motheaten specimen who also had let go of his limbs and the muscles of his face, and picked at his flesh and stared at nothing; the third had one of those thin, obscene mustaches which are disgusting to look at, and black oily hair. All of them were meanly built, unaware, vacant, without joy in body and soul, only a letting-go and perverted self-indulgence. After the beautiful brown bodies in the field, is that what civilization has done to us?

We passed under the bridge and saw an orange barge. Away up a workman on the bridge was no bigger than a pinpoint. I had to indicate him several times before Mrs Watt saw him. We watched the flood of people off the ferry and finally located our bags. We took a taxi to the Women's City Club, 465 Post St, and were nicely welcomed. It is a most airy, pleasant place, done with good taste and restraint, the atmosphere unfussed and friendly. We had breakfast with Mrs Virginia Bunting's mother, Mrs MacCormac, whose husband is a professor at Berkeley. She wasn't important, but kind. I had live figs.

We went to the Canadian Pacific Railway and Mrs Watt brushed me aside. She wanted to present her letter. We waited hours and hours. I was furious and disgruntled. Then we went to the Matson line place and waited hours and hours and wasted vast energy in needless objections. When that was over in self-defence I left. Still mad. I walked up the street. A lot of the women wear black. I found Crockers Bank and went in and got the man to give me $150 without my letter of introduction. This restored me to a good humour. I asked a competent policeman the way to a bookstore and he was helpful and pleasant even though there was one in front of my eyes. I bought a lot of books and more at the White House and ten pair of stockings and *Inside Europe*.

I met Mrs Brodie and her daughter-in-law and her brother Ben

Harding upstairs at the tea-room on the fourth floor. They were friendly and accepted me at once. We had lunch. Then we went to see an exhibition of Gauguin pictures. They made me think that Americans are much more cultured and imaginative and enterprising than Canadians, and they have better taste and sensibilities too. There was also an exhibit of Persian and other rugs of great beauty, and I looked at the American painting which I do like. Minna Davis (?), Simpson (I forget their names, but bright and very alive and vibrating and full of vast energy.)

Then the pretty little Finn, who has huge elephantitis ankles, Ben (driving) and went all over San Francisco, up and down the scenic railway streets, some lined thickly with two three-ribbon threads for the cable cars, steep, and up and down in all directions. The sea stretches around and across are brick red buff coloured mountains, moulded like sand dunes in shadow, and brick red cliffs. We saw the island with the prison where Al Capone is. 'How romantic,' I said. 'Well, I don't think I'd call it romantic,' said Ben bitterly. It all seems prehistorically old, and the scene of some strange happening thousands of years ago. We saw the elegant buildings with the elaborate pink and white stucco fronts and the sloppy wooden backs, and an enormous swimming pool and the Golden Gate and the sun shining on the Pacific and droopy Eucalyptus trees and acacia bushes and far away up on a hill the clean white city below in little light squares for miles and miles. The people burn mostly oil so it is clear. Their houses are wood with stucco on the outside put on top of wire netting. We saw the longest single span bridge in course of construction, the towers eight hundred feet high, and parks with elk, and bison, and deer, and small artificial ponds, and more art galleries, and the Italian section, and Chinatown. The city, counting all the suburbs, is about one and a quarter million population.

September 19: The Pacific

I *adore* André Gide. There isn't even a dull or over-loaded sentence in the whole book – neither vagueness nor hammering. I *adore* him.

September 20

It is teatime, and all I have done all day is read André Gide. And I have finished *The Counterfeiters*. And, I think, by the avidity with which I read it, and by the fact that the *Critical Essays* are still unread, that, after all poetry and the abstract are not my only interest. But by poetry I mean something alive and kicking, the essence, the important core, so perhaps it proves nothing except that anything can be twisted round to the desired shape. Also poetry and the abstract must be personal. Proust is, after all, too long and undivided – place names for instance. Gide is alive in every sentence. He counterpoints and jumps but he always jumps at exactly the moment and to the exact spot you want to jump to. I was not tempted to look ahead or count the pages on my fingers. Golly, what a disjointed thinker I am. Absolutely inarticulate and puerile. I ought to have finished my logic course. I have written a page of disjointed meanderings and forgotten already the urgent point I had in front of my mind before I rushed to get out my book and write it down in time. I'll go and have tea, and when the day, and Gide, have settled down to calm and serenity, I'll take this matter in hand. Also, I'd like to go into the reality of the Frampton situation:[18] whether in reality I was deeply affected by it, perhaps hurt; whether because I really felt intensely then and no longer do; I want to keep up at least the name of my feeling, with a sort of obstinate faithfulness, or a stupid unconscious clinging to youth and youthful passions which it is impossible I could ever feel again. For I *know* him better. I see his thinness and red hands and 'respectability' and mistaken sense of duty, and words like 'juice,' his tea, and umbrella, and use of 'one' – the colourless slang of his era and upbringing. But even that I can't write without a sense of guilt. It's his sense of delicacy, his sensibility and understanding that made me admire him – and are in fact what I always love wherever I find them.

Whenever I have a thought and form it into clear and sensible words and paragraphs I no sooner start to write than I forget what it was and begin wandering and mumbling inanities.

Undoubtedly I had better go to tea.

The sea is blue blue, rich, like a pot of paint.

II

NEW ZEALAND AND AUSTRALIA
September, 1936–January, 1937

September 21: Oahu, Honolulu

The smell of flowers. The intangible, penetrating fragrance. Alegretto morning sunlight. Excitement over the ship. Anticipation. Then the perfume, the sublime, subtle, suggestiveness of flower perfume, and passengers wearing garlands – leis – around their necks, men, women and children, piled high with exquisite live flowers, red carnation ones, hydrangeas, ginger flower, etc. The volcanic shape of Oahu, and the hard green hills. Palms stooping sideways by the water. Manly St Denis slipped four leis over my head, and said sad farewells about ten times.

Waiting for something to happen. Eventual arrival of uninspiring woman. Drive through streets. So many Japanese, also Chinese, Philipino, a few left of the Hawaiians. Palms, palms everywhere, red poinciana trees, hibiscus of every colour, flamboyant mauve blue. Bananas, sausages, royal palm, date palm, sottle palm, breadfruit. Real tropics, white suits, flowers flowers flowers. YMCA Pan-Pacific Union lunch. Speeches. (Miss Zimmerman and Mrs Van Denburgh).

Hot – a boiling sun. A wind. Interviews. Mrs Herrendean, so nice and Mrs Eleanor Wilson. Waikiki Beach and the warm Pacific. Sense of the south. The blue blue light water, red earth, coral sand, Mali Height where the Congress freed the defeated. Green, dark, and rich, and hard. The island exports pineapple (had some – delicious – at Mrs Herrendean) and sugar cane. One hundred and fifty thousand population. Tolerance and free and unqualified mixing of all the diverse races. O to stay in this heavenly spot.

September 24: Past the Equator

I was going to go out behind by the swimming pool and sit in the sun with a large bottle of wine mix, but Mrs Watt telephoned disgruntled and said if I were going to do it I would just have to do it (speeches to prepare for NZ) and that the Diary wasn't ready, etc. So I went up, be-bathing suited, and interviewed her and we went onto B deck and sat in strange chairs and she gave me a lecture, and I came around and agreed with her and said I would.

The lady who owned the chair came along and I said, 'I hope I haven't got olive oil on your chair,' and she looked at me furious and gave me a look to kill. I went out behind and tried to write but it was blowing, so I dressed and wrote in the writing room. Then I typed and read after lunch till 4:15. Then I played with Mr Farquarson. He played badly and we lost. Flying fish pointed out the line of the equator. Intense heat. I eat mostly watermelon and delicious pineapple and sherbets, occasionally vegetables and eggs and orange juice. Bran and figs for breakfast.

After dinner (green taffeta) talk with Breeze Gale (who has been married and divorced twice to the same girl) and told me the story of Belcher Moule of Melbourne University who belched so much that he entered into an inter-college competition and won that by belching God Save the King and became champion, but something went wrong with him and he couldn't stop belching and he wasted away. He is thirty-nine, looks younger, and high praise is to be 'a good son.' He has lived ten years in USA but is Australian. Danced with Stewart Main and Myer and an oniony little fat man who looks like a gargoyle squatting on his victim when he dances with a thin girl. 'A frog he would a-wooing go.' He is so fat, and fleshy. But the smell is overpowering. Stewart and I discussed Gide. He says it's not true. People aren't like that. They'd like to be bad but they aren't. He lived all over the place at the YMCA and knew. He could speak for men. I argued.

After it was all over we were sitting in the drink room about to go to bed when the Boy[1] said almost with a plea, 'I'd like to talk to you. You aren't going to go to bed?' So I said, 'I'll walk around deck with you.' So we went out onto the front and the warm strong tropical wind blew and the moon, sinking low, was yellow and sometimes ruddy in grey red-tipped clouds. And we were truthful and he has a beautiful smile. We moved to the other side and my hair blew straight and my dress kept down better, and I felt full of elation and happiness, and full, and warm towards the dark boy.

September 25: Boat

Once from below he[2] looked so like Donald that I was aghast. He was cheaper and less mysterious today, but undoubtedly physically attractive to me. He can cause me violent overpowering moods and tears or utter happiness in a minute. What a fire, this sex! Never before have I fallen for a pair of velvet eyes and dark untidy hair and white teeth. Sometimes he's like Eddie. He frowns a bit and tries to keep his mouth stern.

Is this business worth its trouble? Here I am sulking in my cabin for no apparent reason. What a destructive force until satisfied! What a consuming monster! Its thoroughness, insidiousness and subtlety astound me every time I suddenly see my puppet-like obedience to it.

I'd like to be richer, fuller, of more use to other people. A drink with a steward here, an old lady's life story there, a shy youth, a sophisticated man, the gay young things. Men manage it. Why can't I? All sorts of adventures other people get by their own easy efforts. Why do I fail to enjoy the fit fruits of the herd?

September 26: Pago-Pago, Samoa

Went ashore with Breeze Gale and Mrs Watt to the lovely island with the steep curious green mountains and the pale, surf-washed, palm-edged beaches, up a road to the native market, where there was a long row of natives, some with umbrellas over their heads, and their legs intricately crossed, selling lovely gay baskets, luncheon mats, skirts, beads, wooden bowls on legs, models of their special sort of boats, etc. It is a very small place, which reveals its charm and atmosphere at once. It was a hot day, and the South Sea sun was very strong. The natives were also selling gay table cloths and cloth of hard material dyed in primitive patterns.

October 1: Past Suva, Fiji and The Last Day in the Boat

It began well because of the anticipation of approaching liberty – where, after all, can you go on a ship? You can't even get to the sea all around you – and ended like hell with a sick pacing on the rear deck under a weakly moon.

After lunch I joined Velvet Eyes and Mr Carney for coffee and we had a gay and independent time. Afterwards, still triumphant, I did a few things for Mrs Watt and again joined Velvet Eyes. We walked on deck, but then his old ploy came out. 'I'm going down to have a sleep.' I didn't like that. It was so defeatist. So I started to pack, disgruntled. But then I went and had my hair done and put a red bow in my hair and talked to Mr B. Jolly, the gargoyle, and wrote postcards, and drank tea alone, and became uncomfortably contrary and temperamental. Velvet Eyes was sitting with the two Lawry girls, Darcy and Judith and their nice grandmother.

Finally I went down and pressed my grey organdy dress and bathed and looked with despair at my limitless packing, and put on unusual artificial things like mascara and cheek rouge and diamonds and whisked down to dinner more contrary and choppy than ever in the world.

It was a farewell dinner and solemn people sat in silly and ugly hats. I clutched my balloon and the American Flag of Independence and ate a little. But not much. I felt like rebelling and leaving the table. I put on a red, white, and blue striped dunce cap. Mrs Watt was gay and sympathetic to my outrageous mood. After dinner we saw the movie *Mr. Deeds Goes to Town* with Gary Cooper and Jean Arthur and it restored a bit of sanity. I stood resigned never again to have the wayward desires of youth and flesh, and listened while Mrs Watt embarrassed me by asking a large Mr Lowry of New Zealand how much to tip. *I* knew perfectly well.

Then I went and packed Mrs Watt's dresses and sang holy songs in a loud piercing voice. Then I went to my own room but still despaired of my own packing so repaired my face and smell and went up to Mrs Watt's room again. At first I was impatient, and wanted to leave before she'd finished telling what I already knew but then I relented and helped her more than I need have and packed for her and kissed her goodnight and went upstairs with my balloon and flag, sober, sad, undesirous, and independent. I ended in the dance room, saw no one I knew so pushed back the heavy door and stepped out on deck. It was windy and there was an almost full moon. I walked a few steps when Mr Morton, the spurious slick, came after me and said I was a funny child, etc. Well, finally we danced, I in control and it was pleasant because it was easy, and because I knew exactly how to deal with him. I joined his table with two undesirable pseudo-men-of-the-world. Velvet Eyes was with the Lawrys at the next table. I saw his twitch. I wasn't sitting long there before they all disappeared to the Smoke room, and then I got into a conversation with Morton when Velvet Eyes came up and asked me to dance and I did and I must say it was good and I enjoyed his soft cheek. He joined us.

I danced with Morton once more, and then talked so exclusively to VE that when I got up to dance again with him, the Mortons (Mrs too – rather sexy but sensible) left for bed. So Velvet Eyes enfolded me in a soft embrace and we danced to old tunes like 'Dinah' and 'Darktown Strutters' Ball.' But he began to get difficult and not want to dance but to leave and spoil it all. So I went out on deck with him and we walked round to the back of the boat. But I began to freeze with the cold wind so we went in, but then VE got more morose and said, 'I'm going to bed,' and I like a fool told him not to instead of making him not by subtle means and we talked or rather he bawled me out (not practical, no feet on the earth, no girl friends, all abstract and parables, mere talk). What would be the use? I wasn't sure I want to anyway.

I really am forced to the opinion that all Australians are suffering from an inferiority complex which vents itself in aggressiveness, rudeness, or cruelty.

On the stairs he gave me a lecture on dignity and not being beaten, or hiding my head. (This reminded me of John and I took it like a fool.) Then, finally, after several false starts, he said 'Goodnight, Betty,' and went, leaving me sad, annoyed, and unsatisfied. So I cried a bit and then went over the ship. I froze, then went to my cabin but when I saw the untidiness and piles of unpacked things, I was full of despair again and cried, and lest I wake Judith put on my fur coat and went up on top and got cooled off by the wind and the cold gibbous moon and excited racing clouds. This worked, sobered and sane, it induced me to realize that without self-deceit, all Hall said was not true and that it was some defect in him that made him say some of these things. Surely, it isn't necessary to decide at once whether you are going to sleep with a man or avoid him altogether, the minute you see him, to be practical? I went down again but still the rebellious waves chopped and changed painfully in my insides, so I went up on the short rear deck behind the deserted dance pavilion and paced up and down beneath a misty tear sick moon till I could stagger off to bed. I left everything lying where it lay and asked central to call me at 5 AM. It was 3 by then.

Still in a mist, still perceptions dull and New Zealand unreal. Still disgruntlement on account of Velvet Eyes and my mismanagement of him.

My complexion has suddenly gone very bad.

Soft air, sunshine.

October 4: Auckland

I simply couldn't make life mean anything all day – life or work. Nothing seemed new or exciting or worth the effort. But I found Hemingway good,[3] and sane and his diary-style encouraging and easy to read, which is a sign of good writing. Hurray for Hemingway! The pall of prejudice is raised in his favour. I will try *Farewell to Arms* again.

Ate apples, and then oranges and NZ grapefruits when Mrs Watt returned from her drive and tea which I refused. She had strange flowers, one like a purple living starfish, and turquoise drops on a stem.

The nice, friendly, modest, intelligent University girls revived me. They had something Foster-Wilsonish about them. And I felt like an uncle as I sat and answered their questions and asked them with the air of an expert. But I must say my strength and sanity have not yet returned, nor have I found an adequate answer for Velvet Eyes.

New Zealand is not yet a reality, but the people have taken on a definite outline in my mind. They are friendly, hospitable, and kind. Not suspicious, not aggressive, not complex. Healthy, robust. A certain type of English with a vigorous pioneer streak. O! I like them.

Think of England, or, think of your various groups of friends, and then think of each type immigrating to a land of their own and multiplying and intensifying their particular characteristics. Australians – New Zealanders, bring this thought into a marvel. Do you see? Each, perhaps exiled for a disagreeable trait, finding justification for it by finding support in similar fellows. We stand together. They can't make us mad. We're US.

October 8: Auckland to Whanganui, New Zealand at last!

Arose to business. Satisfaction of getting everything into bags, at last tidy. Lovely soft sunny day. John with ACWW[4] books. Train. Slow with black shiny seats. On my side only me – double on the other. Quadruple Mrs Watt. Read *Farewell to Arms*. It's winning. It's all right. His diary style is stimulating. Through the greenest country in the world, pastoral green, smooth hills, gorse gullys, bald olive hills, palms and fern trees, mud flats, curious rare colours such as olive green, gold, dull yellow, grey, coffee-coloured streams, dark shiny green of non-deciduous trees. Delicate spring green of willows. 'It doesn't hang together.' Cows and sheep. Then wide green country, hillier, when the water again appeared it was pale pastel blue.

Unlike anything I have ever known. Arum lilies growing in voluptuous virginity on the dirty hill of a railway track.

Whangari. Ladies to meet us. My hostess is Mrs Armstrong (her sisters-in-law are Mrs Wilson and Mrs Clarke).

We had a slight dinner. There are steep abrupt hills around – some bare, some covered with thick growth. Japanese cherries in pink blossom and yellow bushes – and trees completely in red flower. At the back private part of a tea shop the Mayor – Mr Jones met us, and the Deputy Mayor, Mr Worrish. The Mayor is half Irish and half Welsh and I met him at the door and got talking and when I was sitting with Mrs Armstrong and Wilson someone came over and said he would like me to sit with him. So I did and we talked politics and Irish and he is going to give me a letter to the Prime Minister. He had dirty squirrel teeth. The other fellow was small and shrewd. Both sweet and wise. The speech of Mayor, though, was rambling and repetitive.

Afterwards we came home here, through hills and greenery, a steep hill and a view of sand-shadow hills, buff and lime where the gum trees used to be, now bare with only a few green oasis. Birds singing. Small grass daisies yellowed the vast lush green.

October 9: Whanganui to Dargaville

Drive to Dargaville. Lovely sunny day. I found out what the untidy hills we saw yesterday from the daisy-studded hill were like: a relief map, round dome hills, or sharp cornered ones. Trees like a nigger's curly hair over the tops of hills and mountains. Wild yellow lupins. Shiny open trees. Tufts of rata parasite on old great dead trees. Palms. Muddy streams. Short brambles, buttercups.

Fell in a stream and climbed a Hokai tree barefoot. Was cold afterwards. Nearly all the yellow blossoms had fallen off. The lady laughed and laughed. I had fun till Mrs Watt didn't like it. However it blew over. The muddy rivers lined with fresh green weeping willows planted by the early missionaries in memory of home and spreading all over NZ. The country grew wilder somehow, and more remote, but still very fertile.

About 6 we reached Dargaville. A town of two thousand with a wide deserted street and a sense of outlying parts and maybe adventure. Mrs Watt went to bed. We are at the hotel. I bathed, took off my sopping things, and went to a movie with Jay Grump.

Finished *Farewell to Arms* (reminded me of Charlie). Mrs Wilson is the landlady. She is unhealthy and rather sinister.

October 11: Dargaville and down the river

I want to describe this muddy river which Mrs Watt says reminds her of the Nile, which she has never seen. Great tufts of green and white elephant grass grow along the edges. The horizon on the left is bald wavy hills, green-brown, dead looking. A little farther back are some higher hills, dark, deep blue, sharp slopes. But the shapes of these hills are untidy, without purpose. Some are low and smooth. Some are sharp and jagged. The water is a rich coffee brown. Weird-shaped small cabbage palms rise out of the great tufts of grass, with their green puffs of palms. They are a stunted sort of palm – they look like a case of arrested development.

Now we come to a patch of jungly wood with a white bird flying through it. I have specially noticed birds and birdsong since we got to NZ, yet Mrs Watt keeps saying, 'Isn't it strange, Betty, how few birds we've seen since we left Canada?'

The bit of wood has tall piney trees, lower cabbage palms, all with their feet in great clumps of elephant grass growing out of the mud.

On the left some new bare, shadow-marked hills and what looks like a great head of rock.

On the right an expanse of rich green with a herd of cattle feeding.

On the posts of derelict wharves sit gulls, one on each post, motionless. Black-backed gulls and small black-wing-tipped gulls.

I went downstairs and talked to three Maoris. One was a rather pretty woman. She asked me questions. The other was telling her about how he could get drink, and how drunk he had been. The third was the guitar player, sitting on the rails strumming away and occasionally singing. He told me it was a Spanish guitar. It had 'made in Italy' carved on it in black in small letters.

While I was down there I saw Mrs Watt come to the edge of the rail up above and throw something red into the river. She had her spotted green chiffon bandana around her head. I went up. Mrs Watt said, 'Well, I've made my oration to the River-lord. I threw my flowers overboard. We'll be all right for this trip.' She keeps trying to sing 'Old Man River.' ('I didn't realize till I saw that movie how ugly Paul Robeson is. I think he's the ugliest man I've ever seen.') We stopped at a grass-grown wharf to pick up a thin young middle-aged woman. She kissed a farmer with a big droopy mustache and another middle-aged woman. There were two little girls. The older woman looked at me and at once whispered to the other woman who turned around to look at me. When she had got on board the other woman took the man by the arm and I heard her say, 'See that lady there? That's Miss Smart.' So I waved and said to Mrs Watt who was behind, 'That lady's one of your institute women,' and she was waving anyway. They waved excitedly and the woman made the children wave and they waved with both hands and the lady brought a handkerchief and waved and waved. She was very excited. Mrs Watt was pleased.

October 15: Hamilton

Think about dignity and pride wherein they are good and proper, and wherein they ought to be abandoned to the bigger attribute, generosity. But *anyway*, never be coy, coquettish, or flirtatious in a physical way. Never egg a man on to be physical. If he wants to leave, say goodbye. This has always been a principle yet why have I abandoned it at times? Anyway, it defeats its own end. From now on I must be *mental* until I find myself a proper mate. However, may that be soon!

Because my days of virgin *hauteur* are at an end, even as my youth is at an end – the days of Graham when I could scorn what I thought was his meek self-deception. Now I am grateful for a little kindly feeling. That's just my mistake. I ought to be haughty again, self-sufficient, and independent as I was, listening *only* to the inward voices.

October 16: Hamilton to Matamata to Rotorua

Grand Hotel, Rotorua. How I hate sightseeing and admiring undigested facts and never having time to meditate and dream! 'What is this life?'

I've been looking at one of those Round the World prospectus pamphlets – it's vulgar and disgusting and sounds interminably dull. Dull, dull, dull, sightseeing, dutifully, never any time to breathe, to live, to enjoy, to revolt, to be vulgar, to philosophize, to digest, to be flippant, to be irrelevant, to feel, to know, to understand.

I hate facts.

And I'm bored with New Zealand.

Yes I am.

So there!

Wrote a million letters.

I'm lonely for some gaiety.

Some real talk, some genuine stimulation. O for a sophisticated man! An understanding woman! O for Russel! Dear admirable Russel! And Charlie! And Bobbie! And Eddie! Russel and Eddie and Charlie – that would be enough. Tonic for anything.

Jean Batten[5] has arrived in Auckland. We heard her on the radio as we arrived. Everybody was listening, especially the men. She is a lovely girl and sounds capable.

October 17: Rotorua Grand Hotel

'And take more exercise' – as John used to say. Well I did, at Mrs Watt's suggestion (I always forget) and it worked. I walked for miles and it rained in my face. (I still can't understand why John won't allow the inspiration of nature – facing wind and rain – it's reasonable as well as exhilarating.)

Going I was leaden-eyed, stumpy-footed, joyless, too low for despair, with a knowledge that all life is boring, repetitive, known, not worth having. Coming back I knew it was rich, I was full of curiosity. I sang songs. I even felt grateful and saw much beauty and colour in the hills that had only seemed indigestible sightseeing sights before. And I began to understand how, if I stood still for a while and listened and felt New Zealand, itself, the country, would come and permeate me, and I could love it, and start climbing hills again.

So my cheeks became rosy and I decided to go to the party at a Womans' Club for Mrs Watt. It was a small, stiff room and the chairwoman was nervous, a lady with a cracked voice sang – the kind you dare not catch a friend's eye when she's singing for fear you explode, and a couple of people played and so did I, and Mrs Watt gave a talk about how women should be more in public affairs, and a nice girl recited two poems quite well, one by Joyce Kilmer on a deserted house, and there was coffee and cakes and they gave me lilacs and the girl drove us home in an incredibly small car and I bought fruit for Mrs Watt in a store from a Maori half-breed with bad teeth.

Today I swam in the blue bath. It is hot and smooth and smells of sulphur. The whole town, even now in bed, smells of sulphur.

I saw the steam seeping out of the earth and the mud boiling and spluttering and the steam in long streams, and around this open intestine of the earth, Maori huts in a village clustered together. They use the natural heat for cooking. A little indecent this staring at nature's accident, the rude bowels of the earth on display. I thought – all these footpaths over the area, made by sightseers and tourists and curious men, are the scribblings on the side of the wall, as in an outhouse. One bowl of mud made a gurgle like digestion noises, belching and rolling inwardly.

Hills are all about Rotorua, green and rusty brown, sharply con-trasted – cultivated and wild Ti-tree or just bare tangle of fern and bracken. Some of the hills are covered with bush and woods. Gorse, and more broom is in blossom all along the way.

But I have been bored with Rotorua. Only the exercise saved me from death or worse than death – floppiness. When I am bored I am full of despair and hopelessness – 'for if the salt has lost its savour' – O God, but the salt must *not* lose its savour!

They travel from Rotorua to Tauranga, Whakatane, Waimana, Opotiki and Omatua.

October 26: On a Sheep Station, Omatua, Rissington, from Rissington in the rain to Napier and back

Mrs Watt has been saying everything lately as though she were scolding someone. I heard her through the wall telling Mrs Hutchinson how I *promised* to do it etc. My feebly rising morning spirits fell.

I tried to avoid it but had to go in. I yes-yessed everything and then went with Mr Hutchinson to the sheep barns. Sigurd had five sheep in a pen at a little house. He was going to cut the throat of one. Mr H showed me the various and many sheep yards with their many little gates to sort out the sheep, and the narrow runways between;

and he showed me the Dip where the poor animals are pushed right under the disinfectant water to get rid of lice and ticks and they have to swim the whole length of six feet or so, and they even push their heads under. They hate it. And he showed me the sheep-shearing place, where large comb-like razors are machine operated by the shepherd, and where huge sacks hold twice their size because the wool is pressed down with a great weight, and where they sort the whole – some are first class and some are second class.

Five dogs were roaming around. Sigurd came and explained the shearing machine. When we got back to his slaughter shed, the body of the sheep was hung up and skinned, and the bloody head was sitting on the shelf, and the little yard was full of watery blood.

October 29: Napier – Dannevirke – Pahiatua

On awakening: this terrible problem of matrimony! I don't want to get married any more. I dreamt I was married to John. First of all we were all at church singing hymns. Peggy and Lady Pentland behind. John was very sweet and helpful. But then I had to make an enormous bed for Lady Pentland and she didn't like the way I was making it. It had piles and piles of extra blankets and things for padding. I was trying terribly hard, but I couldn't please her. John was somewhere in the background, sympathetic but unable to do more.

How can I possibly marry and sign away my life?

If I married John wouldn't Charles disturb my life? And what if I married Charlie? I suppose it's too late to marry Frampton. Then there are always the velvet eyes of the world. I couldn't consider anyone else. O what about Gilbert? Yes. He's another symbol. Men, careers, one excludes all others for ever. Where is an occupation that embraces all things? And where a *man*?

October 31: Pahiatua

Why do they do it? Why do they drink till they are ugly and unalive? I can see no point at all, no meaning to these hard-faced women, shoulder-strappy, dumpy-figured, shrill-voiced. Even in debauchery and the most abandoned orgies there can be grace, and an even lovable voluptuousness. Why do they need to pound, hard, hard, hard, and force their drunkenness in shrill grating voices?

And the men, greasy and unaware. Ready to maul if you

approach. Their fun is 'a spot' and a few promiscuous unlovely sexual exchanges. But even in these they have no imagination. I saw not one appetizing woman, coarse skin, shapeless figures, fat hips, untouchable hair, crinkled or unnaturally waved. There was one little girl of seventeen who was pretty and still unspoilt. What breeds these unnatural women with no sense of delight? What is their purpose, where may I find the meaning they must contain, the lesson, the cause and effect? They had no grace. They couldn't even dance. The girl at the piano thumped stolidly on, hitting and missing without caring, loud dissonant and unrhythmic.

O! and all the while the large round vibrating moon was out, and the wind was racing through the poplar trees and up and around the dark night-purple hills. And the small river in the valley was moonlit and shining and the little rabbits were skipping across. ('Hard, hard on the earth the machines are rolling')[6]

I went with Dr Paterson to Woodville. He was going to see a woman to see if she was crazy enough to be sent to an institution. She said she had an overpowering urge to 'satisfy herself' on an animal, and she thought this was a dreadful wicked sin, as she had read in the bible, and she was terrified that she would give in to it, as she lived on a farm among animals, and was afraid she couldn't control herself any more. She wanted to be sent away. She couldn't work on the farm any more. She lived in constant dread.

I waited for him while he went with Dr Mules to see her. Dr Mules' daughter Margaret entertained me. She was a very nice girl. She had worked in Wellington in a dental clinic. She had rosy cheeks. Her mother just died. A friend of hers from Wellington came in also. She was nice too, a friend of the Annette Chadwick (Strickland) who was in the play in Napier. She told me her story and more about the 'society' of NZ. They were both friendly and had humour and I said to myself, 'I love New Zealanders.'

Driving over a storm came up on one side over the mountains and made the fields on the other side vibrant green and the hills dark with purple shadows and patches of frantic sunlight.

November 1: Pahiatua

Mrs Watt talked to the Dr about her husband. He was only forty when he died. At twenty-seven he put up a brave fight for disinfecting

Chinamen. The CPR was against him and he was not sure that the government was with him. He held up a whole ship while he disinfected them all. There was a great row. He consulted Mrs Watt and said it might mean he'd lose his job, but they both agreed they must do what they thought right. Another time he knew that one Chinaman out of eight hundred had gone by twice. So he found out that one had died of smallpox and been thrown overboard.

I began to understand at last what has puzzled me so long about Mrs Watt – her rather embitteredness. The shock she got about herself when she was widowed was too much. She must have been through some bitter and terrible things – all the same, there is that weakness in her that made disappointment make her 'bittah' instead of 'bettah.'

I do wish, I do hope I will understand her better, I will find out everything in truth and completeness. Otherwise I am a poor selfish unobservant creature, not fit for my opportunities.

How can I expect to make a Hamlet when I can't even analyse a Watt?

There was a plot against Alfred Watt to bring discredit to him, and he had just cleared himself and then died. The worry of it was too much, he got neurasthenia and died. 'A young and brilliant man only forty years old.'

From Pahiatuta they travel to Palmerston North, Taihape, Martin, Wanganui and Hawera

November 6: Hawera to New Plymouth

Stuffed in a car on a lovely sunny day. I behind with a silent nonentity of a woman and piles of luggage. My stocking begat a ladder which waxed long and irrevocable. Mrs McAsey drove. Then we saw beautiful Mount Egmont with snow on its top. The unsnowed parts streaked up towards the top. I tried to take a picture of a twisted tree black against it but it wouldn't work. We drove around till the mountain was behind us. Lovely entrance to New Plymouth with batches of treeferns and gardens. Mrs Watt's eye was very red and troubling her so we drove straight to a Doctor's which we found after some difficulty. The Doctor was called Doctor Brewster. His wife met us. She was a nice woman, a 'lady,' nicely dressed in a wool suit, grey hair, poise and a friendly manner. There were rows of good books, and nice etchings and prints on the walls, pretty bowls for flowers, and furniture that you dared look at.

The Dr was small, looked very young, with consumptive features; he had darting, sudden movements, a slim build, and a 'bright' manner. Mrs Watt chaffed him. He had marvellous apparatus. She said all Doctors experimented on her. She told him she bet he was trying out his new apparatus on her. He wouldn't admit it, but entered into our spirit of playfulness. He let me look through the magnifier at Mrs Watt's eye. It was like a bunch of pale blue and pink quivering flowers, the centre of a daisy. 'See how it reacts to light,' he said.

He followed us to the gate. He had been at Vienna. They both travelled a lot and had money. There was a Durer (reproduction) and a Medici Botticelli. There was a lovely red-blossoming (completely red) Maunica in the garden. 'Yes, I've been looking at it all the time,' said Mrs Watt. They were a relief to us after our other sort of people. We relaxed and Mrs Watt revived. We had lunch in some rooms by the woman's club. Mrs Smith is huge and disgusting. The other Mrs Smith is petty and tiresome, too fond of being 'kind,' but not as bad as the others, just misdirected. At lunch Mrs Watt was gay and quoted a bit of poetry light-heartedly. The ladies were relieved.

The meeting was a big one. I decided to stay at the back behind. She spoke well and amused them by joking about the MP for the district who was there. The Mayor was there too. An oily Mr Stainton sat with me for a while. I didn't like him. A professional 'kind' man. A nice woman from Glasgow, the assistant secretary, helped me with the orders. They gave me a corsage of pink roses anyway. Eventually I got home.

At the meeting Mrs Watt's eye began to get terribly painful and she sat at a table with her forehead in her hands while distracted ladies hovered around. I remembered what she had said about people having bad breath and breathing in her face. She hates people to touch her or get too near her (except the rare few she loves – she loves Mummy to touch her.) She went off again to the Dr.

Rather cold night, and unhappy dreams. I dreamt Helen was big with Charlie's child. She said she wasn't sure whether it was Charlie's or Terry's. Then she said, 'Which do you think I had better marry, Charlie, or Terry, or Tom?'

They make stops at New Plymouth, Palmerston North, Wellington, Blenheim,
Nelson, Westport, Greymouth, Dorfield and Christchurch; there are meetings
and socializing at each stop.

November 24: At Riccarton House, Christchurch

Whitebait for breakfast – delicious, melting, small slippery and
white from head to toe – all but minute eye.

Sydney Thompson[7] called for me. He has a little pointed beard.
When I came down he was walking over the lovely grounds with
old Mrs Deans. Enormous roses as big as a baby's head. A pale,
sixty-year-old (or more) lime tree. Oh many others and a sunny
morning and the bush around and the garden. Miss Winter sullenly
snipping roses for the house.

We went to Sydney Thompson's studio. Bill came too in his own
car. Sydney Thompson showed us his Brittany chests and bedside
religious figures, and a Maori feather and flox cape, and Maori baler
for boats. He told us how he got it. They wouldn't do one for money or
sell one, but he said he would paint their pictures in exchange. They
agreed and he gave them their pictures and told them to send the
things in three years, for those capes, etc. take a long time to make.
He went away and forgot about it, but sure enough three years later
the things arrived. He said some men had been up among the Maoris
promising to take their pictures, taking ten shillings collected from
them and then never doing anything about it. This is the vilest sort
of thing.

November 27: Christchurch to Orari to Queen's Hotel, Oamaru

Pastoral country. More colourful because of the wheat etc. and
fields. Broom in blossom galore.

Finished *Polynesian Mythology*. Rich and unexpected – but, of
course, choked with too many names, as a fish with too many
bones. Genealogy as in the Bible.

Four ladies met us and had lunch with us. Mrs Watt is very tired.
The county Council was having a lunch. One of them threw a cherry
stone at me. Afterwards the Press came and talked to us. Afterwards,
a small, neat reporter interviewed Mrs Watt and then I interviewed
him. He says New Zealanders always want to be compared with
something – 'How does NZ compare with . . . in . . .' Different news
value in NZ and Australia.

Drive to a beach. Beautiful but unsafe. Picnic behind a hut by the river near where it meets the sea. I walked barefoot along the shore on the pebbles and sang and was happy – O that sudden jumping to be a wave, or wind – the sudden overjoyful 'oneness' which is all strength and enough.

Change to red evening dress for dinner. Meeting in a Churchy hall. I sat on platform. So did the Committee, The Mayor, Mayoress, Girls' High School Representative, Women's City Club Representative, Women's Division of the Farmers' Union Representative, and they all welcomed Mrs Watt who spoke on 'Women in Agriculture' with facts and notes. I played. A lady sang and two ladies duetted. Reception with tea, coffee and cakes at the hotel.

At the meeting the fat Clifford Scott *Times* reporter. Jovial large and red.

Talked to two shy young girls.

Then, when they all left, I played everything on a lovely piano and it sounded well – oh yes really well – and I thought perhaps when I get married I shall take from Katharine Goodson again and write a play in earnest. Again. A lady came in and listened. I didn't stop till 12.

When I was playing at the meeting tonight I had a panic because I realized that the thing was out of my power. *I* don't know what the notes are, or what I should play next, my hands do it all – when I think about it I get paralysed and my hands stop and I stop.

There has to be a flowing and confidence in my well-trained hands. They will do the trick if I only believe.

They travel from Oamaru to Shag Valley, Dunedin, Duvergargil, and back to Dunedin. There are meetings and socializing at each stop.

December 7: Practically the End (of NZ) – Wellington to the SS Awatea

Woke looking like Mickey Mouse. Tickets. The stupid man in Cooks with the pink face and flappy ears, slow, indifferent, and exasperating. Shopping. Soft sun but hat-proof wind. Lunch with Mrs Deans and Mrs Watt. The last gathering. Speeches. Mrs Watt said, 'If it hadn't been for Miss Smart – etc.' Mrs Paterson said nice things about me. I wore my Mary Stuart hat. Mrs Watt says she hates it. Photographed in rows. Giggling women.

O I am old and tired.

More interminable Cooks. Packing. Exhausted. Poor service.

Today I surprised a maid in my room tampering with my perfume. She jumped and began to make excuses and dust furiously. Nice taxi driver. So human.

To the *Awatea* – a gay lively ship, well coloured simply and nicely. Really pleasant. I am alone. A deputation of ladies for Mrs Watt.

The trouble about NZ is that it has no imagination. Even the country, the wild country, doesn't stir you to dream and create, to worship and lean out towards. Rolls and rolls of hills with straight-forward histories, tragedies, and so on, not worth repeating, like the Reports on the 'Woman's Page' of a newspaper.

They say there are no fairies here.

That's what I mean.

The country didn't restore me as Canadian woods do. I admired it from a sense of duty, not from a private or passionate love. I'm afraid New Zealand's dull.

O yes, I know all about the early whalers, and explorers, and missionaries and settlers, the fights, the massacres, the heroism, but that's superimposed or at least not open to the naked eye. That lies in the history books, not in the country.

December 12: Australia! (Sydney) Velvet Eyes Again!

A beautiful sunny day. Early we awoke, with the Heads in sight. I put on my black and white printed silk and stood out in front and watched us sail up into the harbour. The bridge was beautiful. I loved Sydney the minute I saw its clean, white, modern vast expanse. The King's (Edward VIII) broadcast came through while I stood there but they said the static was very bad and they only heard indistinctly.[8]

As Mrs Watt and I were on the gangplank's top, who should meet us but Breezy Gale. I adored him for this. We were photographed, interviewed, and canvassed. Mrs Fairfax met us and a fat man sent to get us through the customs. Much searching for lost suitcases.

To the Macquarrie Club, 15 Casteleagh St. Nice and neat.

I like Mrs Fairfax. She has an abrupt manner, but calls you darling. I like her. Hair done rather well at M. de Augustus and toes red-nailed.

Breezy called for me and took me to lunch at his house where live his deaf mother and brother and sister-in-law and Michael their son aged three. The girl is slim and red-lipped. Very sweet. She has brown fluffy straight hair. The same mould as Margaret Hodson.

After lunch we went to Bondi Beach and surf-bathed. The men aren't allowed to wear trunks, nor ladies brassiere tops. They stared at me. I didn't like it. The sand was glorious.

I love Australia.

We went back to Breezy's and sat around. I was sleepy. Then Velvet Eyes arrived. He came in. I was excited. He had Peter Reid and Dawson with him. He said, 'It's good to see you again Betty Smart.' He was in an Eddiesh mood and he really was glad to see me. He went.

Breezy and I had eggs at a place. I asked for a double milk and the girl came back and apologized and said, 'We have only got the regular size glasses, do you mind if I bring you two glasses instead?' which she did, both full of milk.

After dinner we collected a girl down fifty-six steps. Her name was Margery Thomas. All, or nearly all of the million and a half (or quarter) people in Sydney have a glorious harbour view. There are hills and slopes and the harbour winds in and out for miles.

We went back to Breezy's and there they all were, Velvet Eyes and his friends.

We went miles to Pasadena Road House. Some were in shorts or slacks. Some were in shorts and bare feet. Gay and rather drunken. I liked it but was too sleepy to do my duty so took a drink of neat whisky, and woke up. Danced mostly with Pete Reid though once with Velvet Eyes. I got him off the veranda.

I drove home with Velvet Eyes first in back then in front. I loved it. I sang and was witty. The top was open. I stood up. It was a fine drive home.

Following meetings and socializing in Sydney, they sailed on The Otranto *stopping for an hour in Burnie, Tasmania*

December 21: Melbourne

This diary is getting inexcusably dull. And why? Rich things happen every day. Rich thoughts tumble one upon another.

I must settle my future. The sensitive walls are closing in.

What do I care? Everything jars but the harsh bare truth. Only sprawling vulgarity is authentic. The costumes in *Les Presages* irritated and annoyed me. A joke pleases me. And it pleases me to wriggle my seat.

Ah! What a fall is here! Shall I ever find my right true purpose?

This diary is not worth reading. Dead facts and narcissistic thoughts. Who would bother? My Pollyanna hopes and beliefs remain true, I know, but O so stale! A thousand times I have said Shakespeare, and WJ Turner, and Edna St Vincent, and Humbert Wolfe. O what a cloying prostitution is there!

I grow old – too old. The gates close. The clover is knee deep, full, in seed. The solitary leaves flip to the ground. When shall I awake to work? When shall I ever care?

It's again (O always) a case of the little hand to put the machine in motion. But the reiteration of my one passionate theme is no use. I must be born again.

I can't believe that it is a year today since I came back from Switzerland and found John's cross.[9] Then I saw us walking in Regent's Park after the cocktail party. When there was no one there, only John in his shirt sleeves working and pretending to be surprised when I came in, though he must have heard my taxi drawing up below. My hair had just been done so I didn't like to take off my large hat. It looks too artificial and stiff when it's just been set, but he told me to so I did and I crossed my legs and had a cocktail and didn't know what to say. I was taken aback that there were no other people invited. I thought I was old and in control of all situations. John said afterwards I was very shy. When we walked in the garden he said, 'You must let Bill know you're here.' I said, 'No. I won't. Bill's nothing to me,' and he tried to make me and I got quite cross. Then he put me in the taxi and asked me to Scotland, but I was mad because he hadn't got his mother to ask me, so I drove away disgruntled and told him I didn't think I could go and raced home to Pont St late for Daddy and Jane.

This all sounds silly but the picture is very vivid. Nearly all the things I did with John are intense pictures. Perhaps because nothing was spontaneous. I was always conscious of a tenseness in the air. I was always waiting and listening. I could feel him thinking before he spoke. Everything was thought-out, careful, premeditated.

I'll never understand him unless I love him. I was still rebellious then. Am I older and more magnanimous now? At least I know I can trust him absolutely. My worry now is could he trust me?

O this warm air! This warm air! All my delicious moments come back voluptuously insistent. ('Delicious memories float like perfume through the night' – Cortot on Chopin's 7th Prelude). I think of Charlie because his sympathy was such a rare, exciting and warm thing. But the fly in the ointment at present is Helen. Does she know 'Intangible things are true?' I kill the deer, but she, hyena-like, is not ashamed to take the leavings. I win. But what good does it do me?[10]

O the warm wind. Rationalizing, easing all physical contacts, suggesting, encouraging, teaching, the warm tropical air in the middle of the Indian Ocean. Don't imagine for a moment that I am fighting against anything; I'm not, I'm only lying on my back in bed in the morning and above my bed is a bit of porthole with a grey-white sky all over it and gently a wind warm and heavy is blowing over me. I am loosened, and since it is a sensual wind my mind wanders back among the rare but dear moments of physical sympathy which I have known.

I've never read Mary Astor's diary, but it makes me feel nervous. I must be honest, but as I can't write everything, don't wish to state baldly what the jury might want to know (yes or no) I prefer to take the risk.

Yesterday I skipped through Timothy White's *England Has my Bones* and I remembered him and how I met him at Robin Watt's and then at Stowe. I liked him and his book was helpful. I think I'll learn to fly.

The poets are the most exciting thing I know, – Auden, Archibald McLeish, Conrad Aiken, Emily Dickinson, Spender, etc. At the moment *particularly* Archibald McLeish. (WJ Turner, of course, is a Romantic (?). He is not modern, and not always a poet, but I love him because he has written at least two real poems full of the magic spell.)

I couldn't sleep – I think it was the coffee I had after dinner. I read one hundred pages of Rosamund Lehmann's *The Weather in the Streets*.

January 5: Last Day on Otranto

I have been watching a flamboyant sunset fade, with Hans Reinbach. We talked about individuals vs the state. He is going

Elizabeth Smart at eight years

Elizabeth's mother, Louise Parr, from a portrait of 1902

Russel Smart, Elizabeth's father, in 1928

Left: 'Betty' at eight years

Below: The Smarts' summer house, at Kingsmere, in the Gatineau Hills above Ottawa

Right: With her brother, Russel

Right: With her sister, Jane, at Kingsmere

Below: Elizabeth and John Pentland at a London club in the early 30s

Left: Elizabeth at 20 years

Left: Mrs Watt on her world tour

Below: Elizabeth and her father, in mid Atlantic, during a trip to Sweden and Norway in July 1935

Foot: Sir Stafford, Lady Cripps and their son, John, photographed by Elizabeth

Left: D'Arcy McGee at Kingsmere

Below left: Wolfgang Paalen

Below right: Charles Ritchie at the Smarts' summer cottage

Foot: Graham Spry at Kingsmere

Left: Jean Varda and friends

Below: Alice Paalen

Below: Varda, Elizabeth and friends on the way to Cassis, France

Left: Elizabeth's friend, Maximiliane von Urpani Southwell

Below: George Barker as a young man

Below: In Mexico, just prior to meeting George Barker, 1940

Right: George Barker
with Elizabeth and
Georgina at Willard
Maas' penthouse,
Brooklyn Heights, 1941

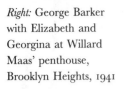

Left: George Barker in 1942

Below: Elizabeth with her children, Sebastian,
Rose, Georgina and Christopher, at Tilty
Mill, England in 1948

home to Germany after nine years in Australia to the New Germany. He says the Germans have that absolute loyalty to and trust in a *leader* once chosen. He says perhaps they are unique in this. It is a very strong trait. He is trying to get into the mood for 'The New Germany.' He is an engineer.

But none of that's what I wanted to say. The perfumes and glamour of the East were in that vibrating sky. A huge double star like two fireflies mating came out. The sky was smooth rich blue. This afternoon at 6:00 a man who died was thrown into the sea. While they pulled long faces over the dead, I played with three little boys. It's coming over me again – this hungry passion for children. Before 6:00 I spoke to the Canon. He was reciting some of Thomas Becket's part from TS Eliot's *Murder in the Cathedral*. He tried to make me tell him what the speech about action and suffering meant – I wouldn't but made him. He explained it and spoilt it of course. Then he began to talk about God and so I asked him questions. I asked what metaphors? And he said the sun. I said, 'The Wind that Bloweth Where it Listeth.' He said, 'yes. Anything. This great vast stretch of sea. But it's not the metaphors we need but the *character* of God. How do we know God is kind? Jesus Christ didn't say I'm like God. He said a much bigger thing. He said God is like me. "I am the Truth and the Light." '

(The Canon said he was sure that if I were going all the way he would have me converted to the Church before we reached England.)

I fell out of sympathy with the Canon. He told me elementary things I knew and couldn't understand things I understood. When he talked about suffering I asked him what things had made him suffer and he said that was too personal, and I said I only meant what *sort* of things. Could he suffer for people he hardly knew? He said no and began to talk about loved ones. Then we talked about Love for a bit but he was only a little man so that when he left I didn't feel soothed so I went upstairs and sat alone looking at the sky until Reinbach came.

Reinbach made me think. So I am sad and philosophic – as always at ends and at beginnings.

III

CEYLON, EGYPT, AND PALESTINE
January–February, 1937

January 6: Colombo, Ceylon

Passports at dawn. Left 'Otranto' by launch with Jimmy.

The rich and sumptuous East: the life, the colour, the dim lights. Mr de Mel talking about the Sinhalese. Jimmy from another world. But he bought me two dresses from the little shop (Ramsamy). They made them in a day, the taffeta evening one in half a day. I wore it to dine and dance with him. We had champagne. Half the boat was there.

I spent all day with Jimmy except the few minutes with the de Mels. I was happy. Very happy. Wrapped around with luxury and love. Well-protected, safe, secure. Jimmy took me for a Rickshaw drive and pulled me himself. The natives got hysterical. Mrs Billy McCollock and the Walsh girl and Maine and Kennington were always joining us for drinks.

Downie was a 'cot case' today. Before we left the ship we went to see him lying limp and damp in his cabin surrounded by empty glasses, bottles, and cigarette ends. He had a woolly throat, and his great round eyes were small and funny without his glasses.

We went ashore in the launch. Before when we were having drinks an officer, Nicholls, said, 'Well I think this is a hell-hole; lying in here surrounded by a lot of smelly niggers.' I despised him. The smell is delicious, rich, fragrant, full of life with warm suggestive winds lapping us as we drove in the taxi.

January 7: Colombo

First curry. Delicious. Ecstatic. Tasty. Hot. Mangos. Taffetas and silks to be made up at fairyland prices. Greed is upon me. The lust and the lure for and of beautiful ravishing cloths – rich silks, taffetas, velvets, chiffons, brocades. You just say 'Like this picture' and he does it and it is and it fits.

The dimly-lit, dark, airy houses.

Dinner party at the de Mel's. A nephew from Cambridge.

A cable from home telling me that Edward Ford[1] is tutor to Khedive in Egypt. (King actually, not Khedive, but Jane made the mistake.)

January 8: Colombo, Kaliniva Temple

The solemnity of an unknown religion.

The young priest, straight, serious, slim, with his shaved head. I worshipped him and turned to the religious life with self-denial, strenuous learning, meditation, prayer, bare boards, truth coming at last. 'The Great Mysteries' kept going through my head. But when we were coming out of the house where all the rich offerings are, the young priest came along and said the Temple was lit up now, and he smiled at me. I was pleased but it was too easy. 'They are not supposed to look at a woman,' said Mrs de Mel. 'But I don't think they keep all these things.'

The priests in orange and yellow stood around in clumps. The nuns shave their heads too.

But it was real, this religion, because it is undisillusioned. I wouldn't touch the leaf fallen from the Bo tree which some beggar offered me. The Bo tree is sacred.

I thought I must reawaken and search for truth, and I remembered my newly-bought luxurious silks and taffetas and velvets and I said, 'It is easier for a camel to enter the eye of a needle, than for a rich man to enter into the Kingdom of Heaven,' and I realized how much I have become attached to my warm voluptuousness, my lent-body. But anyway in this day and age what could I possibly do? How could I possibly find truth by an ostentatious gesture? It is impossible to be alone among people. The world is small and closing in. Is my purpose sincere? I wish I could have met Christ or the Buddha. Where is a Great Teacher? (to resolve these mysteries).

January 9: To Kandy

The Temple of the Truth. Yellow or Orange priests with shaven heads.

Old palm leaf book in Singalese script, etc. Sacred turtles. The Lotus Motif everywhere. Bare feet in the temple. Flower offerings. Bent figures.

Ancient wall drawings in yellow. Pear breasted women. Baby Buddhas. The Buddha in 3 positions: Preaching, thinking and reclining. The Bo tree. They worship where the sacred books are, or the relic, or images of the Buddha, or presents brought as offerings. The sacred bowl of water for pilgrims.

Some men have long hair and do it in a bun. Some wind their heads in a silk or cotton turban. They all wear skirts and bare feet. Same brilliant colours. Bullock carts made of wicker or grain. Gayly hung shops of junk. Women in sarees or with top separate from bottom – a white cotton close fitting blouse. Balanced baskets on head. Their hair is long and drawn back in a bun. Hindus have a spot on the forehead between the eyes. The Priests of the Buddha carry umbrellas for the heat.

January 10: To Nuwara – Eliya and back from Kandy

The day of reckoning has arrived. My hand is trembling. Mrs Watt has complained of my rudeness, especially lately, which she says she can no longer stand. She has also mentioned my selfishness, and lack of sympathy. It is a blow, a shock. I knew I wasn't adequate. I could often feel her resentment, her aggrievedness. But I have in my own way, such as it is, tried to do the right thing by her. My results, I suppose I must admit, have then only been negative. I have refrained from losing my temper, and (I thought) from being positively rude to her, and I have tried to be sympathetic, to go out to join in her joy at least. I can't be sorry when she pretends to be sick – *she's* so sorry for *herself*.

But I have failed dismally. I see myself in the hard, selfish, hateful light which she must see me in – I have pursued a policy of compromise and *laissez-faire* too long. I would have left her many a time but at least I thought I couldn't let her down that way, though I was weak sometimes about the other ways. She is old. She needs someone. She is poor and tired and disappointed. It should be good for me to try and supply all the things she needs. When I undertook this enormous task I thought

I could put love into her life. But that just shows my vanity. She was even unpleasant about money, which she always makes such a fuss about if I spend it, either on her or on myself. She said, 'I can't say that you've been very anxious to spend it on me if it comes to that.' Each time I did spend it on her it was so unpleasant it wasn't worth it.

I *am* selfish. And partly on principle. There have been days (particularly lately) when I have been so far from sympathetic with her that I have come near to hating her. But even for hate there are so many compromises. Her dreadful snobbishness always embarrasses me – particularly with people like Jimmy. Her emotional reactions always go against the grain with me because I can't help feeling them a little pseudo.

And yet she *is* just. She *has* left me tactfully alone. She *does* try to understand the things she doesn't understand.

Perhaps she has tried to do her duty as a Christian as she thinks she understands it.

And I am a Philistine with whom *none* could live.

There are hundreds and hundreds of little things I could have done for her which I didn't do. There were whole days when I forgot her altogether and only thought about myself and my vanity.

If it were a part-time job I should have more hope of being able at least to make a laudable attempt at it. It is living, night and day, month in month out, with her. If I did utterly sympathize with her, I should *be* her. I should be swamped and submerged. I can't have one thing on top to be in control and have my strong personal secret life going on below and in odd moments. She would say, 'That's ridiculous! I have given you every freedom and consideration. Night after night I went to bed with an anguished heart because of your rudeness and indifference. But I left you alone to go your own way. I never interfered. I always wanted you to have a good time wherever it was possible.'

What I say to her always is, 'If you thought I was being rude or selfish or unsympathetic, why didn't you say so at once? Why O why didn't you let me know instead of hardening your heart against me, and bearing me a grievance, and feeling hurt and injured?' – and her answer to that is full of 'wells' – and 'you were paying your own way' – or 'you were sweet to me the next day and I thought you were sorry.'

But all these things I knew before I left home and I prayed often and especially in the train behind the green curtains as I pulled out of Ottawa, that I would have the courage and the strength and the endurance to come through this with a noble character. Well, I haven't. I've failed.

(Poor Daddy! I've disappointed him again!)

But the point is, should I leave her at Port Said? Is it better to stick to her and help her, at *least physically*, until I see her safely to London? Or would it be better, and more honest, to leave her as soon as possible?

When I started to write I wanted to gather my things and rush away out into the rainy night, but having argued myself into feeling it is *my* weakness and error and selfishness, I am inclined to take a less violent view of the matter.

But which way does my duty lie? Should I leave her or stay with her till London? It's hard to help her. If she asks me to do anything she usually does it herself or else is exasperated by my vague methods of doing things. I smile and get things done (incidentally they get done). She stamps her foot or fumes (incidentally they usually don't get done).

But the point is I really am only interested in myself and the salvation of my own immortal soul. I thought that this six months' discipline would be good – but if it is to degenerate into a mutual hate it is only a mischief-maker and a waste of my fast-departing youth. I am the cat that walks by herself – and this experiment in administration, solicitation, and the way the world works is manifestly a mistake. What's gone I don't regret. It only proves what I knew before. I wasn't made for their communal, citizenship, club world. I am a rebel.

Not that there is anything to be proud of in being a rebel – nor yet, I don't see why, anything to be ashamed of. It is a fact. I am not gregarious. My sympathies are with humanity as a whole and with each individual in turn – not a roomful – in a false aspect.

O God! I feel sick I am as I am and so will I be. Should I be bending the knee in pious remorse? Why should I? Well, because I believe in humility and the teaching of Christ – and the other religious teachers. I remember what Lady Reading said, and Jimmy, and no doubt King Edward VIII, and Grisell, and heaps and heaps of others. I can't take their grounds. I have been cursed with 'this New England conscience.'

Have I tried? Well, yes, but only spasmodically. I never was good at endurance. But isn't endurance everything? Will-power? Tenacity of purpose?

But it must be something more positive than just endurance. I must always go out strongly with bright sympathy and new life. O God. O God. I'm weak. We're all weak. I'm specially weak.

Is my alleged goal a self-deception? Is the eternal truth I tell myself I am seeking when I let men caress me, when I jump into the sea, when I dance and flatter myself by the flattery of men, is all this only devil's camouflage, worthless?

I honestly can't think so. Perhaps I am loath to leave my voluptuous pleasures, my conceited delights of the soul, my jealous aloof delights of the mind. Well, I can't know this. I can only go on following the strongest conviction, even if it is only a wolf in sheep's clothing.

But I haven't settled my duty. Time, again, the universal referee, will, I suppose, decide.

I shall go to the Temple and ask about the teachings of Buddha. Christ has been so hackneyed it is hard to hear the great truth above the mess of association, misinterpretation, hypocrisy, and self-deception.

About Kandy

Up the hills, winding through the tea plants and the rubber groves and the palm trees in the misty, tear besmirched day. Past little villages with their market ware hanging out for sale, even on a Sunday. (Sunday, I believe, *is* their market day.) I bought two shawls – one that brilliant pink-red which the natives use so effectively against their dark skin and the dark green palms, of wool, and the other blue and white patterned cotton. Mr Dias thought it rather funny and was rather ashamed that I bought *cotton* – he said that our sort of people only wore silk. I told him not to be silly and not to be ashamed. He said it was alright for me. We lunched at the Grosvenor Hotel. It was rather empty. There were a few English types floating about. Dias talks incessantly, mostly about England and the places he saw, asking me if I have seen them, sort of enumerating them off. It got rather cold and I was glad of the sweater Mrs Watt had forced so peremptorily on my rebellious self.

On the way down I felt slightly sick from the turns, and the unceasing honking, and the cold, and we went through a few pockets of fog. We passed a couple of straight three-storey tea factories. Dias sat behind with me and chattered.

It was when we got back, before dinner, that Mrs Watt's storm of abuse broke and the mutual aggrievedness came to a head. I went down all shaking and desperate with this book to the writing room. The night was black and raining. I wanted to dash out into it and find a hole to cry in. I was just hoping to cry when there was one of the little adolescent girls from the boat. I had to greet her. Then I wrote and wrote.

January 13: Colombo

I've just been reading DH Lawrence's letters and the introduction by Aldous Huxley and my brain's excited and I can't sleep.

But just think how dosed in muddy flesh I am! Eating, sleeping, dozing mentally. My intellect is hopelessly lazy. Once in a long while the wheel turns over.

If I went to Huxley and said 'Advise me' it would be false. I've got past that frantic bewildered urgency. If I said, 'What shall I do to be saved?' it would be more to the point, especially if I added, 'If it's not too difficult.' I have grown so to love luxury and the flattery of social scenes and emotional splurges and soft soporific semi-sex that will anything ever happen to me?

I *think* so seldom. I *feel* so seldom. Mostly I just mope along. I'm cowardly. I'm stupidly polite. I try to make everyone like me. I'm willing to be mediocre and deny my God for the sake of peace. Can't I remember Huxley and Lawrence, Katherine Mansfield, Blake, Whitman, Spender, Eliot, McLeish?

John Middleton Murry is manifestly weak. Why did they all like him so? Too conscious. Too anxious. (Without knowing him externally or internally I dislike him terrifically.)

While I was reading it rained, and a little lizard ran across the floor and snapped a big fly and then ran back; a bug got into bed and bit my toe, and a large green grasshopper landed on my sheet. The rooster started to crow but it was still pitch black and then left off so it must have been a false alarm. The rain has stopped but the insects keep up the hum, and a dog barks a forlorn hysterical bark.

How could I even consider linking up my life forever to John or Jimmy or any of the ones who are not even related to my species?

What puzzles me is why I never meet those ones.[2] Frank Scott is the nearest I know. I'm getting so hypocritical, dull, indifferent. – Or is it just a coal smouldering and able to break forth into flame in a moment? I'm twenty-three. It's too late to be a question mark. I'm still still a question mark. Let me get back to London quickly and meet the ones who know.

Think even of the dishonest, dull, subterfugic letters I write home to my parents. Why can't I be honest and clean-shafted, and direct to Daddy at least? – Because the truth's such a big ball and you can't see it all from one side.

Yes. But why not send the one side, limited but intense, clear, true?

Ah, there's the rub.

My music is used up. My poetry is used up. My patience is used up. My conversation is dissipated. My imagination is dissipated. My inspiration doesn't come like a cloud because I try to think in other people's words on other people's lines. I don't want to do this particularly, but what excuse can I give? They say, 'But you're an intelligent girl, you can see that it's done *this* way, that *that* and *this* is so. You can't ignore the facts.'

You see the things there. You've *got* to learn and follow. Otherwise you're like a child pretending to be a child when you aren't a child any more. It isn't cute any more not to know how the world works. It seems affectation to say, 'there isn't time or I have other things to do' – and if I know, I suppose I must follow – what excuse is there for not following? The world does it like this. The world will point at you and call you eccentric if you don't do it like this. Why don't you do it like this? Appease the world.

And, in appeasing, the vital years slip away, untaut, slack, loose, no use for chiselling the proper arrowy life.

Go my own way thoughtlessly?! But I can't forget that I know. I remember the facts and can avoid trouble *this* way; what possible excuse can there be for going the other? The delusion of self-expression? Surely I'm sane enough to plot it into acceptable channels.

The urge of creative impulse? When was it ever so terribly urgent? I had quiet, peace; I had excitement and noise. When did I ever sit and write and write as I knew I should, as I knew I *must*, to live? But why have I been abasing myself lately? Denying my ego? Saying, 'I must stop talking about myself. People will think I am conceited, or too introspective.' What if they do? I am going against my own principles to deny my ego and its right of cockiness. I am trying to convince myself that I am nothing wonderful or mysterious or potentially great, when secretly I still hope and perhaps even believe I am. Ye Gods! I *should* believe I am.

This false mock modesty. Where did it come from? Being a sidling secretary? Toadying flattery to others? Saying *you* don't need this, give others the great big hand? Yes. Maybe it was extremes of vanity that killed the essential part of my vanity. The necessarily slightly self-deceptive cockiness that is the right, healthy, and natural sign of strident life.

Well, then, fat-head, I am a case. What is the cure? Something physical? – O *The Lives of the Poets*?[3]

More and more questions.

January 17: Galle

To Closenberg, their house by the sea in Galle almost surrounded by water on a hill, with heavenly palm trees, and fernery with an aquarium and strange fishes.

I am ashamed of my neglect of this vital diary. I eat too much and I sleep too much and the heat reduces me to a living lump, but it is the afternoon sleep that demoralizes me. Lately, at Mrs de Mels, and here at Mrs Pereras, I have had to share a bedroom with Mrs Watt, so I couldn't write in bed as usual. Even at Mrs de Souzas I have to get out of bed to turn out the light, so the temptation to go right to sleep is aided and abetted.

I have been reading *Buddhism* by Rhys Davids. It is important. But I haven't quite digested it. He says it is perhaps the most intellectual religion. I think it is the most advanced. But I think I still agree with Leslie Perera, that I believe in all religions, because they are all true, even though I 'have' none. Buddhists don't have to go to church. It is moderation. There is no God as the other religions know it, not individual souls, but only a desire and a striving towards avatarship, or, as Western books call it, Nirvana, a state of peace, bliss, joy, intellectual activity. Ten fetters have to be broken and the escape made from the wheel of life and the wheel of rebirth.

This sounds puerile as I have expounded it. I shall try again after my swim.

Later: I have just been *swimming* in the soft, warm, caressing Indian Ocean. The sun had just gone down. The young moon came out, gradually getting brighter and brighter, and there was a great shining star nearer and nearer. Beyond the sand bar the sky over Galle was pink and orange. The little fishing boats and the palm trees on the two little islands were silhouettes. Some of the sky was mauve. Leslie was with me. He has a short DHL beard and he wore trunks. He completed the picture, dark against the tropical dusk. We each had surfboards. I never swam in water so warm. I jumped back into the joyful pagan worship of the holy things of earth. It's such a beautiful abandonment. What else can most of us know but that blissful, permeating, all-embracing warmth. I don't know whether or not it is sex. I don't think so, because it's complete. It's not a straining after, or desire for, it's a realization, itself, of being alive, or every little bit being alive, here and *now*. It's saying this moment is enough; this is perfect and I am alive in every particle to its perfection.

This morning Garsia Perera took me over the tea factory and rubber factory. Tea is very complicated. It gets withered and shook, and dried and bounced, and cleaned by air blowing heavily or lightly so that the stones and dust drop out, and they are picked over and packed in a jiggly box.

Rubber begins by being sticky white milky stuff like milkweed juice tapped into a coconut shell by a ridge cut into the trunk. Then by acid it turns into curds, then into lumpy white rubber smelling like pigs' food; then it goes into another roller and comes out lacy, then it is hung for four days; then it is put into another roller with acid and comes out thick, rough and yellow. The manufacturers for some reason like it yellow. Then a man cuts it into strips about two feet long.

The tea in small cartons is packed by *hand*!

To get to the various factories we drove through shady coconut groves, with the sun coming through them. If you get a view you see their yellowy green heads in billows. They lean about neatly. In the evening fireflies and stars get mixed up in their untidy symmetrical hair.

On the plantation there were various groups of huts where the workers live. They get their board free and the ones who collect the tapped rubber get fifty or sixty-five cents a day for five hours work. Lots of young girls work in the factory. And women, beautiful straight-backed women with nice round cheeks. They wear the cotton blouses and usually coloured wrapped skirts. Sometimes the babies and very small boys wear nothing but usually they have at least a little G-string.

In Galle, the beggars come up with a wheedling singsong.

Women offer handmade lace, boys offer handmade coconut-sap candy like maple cream. Men with two balanced baskets on their shoulders go by. The sun gleams. Everyone is barefoot.

Old Mrs Perera has no teeth; but she is understanding, comprehensive, adorable, gentle, and she has a lovely colour sense. Her hair is silver grey and she has a very dark bronze skin. One night she wore a silver blouse with her sari, and she wears very dark green. The harmony is marvellous.

January 20: Colombo to the Orford

Awoke rested at de Mels. Packing and the temples with Terence – Asokarama and another. New, gay, and brilliantly, shinily coloured. But the scenes the boy explained to us from the life of Buddha were distorted and corrupted versions of the truth which – surely – would be sufficient in itself. I lost my feeling of reverence in these bright, new, tourist-ridden temples. The only moving thing left was the little single, flowerhead offerings which the people bring when they come to pray.

Nearly all the Sinhalese men I have talked to have been bitter and scornful of the English people, who don't associate with them – Mr de Mel, Eksat, Terence. They just won't mix. A nice Englishman who brought some Sinhalese to tea at his club was forthwith ostracized and resigned and joined a Sinhalese club. The attitude is so stupid, ignorant, narrow, and intolerable that it makes me boil. If I were a Sinhalese I should be leading a red revolt. 'The Governor tells me communism is rife all over the island,' said Mrs Watt. The Sinhalese are cultured, charming, witty, subtle, kind, sensitive, and proud. Those arrogant blockheaded ignoramuses! Lionel Alty, the Australian, made me hate him forever by saying, 'Now, you've never stayed with these people before, Betty, so if you should need anyone

I am at the Galle Face and Mrs Moore Jackson is at the GOH. You'd better take those names down.' If he'd been near enough I would have slapped his face.

It was all so vivid, but so isolated from everything else in my life. I hope it will not fade. These two weeks were complete, utterly new, and utterly delicious. Nothing from the past came dangling over, except that occasionally I met people from the boat in shops or on the street. One day I meet a girl and her mother who greeted me very enthusiastically and warmly till I called Terence over and introduced him, when I could see them taken aback and much less enthusiastic.

The smells, the food, the people, the marvellous big airy old homes, the scenery, the street life were all new, colourful, vital, exciting, stimulating. How can I repay the people of Ceylon? What could I possibly do?

January 24: Orford

Emily of course.[4] What else would cause 'divine visitations' and 'intimations of immortality,' those sudden changes from the loftiest sublimation to the earthiest sex? What else would throw me this way and that, urgently, mysteriously, without cause, walking on the deck alone, saying irrational things to an unknown Scotchman, swishing contrary across the filled-up lounge? And I thought the mental excitement last night was real and true? O Emily! Thy name is the curse of woman!

January 26: Aden

See *The Southern Gates of Arabia* by Freya Stark for perfect pictures of the spirit of Aden.

'The whole place is just one big lavatory,' said Mrs Watt.

Cheap stuff from China in the shops. The native quarters, goats, dirt. The Indian part, more like Ceylon again. Mahommedan Fez, (X) and all other religious hats. Women all covered up.

Intense dazzling heat and dust. This is their 'cold season.' Met the huge fat Colonel Robinson and he motored me to the Arab village, past the long lines of salt tent-piles and the flat desert, away from the striking rocky jagged mountains, lifeless without a vestige of green anywhere. Dyeing cloth in a whole field, held down by stones. He tried to take my arm. Begging everywhere, 'backsheesh.' Camels

drawing carts, etc and lying and sitting in ridiculous positions.
The 'Gentleman's' House with the only (cultivated) palm trees. The
poor shrivelled up 'Gardens.' The bus with all the people from the
boat. All the men well turbaned. To the town of Aden in the Crater.
Various cemeteries. Flat bright white walls with little alleys leading
to colony.

Different from anything.

Utterly.

The native people not so easily contacted as the ordinary Sinhalese,
not so willing to smile, more anxious to get something out of you.
Launch back to the boat. The sharp peaks to the left. The turquoise
sea, a strip of bleached sand. Mrs Watt's libation to Lawrence
(typical).

Lady Harding. I talked to her. Cousin of Aldous Huxley. Sweet.
Easy to tell everything to. In evening sleepy bridge with Lady
Harding and Sir Edward ('EG').

Wire from Charlie – 'Have never found a better.' Darling Charlie. I
grinned excitedly. Jimmy's letter. He's coming to Suez to meet me.

January 30: The Suez Canal and Night Arrival at Port Said

Awoke to the dissipated mysterious moon shining onto my bed.
Looked out to see the lights of Suez, boats and the ancient buildings
against the bare steep mountains. The sun rose red-rimmed and
gradually scattered melting bits of sunlight over my room. I waited
expecting Jimmy at any moment. I got up and powdered my nose.
It is cold for the first time. I wished I had another blanket. Miss
Ommaney, the stewardess, brought me figs, an apple, and an orange
much earlier. I waited and waited. Finally I got up.

Up on deck there were people looking through telescopes and
people taking movies. Suez old and new. Mountains on the Egyptian
side. Vast buff sand deserts on the other with square houses, white-
robed Arabs, and camels. Far away over the desert a faint row of
low sand hills.

'The wickedest city in the world,' said Mrs Watt looking at the
modern silhouette of Suez against the purple blue jagged mountains.
It was distinct in the desert, well knit together with a line of date
palms trailing along to the right.

Then, we moved from the wide flat waters and banks half overflowing, into the Canal proper. Desert on either side. A funeral, body

held high. The pepper (?) trees in rows planted by the narrow river after the open of Bitter Lake.

Sun, and a raging wind across the desert blowing hats and skirts askew.

January 31: To Cairo (Shepherd's Hotel)

Dressed in the dark. Dull trip to Cairo over deserts. Date palms. Donkeys. Dancing children. Handsome people. Fezes. All signs in two or three languages. Later fields green with cultivation. People gathered around a fountain. Veiled women in black, camels, white robes.

At the front of our train was a car marked 'Penal Car,' barred. Clusters of people were round it, harassed women with babies, children. I saw them and wondered at their faces before I looked inside and realized they were convicts behind the bars.

Shepherd's Hotel. Authentic. Civilization again. Delicious food. 'Smart' people. Blasé youth. Nagging dragomen.[5] Exquisite Blue Mosque. Gay children, mischievous, bursting with life. The seething native quarters. Dust blowing in eyes, wind and dirt. New with smells. Roasted peanuts. Many skewgee legs on people. Red running noses of babies carried on shoulder clinging to head. Small boy stuck out tongue and then grinned. Wild happiness in eyes. Sensual people. Some fishnet veils over the women's faces (Arabs). Marvellous, indescribably beautiful mosques, outside. Round domes, minarets. Moccasins over shoes in the temple. One and one half hours drive with horse and carriage. Freezing when we returned. Tea and exciting *Harper's Bazaar*, etc.

Delicious dinner and to movie *Clo-Clo* with Martha Eggart at *the Diana* (German). Beggars, staring men, sellers. Getting lost on the way. Mrs Watt's rage, confusion, ungraciousness, roughness.

A clean bath.

February 2: Cairo

Alone. Cairo Museum. Seeing Mrs Watt off. Alone in a Big Hotel. Movie of the Crusades.

The illustrative and the coloured designs were so exhilarating that I wanted to cry from joy at perfection. But I didn't because I didn't want my highest lowered. I was really trembling with satisfaction. This is what you give *worlds* for, throw all in, work years.

Alabaster lamps and bowls. Faïence. Design is at its most perfect in this Egyptian art. Sculpture. Mummies. Jewellery. Shoes.

It's rather dreary not knowing anyone in a luxurious hotel. When the waiters asked if 'my mother' were not coming down to dinner I said that she had left and they were very surprised and overjoyed and smiled and grinned and told each other with glee. After she left the sense of fear and of being cheated left me, and everyone was nice to me, even the dragomen. The whole atmosphere was different. When I drove home from the movie in a cab and asked how much, a whole gang of people gathered around to see that I wasn't cheated, an Egyptian from the hotel (in uniform), two English soldiers, a couple of dragomen and the Egyptians that stand around. The manager always exchanged words with me. He asked me if I would like to go to a cabaret with him. Mrs Watt confuses people by hating them and mistrusting them so violently.

I can't *feel* Egypt much; I am confused with so many countries. I can't disassociate the pyramids from the cruising tourists, nor Cairo from Elizabeth Copel-Cure and her last desperate attempt to find a husband.

Cream-green cactus hedges with their flat oval prickly paddles and satisfactory curves spreading in formidable tangle.

February 4: The Pyramids

Sore knees from scrambling over the huge rocks, powdery in their decadence. When we were on top with the guide who refused not to come with us, another man reached the top triumphant and took pictures. He had a camera with an automatic shutter and stood on the edge of the pyramid with his back to the other while it took his picture with a burring sound. Another youth, fat, with a pimply face came up too with a guide and took pictures with a small camera that clicked. Edward in his inimitable way joked with the guides and asked them questions. 'Well anyway he's got a very illuminating idea of Egyptian history,' said Edward. The guide loved him. But when Edward was talking to the fat man's guide he said:

'Do any people ever climb this pyramid by moonlight?'

'Yes,' said the guide.

'Who does?'

'Soldiers come from hotel. Drink. Come up. Other times lots come up here bury many things. Spread things to eat. Many many.'

'And do you have to clear away the rubbish?' said Edward.

At this the little man flew into a terrible rage and said 'No.' He spoke good English. He was a guide and abused Edward and strode away insulted. Edward said he was sorry and laughed, and the other guide laughed too, but acted as peacemaker. They love a joke.

I was almost dizzy and a little scared when I looked down the steep ascent to the minute people below. The stones to get over were so huge and precarious. Besides I only had on my party pants because I had locked up my suitcase and then lost the key just before I set out, and I don't think I was decent but I decided, as it was irredeemable not to care.

Inside the great pyramid we bent double and went up small uncomfortable tin stairs, airless, dusty, smelly, and suffocating. It was like a dream of hell. Going nowhere bent double down an airless passage. The high room reechoed to shouts. The Queen's room has an empty stone coffin. I felt nothing. But Edward and I decided to go to see the sewers in London next April. Edward made me laugh when I was out of breath. He is a good companion. He gave our unwanted guide more than he asked for. There is no atmosphere left about these ancient tombs. Too many tourists have trod that dead dust. Electric light (subdued, true, but there) lights the way to the gaping spots. And after all what is there to gape at? A hole in the wall where the jewels were stored. It needs imagination colossal to restore life to such very dead mementos of an unrealizable past. It smelt like a latrine.

I don't know why I have suddenly got so ugly looking and dull. Life today seems empty, though Edward is good. It's not rich. I look but don't see. I know but don't realize.

I was awfully tired after the climb and I ate too much dinner at too late an hour at Shepherd's. I started before Edward because I couldn't find him and that spoilt things.

Boys bawling shoes shined!

February 5: Cairo to Kantara East

Why do goodbyes revive everything? I became garrulous and teeming and Edward affectionate and Canadian. He gave me a bracelet of wide elaborate stones. 'A l'il souvenir of your visit to Cairo,' he said. I love trains. My brain sprang to life and I thought and meditated, and things were worth looking at.

This morning I went for a walk by myself through the teeming markets and under the arches of the market streets. I passed up narrow alleyways where children tumbled about and everyone carried on his life and business right there before the eyes. I saw a woman passionately sucking the chin of her baby. Men go by with trays of those enormous blown up cookie biscuits. Meat and fish hang in the doorways. Mangy dogs skulk about. In some places very unsavoury-looking food lies waiting for buyers. On some steps in a steep alleyway sit a group of women veiled in the Arab fashion from the nose down, the veil suspended by a spool over their forehead, made of fishnet, black voile over their heads. Their eyes are rimmed heavily with black on the lower rim. There is a real sense of filth in Cairo. You dare not put your hand to your eye. So many of them have eyes gone funny. Edward says it is on account of the flies. They don't seem to mind. They let as many as three settle on the baby's eyes and never bother to shew them away, and their noses run unhindered.

Under the more respectable arches are the jewellery, antiquity, and persian carpet shops, full of fascinating but expensive things, little statues in that dream blue of Egypt, half turquoise, half china. If you don't loiter, no one bothers you. If you do, a swarm of merchants buzz around you entreating you to go in.

The sense of life in Cairo, though so prolific, has a sense of despair. It is like the life of maggots swarming in the dust of the dead, on the mighty corpse of Egypt. But the people are not a 'subject' race, like perhaps (sometimes distressingly) the Indian people are. They don't take things lying down. They are impudent, suspicious, cunning, and merry. For instance the little boy who stuck out his tongue at me in sheer devilment, or the guide who flared up at Edward because he asked him if he had to collect the rubbish. The children have alert shining faces and eyes (if their eyes are not skewgee, and even if they are skewgee). They always seem to have immensely exciting business in hand. You can share a joke with anyone almost without speaking to them. When I told the waiters at the hotel the 'Madam' was not ill but had left (for Palestine), they got together and thought it a huge joke.

In the alleyways some sucked split sugar cane. Peanuts were for sale. Funny unwearable shoes hung up in rows. I drove to the Museum in an open carriage, an old one that reminded me of Brackly Beach, the cabman gently lashing the horse all the way.

At one o'clock King Farouk drove by Shepherd's Hotel. Whenever he goes anywhere policemen are stationed along the route every few yards, for at *least* half an hour before. When he rides by a motorcycle rides before, then perhaps an open car with a man behind, then the King in a closed car, with a companion. As he passes by, people line the route and clap and raise their voices, not in a shout, but more in admiration. He raises his hat and smiles slightly. Edward says that he is precocious and intelligent but that he is going to be spoilt. He is at the stage where, if he worked hard for another year, he might be able to get into the army. His passion is for collecting. 'He likes to think he's got something which nobody else has. But often he hasn't at all. It's something quite commonplace.' Edward tried disciplining him one day but he couldn't take it. Edward only goes when he is sent for. The King only sends for him when he feels like it, and then dismisses him when he feels like it. And always it's the position of King and guest, not pupil and teacher. At the palace they steamed open one of Edward's letters from his mother because she had written it while staying at the Archbishop of Canterbury's. The King lives with his mother and sister in the palace a little on the outside and does official business at Abdin Palace.

Edward and I sat out on the open veranda behind the railing at Shepherd's Hotel and had tea and read the letters. Funny how lifeless this whole Cairo visit has been. It's been only waiting for Edward, without any particular anticipation or day-dreaming. It's just that I felt incapable of doing anything alone, or having any initiative when he was with me.

The pullman was luxurious with every armchair covered in white. I was alone in my state. I ordered a large and expensive dinner.

I finished *The Home and the World* by Rabindranath Tagore – it was very interesting. There were some lovable characters. The idea of the treatment was excellent. And the whole thing got put across. Perhaps it was a little too long in spots, but always absorbing because it's so personal. You get what they thought as well as what they did and even how it seemed to several other people. At one point while I was reading it I thought I would run across to the Anglo-Egyptian building and buy both the others in the Tauchnitz Edition, but later on something stopped just a fraction behind, my making Tagore another great discovery. But he is my friend. I tried to read Richard Aldington's collection of short stories *Soft Answers* but found them laboured and dull. I do find bitterness, sarcasm, and hate dull. So *young*. There's never any need to batter the fists against things. Move away, see all. Be paternal, maternal, full of humanity. Grow up and grow wise to a sweet large acquiescent philosophy.

I returned to my Proust. A curious thing about Proust's Mme Swann is that both Charlie and Frank Brown (the little boy on the *Orford*) said, 'Wasn't Madam Swann a fascinating creature?' Charlie said, 'An absolutely perfect picture of a beautiful woman.' I never more felt really attracted to Mme Swann, or in love with her. Edward said, "Do you think my sister of sixteen is too young to read *Swann's Way?*' I said Yes. Huxley says Proust gets into a bath and execrates it from his eyes and nose and ears. Strange from Huxley.

February 7: Haifa to Nahalal settlement (co-operative) and Wizo Girls' Agricultural School.

What was this day? The sudden upheaval of all the questions ever asked. Life-values. Desperate breathless decisions. Should I stay for two months at the Agricultural College and live a life of outdoor labour and intellectual study? At first the warm sun, the hens crowing, the smell of cows and earth, the marvellously healthy girls in overalls, rolled-up sleeves, and handkerchiefs tied over their heads, quite convinced me, drunken with the idea, and the wine from the corner-stone laying, and the unwanted morning coffee. There seemed nothing against it. My trip is over, my responsibilities at an end. London sank to a dull waiting-place. Waiting for what? Waiting for things to happen and without the strength to make them. Loneliness along deserted streets. Emptiness in an ugly room. What, after all, was I going to London for? Here I could work, physically, and write in the late afternoons and evenings. I could grow healthy and strong and in control. I would be preparing myself for my future form. This would be real discipline and worth anything. I loved all these marvellous refugees. Jewish girls, German, Romanian, Russian. Beautiful. Liberated. Shining. I found it was possible to stay. They would take me. I was so excited I could hardly eat lunch. The soft blue hills of Carmel looked dreamy and poetic, strong, full of inspiration. The rooms were simple, bare, but sunny and modern. There were Van Gogh and other reproductions and several good drawings on various walls. Huxley, Virginia Woolf, Oscar Wilde lay in one room among the Hebrew books. Botany is taught. Sometimes there are special lectures in the evening. It would be simple living and high thinking.

Why didn't I?

When I first found I was weakening and that London had risen again from the flatness and squalidness to which I had shrunk it and was pulling with undue and irresistible force I thought it was wicked weakness of character, my drifting indecision, and a sign that my life was never to be of any use. But later on, after the tiredness from walking so far had gone away, I began to dissect the reasons, and I came to a conclusion, which is this: that I seek a mate, not a way of life. I must satisfy Nature before I invite God. That settled it for a while. But it was not settled. It rose again, as we drove back in the twilight, with a cold orange glow over the Carmel Range and Miss Hauser singing sad Hebrew songs about Elijah the Prophet. Here, I was puzzled for a while by the greyness of the trees, but of course it is winter again, and they have lost their leaves!

This morning we saw the 'Women's League for Palestine' where they hand-weave and fit girls for work, and Mrs Watt laid the first bit of concrete in a building and we drank to its health in sweet wine and cakes, and then we drove over the hills and bare dales to Nahalal, the Girls' Agricultural School and the cooperative settlement built in a circle.

As I was weakening about staying I looked at Mrs Watt in the midst of her country-woman gathering, making a speech, and I realized that you have to be slightly blind to *thoroughly* believe in *any* cause.

What beautiful breasts Jewish women have!

The settlement is for those who want to be more individualistic than the communal ones. They build and plant as they like on their bit of property, but buying and selling is cooperative; sick man's property is cared for by the others in rotation, and no hired labour is allowed. 'Social Justice' was the keynote of the young girls' information.

This was a rather drunken day.

I never drink a cup of tea now, or smell its delicate smell without seeing again the light airy tea factory in Ceylon, the beautiful native girls squatting on the floor, sorting, the lazy sun streaming in onto the intimate complications of tea preparation or the winding drive through the illuminated shade of the coconut palms.

They visit Tiberias and Nazareth before arriving at Darania, the first Jewish communal settlement founded in Palestine.

February 8

We arrived at Darania and picked our way over the hardened mud. A woman with her hair cut off like a man, dressed in blue trousers and shirt and with strong arms and ample figure met us with a warm handshake. Young people and girls dressed in blue blouses and skirts and rubber boots were running around.

Inside the house people were eating at tables in rows. Everything was clean and new and understandable. No cloudy hangings from the vague past, tradition obsessed for no known reason.

Around a yard were a row of WC surprisingly modern inside, with stone floors. I wiped myself on a Jewish newspaper.

On the oil-clothed table we had cauliflower out of a big bowl, tomato, grapefruits, bread in a basket, and apples, and prunes, and juice in a cup. Mrs Watt only ate bread. The women came and talked to Mrs Watt. One was Polish. She came many years ago in one of the first waves of Zionism, from idealism purely and not from persecution; the other was Russian. She had come from a well-off family. As early as sixteen she had been affected by Zionism and wanted to find a way to work on the land. There are about two hundred people. Nearly all the people came there long ago from idealism not necessity. Mostly from Russia. But we all spoke German as usual.

Funny – here, too, the Van Gogh reproductions everywhere.

We were shown the communal laundry, sewing, school, and the agricultural museum just begun, called after Gordon, whose ideals were for the Jewish people to return to the land to simple peasant people for three or four generations, not doctors, lawyers, or university professors. That is why *land* is stressed above all else.

Everything is communal and nobody is paid.

From the museum we looked to the hills, to Galilee Lake, and beyond the hills of Syria and Trans-Jordan. Grapefruit and olive and citrus trees. Cypress in rows for wind break. The children do the work on their own school. Schnizterlink was my guide. This was exciting. *Great*. Pictures of Herzl the Zionist, everywhere.

When I recited 'The Donkey'[6] this morning Mrs Watt said, 'O yes. When he rode in triumph into Jerusalem and they spread the palms before him. Poor Christ! It was the only little bit of triumph he ever had!'

'How still it is,' said Mrs Watt as we drove back by the Sea of Galilee.

This day has been rich and alive. The spirit was upon it, and truth left it unperplexed, only grateful, grateful and alive, but alas! inarticulate. O if I could only speak! If I could only convey, express, reveal, what has been revealed to me!

God is with me.

It is still and silhouetty. I accept all. It is an overflowing hour. There are not many such hours. God – Remain with me.

This is a land for Keats. 'When, sick for home, she stood in tears amid the alien corn.' When I undid my shutters and opened them slowly out I thought, 'magic casements opening on the foam of perilous seas, in fairylands forlorn'[7] and now comes 'Beauty is truth, truth beauty, that is all ye know on earth and all ye need to know'.[8] Old, repeated, said a million times, but only realized in a rare rich moment.

Dogs bark in the distance. Birds' wings flutter in the nearby tree. A moth's rattle grows and fades. The lake fades out, the lake. The lake and the sky become more and more one.

February 12: Jerusalem, Jericho, and the Dead Sea

Agricultural School Farm. (NB Remind Mrs Watt to send brass plate for trees planted today.) For youngsters, not for grown-up girls. Farm belongs to Jewish National Fund.

We stood on the high balcony on top of the roof among the sandbags left from the Arab raids, overlooking Trans-Jordan hills with Dead Sea mistily visible. On the left rises the modern building of the High Commission, to the left further back the greyness of Jerusalem.

The poet Bialik. The open air amphitheatre (Greekish where they sometimes have symphonies and music) overlooks the Trans-Jordanie hills.

A land where prophets would naturally arise. On the right, Jerusalem and Omar's Mosque. The wall running round is easily seen.

Young pine trees grow around terraces. There are seven hundred students. The ideals and the spirit. They have a place with all the flowers in the Bible.

It is extraordinary. I am a different person. It is not just the usual up after the usual and boring down. I can suddenly see the result of my six-month experiment and the things I have learnt on my travels. I am new-made. And I am pleased. O, if it can only continue!

This is an alive and most stimulating place. I must write Jane and tell her to come here. I must. After about six weeks in London (which now seem dull), work my way back here, or come tramp steerage. The enthusiasm is not just the immaturity of under-graduate youth awakening to the delights of the mind and the realities of life; it is a real and spiritual movement – the Jews back into their own country. It is exciting. It is thrilling. It is poetic. I haven't heard a false note. Not once have the 'ideals' been hammered at me, nor have platitudes played any part in the explanations. What they say comes simply from the heart. There is no hypocrisy. You see, they really *are* an intellectual people with 'Torah' and music in their souls. They have been persecuted and it is the great ones who have been the first to find their way back here. This Spirit of a new birth is not just a small incubator baby, to be forced with desperate abortive efforts into a flutter of a life. It shines from the Jewish faces in the streets, the girls on the agricultural school, the old workers in the settlements, Stuck, Hermann, Ginsberg. I never met a thing so alive. It wakens me. I never felt so omniscient, so full of understanding, comprehension, realization of how the world works, and grasp of great human movements. I feel wittier, more sympathetic, more powerful. I am coming back: I must. Where else has this happened? Or ever?

They sail from Jerusalem on The Ranpura *to Port Said stopping at Malta and Marseilles.*

February 20: Ranpura, The Lowest Ebb

How I hate the sea and the interminable, long, dull days. The cold, the food, the insufferable passengers who never smile, England and the bloody English, and the utter emptiness and futility of the whole thing. Barren, sterile, and stale is the smell of the ship. I have met two people in two days whom I would like to kill. I didn't know my repugnance and hate were still so fierce. I hate Mrs Watt too though she is being very gentle and kind too, and it is much harder for her than for me, and she is going home to an upset office and unions and she will have to make rows, while I am going to have months of friends and the delights of civilization again. But I am dead now, waiting for Emily (the evil spirit precursing her), and generosity and fire and love flow out into the desert. I had meant this last unfilled trip by sea to be a résumé of the six months but somehow I never can exude proper emotion at place and time. I had so looked forward to looking back that the present is null and void. And the anticipation of London was more exciting than anything that could possibly happen to me. I have had that thrill before – but it can only take place at an unalterable distance from London, when to get to London must take weeks, and it never never never could endure right up to the cliffs of Dover.

Now I can see all too plainly the emptiness which I have also felt in London – deserted Piccadilly, a left-out feeling. I remember John lamenting once because Clive Pearson, his hero and chief, got back a week or so early from New York before John had had time to think up what attitude he would take up, or in what way he could subtly alter their relationship.

I feel no anticipation about John at all – only a determination to be independent and not browbeaten again. It's to Grisell I look when I think of London, and Charlie when I think of life. As for love, I don't think of it.

I think the English people (Indian Army, lower middle class who think they're upper and all snobs who haven't got taste (Golly! what a snobbish statement) are the rudest, unkindest, most unimaginative and ill-mannered people in the world.)

And yet nearly all the people I love best are English.

The American youth Wager (Philadelphia) with spectacles gave me, in all seriousness, a lecture on how to be attractive to men. He said I must be *feminine*!! and not to wear trousers, etc. Such insolence, or rather ignorance! He thought he was being kind.

Bridge first with Mrs Giles and a beast called Sir Benjamin Robertson, rude, rough, and ignorant (to be avoided). I won six shillings. Mrs Watt and he nearly came to blows. He corrected her, told her to speak up, told her he'd been waiting a long time, and told her everything was her fault. The universal ill humour round the bridge table almost restored me.

The American got me from my cabin where I had gone down and we danced a bit on the cold, glassed-in deck dance floor.

February 25: Ranpura, Stop at Plymouth 6:30 AM

From the most delicious dreams I woke to the most delicious smell of England – and even (wafted from afar) London. I got up and stood to look at Plymouth in the foggy dawn, damp, misty, nothing but a rich suggestion. And then the sounds of departure, change, anticipation. It was rich and warm to lie in bed dreaming of things to come, warm, smelling the mixed smells of the beloved land after the sea, having a pleasantly cool damp nose from the fog.

Nothing happened in the day at all, but I was supremely happy waiting.

In the wet moistness of the distance I saw the Isle of Wight, with its white sheer cliffs and ill-named needles. At night rows of lights appeared in patches – long steady rows of Brighton? Hove?

People have relaxed. They begin to smile without provocation. Today at teatime I played the piano and many people came in until the room was full and sat quite still and listened and when I stopped they clapped and begged me to go on and they clapped after every piece and when I stopped altogether they thanked me, solemnly, simply and sincerely. It was elating. One lady confided in sobs about to burst that her daughter would have been my age if she had lived but she died six years ago. I realized something about my music – and it is this – that I can play, as they should be played, the pieces that the average musically uneducated people want to hear, that means something to them. They don't understand the great and subtle music. *To a Wild Rose* is what moves them. That I can give them. So that, inadequately equipped as I am, musically, I am in a position to give more people in this world pleasure by my playing than most musicians are. Ten years of intensive study couldn't make me better fitted for this particular job. They only understand the feeling sent through a simple instrument.

Today I was very fond of Mrs Watt and I felt tender and motherly towards her.

Before dinner she felt a chill so immediately afterwards she went to bed and I brought her a huge glass of hot lemonade and a lady gave her brandy and she had hot water bags and woollies on, but she had an unsatisfactory letter from Sholto saying he hadn't found a suitable house and that Joan White, the ACWW secretary, had been sent to Geneva. I *felt* so for her, but there wasn't much I could do.

The Albatross Book of American Short Stories is *good* – really American, well-written, representative and varied.

It was a joy to get everything neatly stored away, to do my nails and curl my lashes and lay out my clean clothes in preparation for too-exciting-to-be-thought-of London.

February 26: Tilbury to London

Undertones: John, Frampton, Jimmy. Now that I'm here I've never been away. It's unnecessary to call friends. It can't be a year! John telegraphed (dine tomorrow – typically). Jimmy a sweet typical letter waiting ('the bluebells of Kew, and the neat bushes of Virginia Water').

London again, but not anticipation, not excitement, just acceptance, a generous repletion. Just a thankful sigh of contentment. What moves me to tears of joy and sadness with meaning are the black stunted trees that grow by the grey rows of dark houses, half mist covered, the street wet and shining and deserted, the mystic, significant, suggestive *smell* everywhere.

Once the nostrils get accustomed to the rich conglomeration of moist smells the excitement of London gets lost in its days threading in and out, and is only discovered by surprise, suddenly, or by love, or by a soft insistent spring day.

'Not England
But the desire I once felt there.'

PART THREE

1937–1939

I

LONDON
1937

*On her return to London, following her trip around the world, Smart resumed her
social life and her relationship with John which soon ends. On June 11, 1937,
again she returned to Canada to spend the summer at Kingsmere. On August
19, she returned to London and in August made another visit to Scotland. She
returned to Canada in the fall but was back in England by January, 1938.*

*There are three notebooks for this period. The entries from February to April
are an account of her days in London following her trip. Journal entries from
May to January are poems. One notebook contains the story 'My Lover John,' an
apprenticeship work on which she had been working during her trip. This version
is in process, and makes use of material from her past journals. She fuses details
of her relationship with Lord Pentland and incidents from the summer before
she leaves Canada to travel around the world, with incidents from her trip with
Mrs Watt. There is a disparity in the voice of the narrator, which fluctuates
between the voice of a fictional narrator and the voice of Smart herself.*

February 27: London (8 Lowndes Street)

Oo the cold on emerging from bed where I just managed to keep
warm by squashing myself to myself.

All morning unpacking in overalls and tidying a hopelessly untidy
room. There is nowhere to put anything at all except dresses and
bottles (no hangers though), no bureau, no dressing table, no chest
of drawers, no bookcases. It was a mathematical problem.

Victor[1] telephones to say the doctor has ordered him to bed –
would I go there for lunch?

At once I went, in my frilly French collar. The rain rained. Chill
sharp penetrating through the taxi. Victor was miles upstairs lying
flat. I sat by his electric fire and had lunch off a tray on a little table.
When he even sees me coming he thinks it is a huge joke and laughs
and laughs. He smiles and smiles. It was good and I felt enriched.

I dropped in to Patrick Rolleston's and met Joan Bonnycastle there. This was nice too, but I felt disgruntled. Patrick is so invulnerable. But at least I have at last achieved – or rather regained – independence of all people's moods.

Then – I hurried home and bathed and changed in a terrible rush, as the hour began to draw near I began to be terrified with excitement but more nervousness. I felt as a child going up for an examination, or as before my first speech.

I got a more universal view as I went round the glistening darkness of Hyde Park Corner, but cold began to penetrate. London is so usual, nothing strikes you anew – you don't say O *look! That* again, I'd forgotten. You just drive along and think new thoughts as if it were the same chain of taxiing through the years.

I arrived out of breath from nervousness at John's door and he opened it and I said, 'Hullow how are you' in an artificial high voice which I tried to keep calm and he said, 'Kitty's sick I'm all alone.' We talked in front of his fire. I forgot I was nervous. I wasn't a bit any more. I was too sure almost, and we talked like two interested but impersonal friends. He put on jazz. He had the mud postcard and the songs I sent on the mantle. He looked at the pin I wore which he gave me. After a while, pleasant, smooth, untroubled and conversational, an intense upper froth being absorbed first, the Makins (Foreign Office – she American) arrived. She is American gone Englishy. I didn't take to her. But I adored him.

After a bit of waiting for Bill we went to Prunier's, women behind in John's car. Kenneth Lindsay joined us for drinks and Bill came. I had Makins beside me. He talked well and let me too. I like chaffing Bill. Bill is extraordinarily stupid in some ways. He has just discovered David B. Milne.

After a long but very pleasant meal we went back to John's and the Salmons were there and we had more conversation till about one, then Bill drove me home and I shivered and chattered, but when I got home I was disturbed because I thought I hadn't thanked John properly or talked to him and I looked in the glass and said: Is this misery going to start again? But I didn't think so, so I did my face and tidied for night and here I am – London begun, the rare delicious moment of imminence and anticipation grown to a full accepted day.

'Nothing's so beautiful now as it used to be.'

I see *all* now with one of those sweet sad smiles as Charlie would say.

John is sweet but sometimes I turn against him disloyally. I *saw* him again – shy and easily wounded and on the defensive – so I must be unendingly generous and gentle and understanding, not demand anything of him, never be dissatisfied with the little he gives even if I think it inadequate for I am strong now and I think he has great courage.

Anyway I should be kind and unselfish to everyone.

But soon I felt the pull of the early hours I have been keeping and wanted to close my eyes and sleep.

But now, the turmoil within won't lie down and rest.

First thing in the morning I shall telephone and thank him.

(Bill said to, too. Bill has that straightforward sort of loyalty.)

John, do you need me? Do I need you? Am I a fraud? Questions not yet again problems.

A picture this morning when the two maids made my bed and told their views about what it must be like to go round the world and see 'black people' and the different way they eat, etc.

February 28: London

I phoned John first thing. It was tragically impersonal. He would like to have a drink with me sometime. Next Wednesday or Thursday? I fixed Thursday. So long! I lay disgruntled. His iron will is hypnotic.

However, when warmed with three cups of coffee and various phone calls, including Victor's rather sad voice from bed, I got up and wrote a myriad of letters. John Davies has a cold and is in bed so we won't walk. I had lunch here on a tray, soup, bread and cheese and milk, and grapefruit. The snow was snowing. When I set out towards the Knightsbridge tube the wind was wild and piercing and the snow whirling in icy abandon. I clutched my coat and hat and made a nasty face as did all the passers-by. Going down the tube escalator I felt independent and elated, or was it the echo of a John-feeling I once had, lovely, on my way to Hampstead to practise. I walked down the wet streets in the hurly-burly snow, wet flakes to Ellerton Road 7A. (I got muddled in the tube, but a vivacious little Northerner helped me out with dignity.) I went in. Mike was sitting by the fire, untidy, with long hair over his brow. He said, 'Hullo, Betty,' but didn't get up. (I am bound to say his attitude improved during the evening and he almost began to get on his toes.) We talked. People can't easily deflate me now. Maryon came in. The room is hung with David B. Milnes. I bought one (for they are selling them for the Masseys). Mike has rather broadened and reddened out. Maryon has a sharp face, not beautiful from inside. But we get on easily. I love being Canadian vulgar with her.

These days good things tumble so upon each other that I can taste nothing and I become either full with satiety or disgruntled for never savouring as I love to do.

Patrick and Marjorie Gordon and a Ralph Connor came in. It was full of laughter, till it hurt. Marjorie is charming with aliveness bursting from her eyes and great sweetness and comprehension on her mouth. She is pretty except when she laughs. Her eyes are beautiful. Her strong upturned nostrilly nose reminds me of Jane and Katherine Hepburn. She loves laughing silliness and is full of comeback. Yes – I do like her.

After supper we had more easy sitting and laughing and talking and for a bit I read a *Forum* where were two wee poems by Jane.

There was a moment with Mike before the others came up when I was glad of my physical womanly growth and rejoiced to own such a powerful and easy weapon. Because Mike can be so rude when he is bored.

He dislikes Kenneth Lindsay and says he's ambitious in the wrong sense and full of himself and thinks he's arrived.

Maryon drove us all home in the cold and Mike let her. He stayed behind.

Hampstead still has that air of concealing just around the corner, the house I read about in some old book when I was a child, a different *life*. I know someday I shall find that family whose smell is in the very Hampstead mists, behind the clipped hedges, under the arched doorways. Keats walking with Leigh Hunt, or the whole Sanger family sitting in the sunshine in an untidy studio making music in the middle of the afternoon.

This so intangible thing runs richly up my back tingling and keeping alive even the spirit on a cold deserted street.

John disturbed me for at least eight hours after I talked to him. What *is* that magical tragical power anyway? I am drawn to him, compelled to be miserable, chastened, subdued, humbled, curtailed,

bound. Why? Is it some divine idea to discipline and tutor my easily
inflated self-esteem? Would fate dare to interfere?

March 3: London

This whole day was nothing but a waiting and a preparation for
John. I did a bit of 'Details,'[2] but lay too long in bed. About one I
went shopping to buy sherry (Bristol Milk) and sherry glasses and
biscuits and I had lunch in a cheerless cafe or tea shop. I carried
the Bristol Milk and biscuits home so that they would be sure to be
there when John arrived.

I went to the Canadian Club tea but it was dull and the selfishness
and avidity to be smart of the women put me out of sympathy. I saw
Mrs Grace Gordon Bell, KKB, Mrs Tustin, a Miss Denison, and, of
course, Mrs Edgar who paid for me. We sat with a Mrs Hancock.
But soon I left (after the ice cream).

I went home. Did and re-did my nose. Sat waiting. Played records.
Tried to read but it got too dark to see near the fire and too cold away
from it. About seven he came. We had a nice long easy talk about him
and I was elated. Then we went out to dinner (unpremeditated) at *Au
Jardin Des Gourmets* and that was good too. Then after indecision as
usual and vagueness we came back here and all was well. Then I read
him my diaries and he said he thought they were good. But then he
got up to go and intimated that he wouldn't see me again. My heart
slithered sickeningly down to my wobbly feet and then the tenseness,
emotion, and utterly despairful time began. John wanting to go but
tied here by my abjectness at his unnecessary stern decisions.

O what is this? Is it because he likes me? Or because he doesn't?
Because I disturb him? Or because I tire him? Or because of another
woman, or man, or interest? Are these extremes necessary? And yet
what right have I to detain him if I can't even say I love him? Yet
why should I lose and let go my dear dear friend, my necessary part
of London, part of myself. It is quite possible to be warm and mutual
and rich without the end of sex. Affection, not stern denial, like Jane
and Mummy. Fondness, not disrupting and disregardful passion.

Yet now I feel more at peace. It is the sickening waste and futility
that I can't bear. And now, *honestly*, it is from John's point of view
that I worry. I could really help him.

Yet even now I have sobered down, with sleep and warmth and
realize that perhaps it would be a good thing not to see him.

I can become adjusted to anything.

O but only remember the walks through the wet woods! What they might have been! The misery of the thought of what they might have been! O the wild dreams! Was it really the end, then, when I sailed, sick and exhausted, for Canada last year? What have I done? Is the fault mine or his? He said he had learnt that he couldn't teach me anything, nor he learn anything.

March 4: London

An enormous black cat met me at the door tonight about midnight, whined to be let in, followed me politely upstairs. I went in and shut the door on him, but he complained loudly so I let him in, and he nosed about looking for something to eat, tried my stocking and all the chairs, sharpened his claws on the upholstery and then left through the door which I had left open. He had great yellow eyes, and long puffy fluffy black fur. When I went out into the hall he was lying in beautiful elaborately abandoned repose, waiting. He followed me down the stairs and I let him out. Our pleasant, curious, impersonal relationship at an end.

I woke early with a sense of loss this morning, but as I was lying preparing to have a pale reaction, Mrs Watt phoned, in the most cheerful spirits and gay good humour. She asked me to be at the offices at 11:30 to see about the money I owed them. I saw Mary Morrell. It was rather uncomfortable. I can't respond to artificially enthusiastic people. And I always feel that she is pumping me or trying to squelch me. But impersonally or is it personally, I quite like her.

Mrs Watt completely cheered me. I said, 'You seem in very gay spirits today. What is it?' She said, 'It's seeing you again.' I dropped her by taxi at the doctor's.

By lunch time at Tom Davies, I was quite cured and in exuberant form. Gilbert Yates and 'Jasper' were there too – Tom was surprisingly delighted to see me and kept referring to my 'family,' meaning, of course, Helen. 'Write to them and persuade them to come over,' he kept saying. I talked about my trip and made them laugh. I had bought a new hat (actually two) in Army and Navy Stores (!) while I was using up the extra time.

Tom took my arm walking to Whitehall and I felt gay, but I was thinking about John with vague (definite but not disturbing) regret that I shall not have the pleasure and education and stimulation of his company. However, I came home pleasantly and waited for Diana Battye.[3] I bought daffodils and white lilac to make it smell beautiful. She was nearly two hours late. She was looking absolutely beautiful. Fragile, sincere, breakable, innocent, incredible. I adored her. She is doing some work in the films, also posing for photographs (at 10 shillings a sitting) and a bit of mannequin work. She can cry in the movies when they want her to. She thinks of a 'romantic story with an unhappy ending.' She is writing a book about a girl who was disillusioned, whose parents were divorced (hers were). She says she is to be married next September. Then, the following June, she would like to go back to Canada alone. She had a little round cap on the back of her head and a wavy bit of brown hair kept falling over one eye. She had on a very simple dress with buffalo-nickel buttons down the front. She stimulated and excited me. Her movie name is Doone Layman.

She stayed till nearly seven so I was late for John Davies at his chambers. I went by taxi by mistake to the Temple first. Tanya, Katherine Ridley, Edward Charles and Ross McLean were there. We had beer and sandwiches and cake. The office was bare. You go up a spiral stone staircase. The unshaded bulb throws a hard light onto the exposed room.

We went to Sadlers Wells running up the street till we got stitches because we got on the wrong streetcar.

We saw *The Marriage of Figaro* by Mozart. Quite good. Pleasant. But never yet has an opera moved me. I always like the Overtures best. John loved it. He responded alively. We came home by bus. The night air was nippy and the atmosphere impecuniously intellectual.

From Pont Street I ran happily and at my door met the cat.

From today I got the desire for Diana and her company. I thought I hadn't taken enough trouble to have women friends. Her life is so right, true, and unvain. With her as fortification perhaps I shall not even need John. Tonight John Davies was special to me.

I felt aloof from everything, passive, contented enough, but undesirous. Probably just sleepy.

As Graham said of me once, Diana is a rare flower. Why couldn't Eric abide her?

March 10: London

John Davies cured me.[4] I awoke alive and worked all day. Lunch on a tray. Up to chapter twenty-eight of 'Details.' O it was good! I have a cold but that doesn't matter.

I worked all day. I swallowed a lemon drop whole by mistake. Maryon phoned and I went out there to dinner with her, by underground. We went to see Elizabeth Berginan in *As You Like It*. I loved it. I wished it could have gone on and on. 'Audrey' was especially good and pretty. There were many delicious little touches (Treatment suggested by JM Barrie).

A good and moral day with beginning, imagination, birth, and end, all enough.

I am free. Also free of my tyrant John. He is pleasant enough still to think about. I am free.

March 21: Diana Battye's, Billingbear Lodge, Binfield, Berkshire

The sky caught glassily in puddles.

Almost dizzy with so much sleep, I at last took resolution and thrust aside the warm soft deep covers and dressed shivery in the cold, without preliminary. But then I heard Diana's breakfast going in to her and Nannie came in and said, 'O you're dressed. You were to have your breakfast in bed.' So I sat on the end of Diana's bed with her fur-lined coat over me. She looked adorable in the early morning, sitting up in bed in her baby pink bed jacket. She was sleepy and tousled but still starry-eyed. She is quite physically unconscious, so that she even looks more attractive for having her nose running, or her face all shiny. With Nannie, and in the early morning, she has a humourous look about her mouth which kept reminding me of someone whom I finally found out to be Ruth Stevenson.

After breakfast I read Virginia Woolf's *The Years* by the fire and she wrote at her desk, and sent postcards to her Crofters about the tweeds, etc.

The morning sky was a dull, damp, white-grey, and cold.

We went in her car along the behedged lanes to a station to meet Graham Grant, a Canadian, her agent, and a Miss Bell. I didn't like them the minute I saw them. He had a green hat, tan shoes, and slinky eyes. She was small, with sleek black hair and a thin face, pencil eyebrows, enormous eyes, thin wet lips and slightly sticking out teeth. She had on large check 'smart' tweeds and an imitation 'county' hat. He ignored me. I sat behind with him. I was sleepy. But when he ignored me I became furious and did nothing. The whole day they were both influencing me so strongly that the mood was unmemorable. We went to the bungalow on the airdrome where Diana's mother and her husband live.

When we opened the door they raised a shout of joy and said, 'Here's Didy.' Leonard Hackett was the husband. I felt awkward and silent. I drank tomato juice by the fire in a stiff chair. Diana's mother looked at her adoringly and admiringly. She was pretty in a slightly gone to seed way, and largely built, grown fat and flowing, generous and genial with little ridiculous feminine ways. The sort of woman you are bound to be fond of no matter how silly she is, and she probably is. Leonard was younger and jovial and generous and enthusiastic. A typical sort of man of the playing kind. He talked about when he and she were engaged, rather sentimental, and they had chairs put out in the garden to watch the sunset. It was the first time she had sat in the garden, and he told me how when he got engaged Nannie disapproved terribly, so he bought her a huge bottle of boiled sweets which were her weakness and she said, 'Humph! I don't know what you want to give me all those sweets for. I'll never be able to eat them.' But the layers got lower and lower.

She had a set of Penguin books in her bedroom. She saw an advertisement saying sixty novels in bookcase for thirty shillings, and they sent for them but had to pay postage and carriage, etc. and the bookcase was only cardboard and had already started busting.

We left and came home to lunch, which we had in the dining room. I didn't talk much. Mr Grant said a few more words to me and was slightly nicer. He asked a bit about Canadians we both knew. Miss Bell talked insincerely and enthusiastically and began to get on my nerves. (Emily is today or tomorrow.) Her voice jars. It has a trace of cockney. I hate her. She is artificial, and thinks she has to give her platitudinous opinion about everything. Her voice is like metal clattering. Diana was adorable and talked to him and her with full and generous measure and with her innocent wide-eyed look and sympathetic interest. After lunch we sat by the fire, until Maurice Cardiff (paints) and Leonora, and Johnny (actor) arrived and then we went for a walk. Diana getting beer out of hours at the pub. The mossy red bricks and green red water. The mud. The pine trees. My out feeling. Out of it, suspected outwards feeling. Tea here. I still dumb. The jawing woman and Diana mostly saying things, and Mr Grant. Then Diana remembered she had forgotten to take Mr Grant to the stables and they rushed off, and Maurice and Leonora (in love) left and I was alone with Johnny and Miss Bell. I got so I couldn't *stand* Miss Bell so I went off and helped Nannie dry the dishes, then I went in D's rubber boots with Johnny the dog across the fields, running through the mud, for a walk.

I crossed the cows' field, scared, and walked through a wood and felt better and saw the buds ready to burst, and primroses, birds twittering, and I sang loud mournful songs and thanked God when I suddenly realized I was 'free of love and hate' and quite independent and calm and tranquil in my soul. No tragedy does the word have to balm. No healing, no mournful romantic dreams. I was always wanting to bust my sad songs to joyful ones, but I can't sing the joyful ones, they get too robust. I walked in the bushy wood and the little excited muddy dog tore around. It grew dusky. I met a man who altered his course when he saw me. There was a race track and abandoned carts. I walked along a grassgrown track path. The sky was caught glassily in puddles. It was rich and English and rare. The whole great loveableness and mystery and soul of England was there. I walked under a room of great trees, across the fields, up the muddy field to the little house, now in the dark, light only from the kitchen windows.

I took off my boots and put on my silk stockings and shoes and washed.

But when I joined them again it was just the same.

There was a knock at the door and with great noise and laughter I heard a merry voice say, 'We've come to return your call.' It was D's mother and husband. They only stayed a minute.

We drove through floods to Maidenhead and had supper in a movie tearoom upstairs. Diana read Johnny's hand. Johnny is beautiful and sensitive. I wanted to talk to him. I hated the other worthless pair. He had to catch the train. Diana took him. Then she came back and we took the others. Then we drove home together and talked and I relaxed again, and felt rich and full and loved her. We sat in the warm kitchen with the stove and Nannie talked. It was pleasant and rich and real and flowing and as a result stimulating.

I had a bath and mounted the stairs with my oil lamp.

There is a hot water bottle like a sheep dog in my bed and I have just put out the oil stove and opened my windows looking out onto the field.

The trampled English wood was like the crumpled bed where two lovers had thrashed themselves in vain against each other, searching for the unattainable fulfilment without success. Man has beaten himself against Nature, trying in tragic vain to rouse her to her great revelation, and give satisfaction for the endless disturbing potentialities.

March 25: To The Cripps, Goodfellows, Filkins, Oxfordshire

Late bed. Shopping for Felicity. Too late to see her. Lunch milk bar. Bumped into Ross McLean. Shopping Peter Jones. Hair around the corner. Frantic packing. Taxi to Paddington 4:45. Full Train. No money. Sat on suitcase in corridor. Poplar trees in the mist beyond the graveyard. Out at Oxford.

John Cripps' shining round rosy face, and tall Theresa (Ter-eeza) and little child-faced Ursula, John's bride. Motor in gathering dark to Goodfellows. Pale, sad, tired Lady Cripps, kissed me. Sir Stafford, looking still boyish coming into the hall said, 'Hullo! Here's Betty. How are you? It's years since we've met.' Central heating in my room. Lady Cripps' pale washed-out sadness. Dinner – 'We mustn't talk about food at the table – you see we each have our own diets and if we talk about food each gets arguing about the relative merits of his own.'

John and Ursula's house discussed. The lateness of the three other expected ones (Geoffrey Wilson, Michael Foot[5], and a girl Barbara). Things John was doing. Sir Stafford's meetings. Ursula was sweet and solicitous and asked Sir Stafford about things he had done in a little childish voice. Sir Stafford and Lady Cripps both have nerves and Theresa was not calm but rather imperturbable and independent. 'Nannie' was at the table. After dinner by the great fire Sir Stafford asked me about my book and each of my family. He is a scholar, thinker, philosopher, intellectual, by his face. 'I wonder what our friend Muss[6] is saying tonight,' said Sir S.

'I don't want to but I think we *ought* to put it on,' said Lady C.

I can't imagine how anyone could ever be with Sir Stafford Cripps for very long without becoming one of his disciples. He is so sincere, natural, simple, charming, full of sense of humour and human sanity, young, gay, disinterested, and unselfish. He is rare. Beside him the others seem fakes. With the Cripps, I always feel humble and unworthy. Yet they are sweet and kind and tender and merry to all the friends. Lady Cripps is tragically broken up with sadness and despair. Yet it is only her weak health and sickness. She is still gentle and warm and understanding and spiritual. She loves Ursula and hugged her and kissed her twice goodnight.

O! I do wish I could write this whole Cripps family suitably. If I could make you feel the way I feel, see what I see in them! All evening the ugly tune and the words, 'Sir Stafford Cripps should get one and wear it all the time,' kept going through my head.[7]

March 26: Goodfellows

'It's just trivial things.'

What are trivial things? That's all that ever happens in life. A woman of fifty-five looking into her glass and finding that she's got one more wrinkle.

'The Germans were defeated' means nothing unless you translate it into the effect it had on each individual German, unless you see the trivialities it produced or ended.

Ursula, always dressed in tunic effect with blouse or sweater beneath, playing the piano; I thinking, 'John loves her, he runs his hand through her hair.' Do I want to be loved? No. I can't ever imagine love now. I watch Ursula and John with wonder. John came in from a walk, surrounded by gusts of cold air and kissed Ursula's forehead while she was playing. Ursula stitching a peasant vest of printed blue cotton by the fire.

Sir Stafford keeping the bank in Monopoly.

Theresa, young and uncompromising, and stern and triumphant about her mouth. I don't think she likes me.

Up in the cold studio peeling grapes, Ursula told me about her musical education, her job teaching in Wales and at her old school.

There is never any general conversation at the table.

It is generous of the Cripps to have us here, Michael and Geoffrey and Barbara, who work for the Labour Party, and encourage them and me.

As for me, I begin to feel guilty, and flippant, and vain.

Sir Stafford and Lady Cripps are the only ones I feel close to. The others are obstreperously absorbed in their revolving worlds. The talk is all of Ursula and John's new house, the diets, arrangements and people I don't know.

I hate to take and not give; but what could I give that they want? When I played the piano to Ursula it was stupid and childish and sounded stale and dull. I felt ashamed.

It is this young love between John, whose face is always shining, and whose eyes light up with embarrassed humour, and little, good, child-like Ursula, that absorbs me. Is it half jealousy, thinking of their warm and comfortable intimacy? The little loving ways John has towards her? No . . . Sometimes I love her, thinking how he must love her and watching his serious, spiritual face. But she has no weaknesses. She is sure. Weakness is so lovable.

They are most unselfish, the Cripps. I almost feel a traitor to their great cause. I feel they think I am a deceiving, gay capitalist, pleasure loving, pretending to be more serious than I am. Yet, of course, I know they don't think that.

England this morning, driving through the rolling red-brown fields, orange, tan, and walking across muddy fields and in woods and over stiles. Green helibore, white violets, pink daisies, Dog's mercury, lesser celandine.

Theresa learning to drive with a big L on her car.

The moon in the cold night shining onto the lily pond.

Lots of dogs and a pet goat and a swing.

Barbara is gay and individual and easy to get on with, and so are Michael and Geoffrey.

Theresa is a bit authoritative.

Lady Cripps said of Graham Spry, 'That man is a saint. Are they married yet?' She asked me twice.

'Were you writing your book?' said Ursula to me when I went down to the dining room for tea.

'Yes.'

'I thought you were,' she said.

The house ceilings are low with beams. The house wanders and I get lost in it. Outside it is grey landscape stone, and goes in all directions.

Sir Stafford is fascinating, charming, irresistible, so simple, so interested. Sometimes Lady C reminds me of Mummy – what

Mummy might have been if she had been less hysterical and highly strung. Lady C is more reasonable and less selfish and quite unvain. She has the same warmth, suffered but beautiful face, gentle motherliness and graciousness.

I wrote eight pages of 'Details' in the still, sleepy hour after lunch and also some letters. I wore my velvet dress and no one else had on long dresses except Lady C.

Sir S said, 'You're very grand.' I wished I weren't. But Ursula said by the fire, 'I love the colour of your dress.'

Monopoly is a harassing game. I don't like it. It is unsatisfactory even if you win. I never do. Theresa won. She is so competent.

March 27: At Goodfellows

This 'trivial' still upsets me. Because it affects my work. Naturally it doesn't affect Virginia Woolf. Is the overlying purpose shown, the meaning, the epic pattern? I feel so loose and unknowing, just feelings, laziness, egotism. The labour, the labour. I must labour.

O that I knew as my comfortable friends Yeats, McNeice, Roger Fry, Virginia Woolf, A. Huxley, Spender, Auden, McLeish, GB Shaw, etc!

Barbara is obsessed by the evils of the present economic system. It's the poetry I want to abstract and shout from the rooftops.

Swinging in the swing, the light on the pale reddening willow trees and the patch of bright rich grass, and the grey stone walls with their brilliant yellow doilies of lichen – the past. I say, 'We have got this far from the beginning of time' – with pleasure I say it – as one who should say, 'See – I have got to the sleeves in the knitting of this sweater.' So from the oozing bogs to the orange lichen on grey and ancient stones.

England – what colour is that? Russet brown? It's redder, it's paler. And that? Redder, brighter, tan. Leaves wet and fallen in the wood. And the orange, pale creamy brown orange fields, ploughed.

The winding lanes, brambles, the grass banks, the tangled hedges, wolds, a square tower on a church, the orchard and double snowdrops, the pool glimmering like cut glass, clogged with waterweeds.

Escaped periwinkle, purple. Grey stone houses and buildings part of the land, fences of stone, overlying, indefinite, rising around.

At the pool: marks where hoofs had slid down the slope in the mud to the water.

The top of a tree that has no leaves and is high, lofty and spreading. What inspirations from childhood, swinging in the swing, the wind lifting hair – cold and richness in the bleakness.

My words run dry. Repetitive grew my feminine words.

Daffodils spearing up in the cold, carelessly in any spot. Was it planned and left untidy on purpose? The daffodils look as if it were quite by chance.

Red whips of the willow. Soft earthy red – against live green. O that I were a poet – such conglomerating, life form surfeit, running richly waste. I begin to see life – however little I know. Knowledge now – wisdom distilled – sudden understanding. But ah! inarticulate – urgent sympathy unsaid – lame uttered, in vain. Never conveyed. Write, speak, search. The Word – in the beginning was the Word.

Whatever meaning, search. Never any rest.

Blake felt and spoke. Follow the days with accepted organized work? Today ten pages – on, on.

It is getting dull. It is all flippant and vain. I could make it better.

The thousand possibilities and potentialities – what it might be – paralyse me.

I leave it as it is.

Each word enlarged could make an essay – but would that be tedious, or would it arouse more interest, elucidate and give continuity and be less jerky and new and sudden?

I left out 'The Parrs'[8] because they were too big. They are a whole book – or at least a Katherine Mansfield. I thought they needed inspiration and special concentrated preparatory thought. Because, you see, I mentioned Aunt Ellen and they seemed somehow connected with her.

Could I make her a great character, always influencing but never appearing?

WORK MORE.

Each bit could be so much better, if I sat and thought and turned over before I wrote.

But it is a diary.

It is preparation.

I feel I could do so much better. I feel I am not doing my best.

John and Ursula's cottage near Witney, and their enchanting Granny. We danced in the evening.

Looking at the lovely special editions. 'This family seems to be Blake fiends too.' Ursula: 'Oh do you like Blake?' Me: 'He's my very favourite man.' U: 'How funny! He's mine too.'

We looked at Arthur Rackham's Undine illustrations together. It made Ursula seem more romantic and glamorous when I thought of her together with her Rackham and Blake dreams.

She wore a long brocade dress with short puff sleeves and square neck and old-fashioned modelled gold necklace.

'That's the dress she wore at her wedding – I mean the reception we gave for them.' 'She looks well in those peasant styles. They suit her.'

Theresa came down in a real peasant costume with organdy blouse, but thoroughly resented all the many comments. She is at an age of too sure knowledge. She has just got her scholarship. It is almost as if she despised the rest of us inefficient vague people.

Not even Barrie's mother had a softer face than Lady Cripps.

March 29: At Goodfellows

Slept late. Muffled and doused with sleep. Breakfast alone. The sun wasn't up. I don't like getting up when the sun isn't up. 'Like the actress who said in some interview that she never got up before the sun had warmed the streets,' said Barbara.

Diana drove us a ways and Barbara and I walked back over the fields.

'Tell me about yourself,' said B.

'No. You tell me about yourself,' said I.

She told me about her scholarship, her hard work, and then her tired-out-ness when she went up to Oxford.

'What did you do?'

'Danced and flirted.'

She would lie awake in agony at the thought of approaching exams and then get up and go out dancing again to forget about it. Understandable. A human story. But she got a third. She does work on the Tribune paper now (Michael too) and has meetings, etc. She told me she wanted to marry a man who was heart and soul in politics as she was.

'I'm very feminine,' she said, as we walked along a high little lane in the sun, 'and I need a man to work with me and sympathize.' Her pale red hair shone in the sun. But it was caught in with bobby pins.

She said that she had found that man (Michael I suppose) but that that made it more difficult (money I suppose).

'You're not interested in politics. You're more interested in the little things of life. Watching people. Not in the great issues and underlying ideas.'

'It's because I'm only interested in the big things that I'm not interested in politics.'

'I want nice things, dancing, pleasure, love, romance, fine clothes, but I don't feel I have a right to them when I am working to get them for everyone else. I want everyone else to have nice things, love, romance, the pleasures of life,' etc. etc.

'What a wonderful thing it is to have so many things that you believe in,' I said.

'What things?'

'Well you believe in the cause. You believe that things can be cured and that you can help them to be cured. That's two big things. Then you believe that material things will change and help people. And you believe in love.'

'One has one's moments of profound doubt.'

'Ah! But with four things you can't doubt them all at once.'

'But they're so woven together. If one went, the others would go too.'

'Even love?'

'Yes.'

We passed the Rook wood and a great clatter and chatter was still coming from the tops of the trees.

It was cold. I finished *The Years*. Not as good as *The Waves* but full of allusive meaning. And a great example. I love VW.

After lunch, papers by the fire and Sir Stafford and Geoffrey and Michael and Barbara talking about politics.

Sir Stafford on Victor Gollancz's Book Club and the books he had brought out and their merits and how poor they were getting.

'Twelve books of political propaganda is too much to expect the ordinary person to absorb in twelve months.'

He spoke highly of Neville Chamberlain and said that he was the best man and that his austerity, his lack of charm, might go over very well now – people would say, 'we don't like him, but it's all for the best.'

Some of Barbara's opinions were immature. She sometimes leads herself in the wrong directions. When she dances her hand is placed so – in a rigid manner on her partner and her elbow goes up and down – she is moving as much as her partner and leading him – or doing 'steps' *with* him – with serious, concentrating face.

Then I wrote in my room twenty-four pages and someone came and told me to come to tea and I went down and some more Crippses were there. I felt gay and irresponsible and irrepressible. I talked and chaffed to twenty-year-old Charles, and the father who had been to Hollywood for three hours, and when they left I teased Stafford and everybody else I saw and I felt in control and loved and loving and gay.

This morning Sir S said, 'Good morning, Beatrice.' (Last night he said goodnight Beatrice.)

So I said, 'Good morning, Dante,' and was one up.

Then I wrote more until dinner. John came to get me. I didn't know it was early. Some new people were there.

I got talking well at last with Sir Stafford.

'The trouble is you have to be such an editor,' I said. 'Everything in the day can be equally valuable artistically if you spend energy on it.'

'No. I don't agree,' he said. 'Some things are more important than others. Working for peace, for instance, is very important.'

'Yes,' I said. 'But what's that to do with it? You're confusing me. I'll tell you tomorrow when I've written my diary and "clarified my thoughts".'

So –

Working for peace – naturally, the most important external thing today – but in the fullness of time – non-existent, as votes for women and all the things we strive so fiercely for if we haven't got, but think dull and forget if we have – and rightly, for they should be so accepted and taken for granted that no protestation is ever needed on their behalf.

But universal things cannot have protestation or propaganda in them.

Toby Weaver arrived tonight. Round flappy sticking-out ears. Diana has a beautiful, pale, spiritual face. I love her without reservations and her mother. She and Theresa and Ursula all had on their Viennese dresses and aprons tonight.

March 30: Back to London

Sitting on top of a bus, eating dried fruit and chestnuts with happiness pouring over me.

April 7

This reading all day in bed makes my senses *clotted*.

But yes – Henry James had something. From what his admirers had said of him I had hated him before I ever read a word of his. I expected to be bored and resentful, but instead I twiddled the pages in eager gobbling of succeeding words. Afterwards, I suppose I can walk back critically and pooh-pooh the crumpled bed of passion – that is what they do, the critics. But what does it gain them? Are they any nearer the truth? Perhaps not, but perhaps – because look at Ethel MacDell. I've only read, so far, *The Turn of the Screw*.

Clifford Curzon playing John Leland's Concerto in E with Sir Thomas Beecham. I had no hat. The man beside me smelt. I had a sore throat. I was alone. It was wonderful. But when the sudden loud and energetic bits came after the soft gentleness it was a terrible shock. I wanted to cry out 'DONT!'

II

FRANCE
1938

Between January and April, 1938, there is only one journal entry. On May 5, 1938, Smart left London with a group of friends for Jean Varda's home in Cassis, in the south of France, where they intended to work. They stopped in Paris on the way and Smart met Alice and Wolfgang Paalen, an unconventional couple she later visited in Mexico. She spent two months in Cassis during which time she began a relationship with Jean Varda. In July she returned to Paris, returning to Canada in August.

The journal entries for this period are sporadic. However, the entries begin to show a change in the style of her writing: there is a shift from an external focus to an internal one, the tone becomes meditative, and the language imagistic and metaphoric.

There are two notebooks for 1938 and they contain some overlapping. They are full of lists of the books she is reading and has read, lists of the names of plants, flowers, and the French vocabulary she is learning as well as French poems, and the poems of George Herbert, Henry Vaughan, and Andrew Marvell, the poets who influence her writing. In both the poetry and prose she is beginning to find her voice.

January 9

Beauty is rare.

You strain after it. You grope. Often you say to yourself, This is beautiful. But it is not beauty. It is dead. On your awakening to its reality, it is dead.

Beauty is not sight or sound. It is a feeling. It is a spirit. It permeates through you. It urges you out in a gesture of abandonment or surrender. Yet it leaves you impotent. There is no end for beauty. The fixed gasps of a million poets fall dead at the heel. It is a melting.

Beauty is holy. Beauty is earthly. It is God. It is sex. It is the momentary harmonious union of God with nature.

May 7

What is a 'vamp' then?[1] One who must have the submission, the homage perhaps, even the prostration of every man she meets? Who draws, who sucks to herself with world-without-end promising looks, and who, when they are come, all eager and trembling with a mighty expectation, turns them away scornful, the successful execution of her subtle arts her only end? Who delights in bringing death and destruction, and whose life-blood is power? And who, naturally naturally naturally must forever be flattered?

Yes. I suppose so. And she must have no heart. She never must throb for an alien throe. Her only frustrations are her own cool scientific miscalculations.

Am I vamp? Or how many seeds lie on the wet ground? How hard is the clay in this despicable mold? It is true my machine needs the petrol of flattery, but does that amount to more than a desire to be in harmony with my surroundings? To have a sympathetic contact, a tune which does not strike a discord, with the human beings whose lives by chance overlap mine? Their adjacent bodies mean nothing, their nearness might as well be eternal absence, if there is no flow. Even the stones give me a synchronization of mood, a harmony of inside song.

Power – that I deny. I do not want power. Power over myself – a steely control, which is all positive and can *do* and *see* the desired-to-do, at will. (Perhaps this shirking of power is weakness, dislike of responsibility, but still *I do not desire* power. I do not want to bend the wills of others to my own. For what is my own? Do I even know?)

'To draw all' – well, naturally I should desire (again) to establish contact with every living thing, to have a universal and impersonal love for every living thing, to *feel* for them, and perhaps (and perhaps arrogantly – Oh! these points grow too hair-thin) to help them. If my mind has found a formula which works when my receiving set of instinctive sympathy is dead, I am glad, I can perhaps be alive again by this artificial stimulus – But is that bad – To seek a paved path in the wilderness of my own emotional floppiness?

'She must not feel' – well, sometimes I am dead. But I suffer for my deadness. I pay by my paralytic agony, my awareness of my unawareness.

The germs of every evil – *and* of every good – lie in me. But I am not a vamp. I am much too nebulous as yet.

These accusations were by him to me because I refused the body. It is true that when the heart expands the hand reaches out to follow. The gesture towards wants an outward sign as well. But the body is finite, it is unnecessary and it is a detour, for it fences in, and tries to contain an overwhelming ocean. The body binds, curtails. (The body without complete love, I mean, I am no advocate of sexlessness.)

I want to flow towards everyone. But if I give in today as the natural accompaniment to my flow towards, the unseparate following, what is to prevent me from giving my body to every sympathetic man I meet? That, surely, would be wrong, there would be a spuriousness, a deceit in each giving, there would be a sentimental veiling of truth, an escape, a shutting out.

Then, if for the sake of form, outward form, finality, I chose one, one who is more to me, whose contact is more complete, from the rest of the world, I still have to pretend, for that one spot could not contain the world. No spot could contain the world except through the rare miracle of complete love.

Sometimes isolation and proximity wipe out the other, and then the body is right and inevitable, for then it does contain the world, and there is no deceitful self-deception. But oh the hard words man has made for himself to condemn his own bewildered actions. 'You say this to all the girls.' Ah! Perhaps there is that small inward gloating at a successful sally, a following-up of that spontaneous and unpremeditated coup – a 'Here lies the touchstone – touch it and it shall be opened.' The milky baby's shy smile finds the stone too, and who condemns? But we grow too wise. We see. We cannot deny our own selfconsciousness.

O floating world, like a great shy bird I strive in vain to stroke! I *will* be good.

The truth I *will* have.

May 8: à Paris

Yesterday was soft and holy because it was made of sympathy and *felt* emotion. Today had an intoxicating excitement of the brain which fired it to action.

Both days contained new worlds.

Varda in changing shapes and colours moves in and out like a tune on the radio which fades and grows sometimes disturbingly loud. The fading and increasing seem for no reason, and the images are endless.

Paalen[2] was trembling when we looked at his pictures, and drinking coffee, the excitement of communication through even laboured and unknown words, rose to a pitch. But running in the wood he grew smaller, and softer. And for me going home coldness and shooting cramps shut out the flow.

Varda faded in the evening. I am alone again and displeased with myself. After great riches, extreme poverty. A low loop ends the day. But how (watching the others too) small physical discomforts such as cold, tiredness, late food, sudden fresh air, govern us all! I am glad it is not only me, but at the time I think it is only me and despair, blaming my death.

May 9

The fluctuations of our threading lives! The words like mountainous waves flood over and dash high in castles of foam, then suddenly recoiling leave the rocks bone bare and the seaweed drying in the unwelcoming sun. Who can avoid this? I look around. Not only the contrariness of my own always reacting words, but the steadier ones, yes the calm calculators sit silent at the table, nibbling a piece of bread, staring staring at their inward unaliveness.

I had a dream last night and it contained all terror and all despair. All things converged. From my two old and from my one strange new world the seeds came, more forceful than in their own wearily-beating day.

Varda symbolized the new. Always, in times of doubt and emotion in my dreams, I walk down Elgin Street[3] in a snowstorm, the whole world shrouded in a sort of pale twilight. The lights from the Roxborough[4] shine and it is always towards that that we are walking. There we part. But I feel that I am wrong to part – to send away thus – I am strangling and wondering which is true. He turns, hurt, proud, shut up, and goes down the lift – or up. Last night he lived up on the next floor. It was an open lift. I repented. I grew desperate to dispel the hard knots he was creating. I rushed to stop the lift and my hand got squashed.

I went into my flat. It was huge, and the glaring lights above shone on the ugly furniture, some of it in dust covers. I am full of remorse now for I see the sin I have committed against a gentle suffering man. Suddenly I love. Then (dreams collecting always from the secretive dreariness of the day before) I look for a place to remove my tampax. There is a large room on one side behind, full of packing cases, and amongst them a toilet with a brown seat. I go towards it and sit down, bare. Then I look up and to the left are iron bars and all the girls from the LTS[5] holding the grating looking in and suddenly there are workmen all around. I rise quickly (perhaps pulling 'T' but somehow later it reappeared in) and leave this cement floor place.

I am just about to remove T in the dust-covered drawing room when Mummy and Daddy and Russel and Jane arrive and I am in an agony of guilt. I try to explain why I am in Paris. They believe me and love me. The room is filled with adolescent boys, friends of Russel's. This I remember made me draw some conclusion; I forget what.

Later though, Mummy fell over the banister and I just caught her in time by the tip of her coat (my black coat with the safety pins) and Daddy helped me draw her back. We kissed her, Daddy and I, but all the time Daddy was really kissing me, passionately. Mummy's face was red in patches marked off by ridges like a rose garden. We flattered her. She beamed. Our flattering saved her just in time but I remember the fact that it did utterly sicken me.

It went on for a long time, full of terrors and doubts and despairs. Varda always appeared walking by sad in the distance. There were always misunderstandings. I was trying always to make him understand. But he believed in my evil intent. Michael[6] soothed something between us.

I woke up in the middle of the night and I was terrified and trembling. It was still pitch dark. I was afraid. I was alone. I was in a strange country. Unknowns surrounded me. A baby bewilderingly came out of the womb. My feather mattress cover was on the floor. I drew it up and around to be the ultimate comforter.

May 14: Cassis

There was a question mark in the sky only it was backwards.

There was a pine tree and the rest was blue. This is all. This is the key.

The yellow eyes are glaring at me without a melting.

'D'ou viens-tu Bergère?'

From the beating of the heart O! like a pulse of the sea, uncontrollable, for a vision upwards through the thorns.

Should I have expected these tearings of the flesh by the way? For the *toiling* I had set my teeth against. Rip! Rip! The disobedient flesh and on top at last a soiled remnant gasping its goodbye. For me, these visions are a consummation worth the world beside. All I would give away and accept fiend's puny jeers. Then that unspeakable largeness wipes away those cloistral pickings of the nose, less than my sporting with the eight-day long Atlantic.

You see, even now, through tears just defeated, comes the balm, aerial souls of pine.

This this is enough, and the upward mingling of the sun.

O you cricket, whom I agonized in vain to recreate on those too calm fields (fearful with impotent vision in the rain but treacherously soothing to the unwilling liar). O you cricket! *Now* – and among the flowering rocks!

Out of these rocks comes the saving essence – and by saving I mean no blasphemous poster on the summer road, but an overwhelming force of spirit that may be fierce wanting, by an uncondensed and unadulterated throe of upward desire, enter, enter the body and purge. O glorifying! O glorifying with a full full sweep of conscious space, as they say before leaving us no word, less than no word, for they left untruth in the old.

Sometimes the rocks bleed. Knowing too much, gathering such greatness from the pouring good I bleed. I bleed to attain my God, not impotent but manifest by a sign. Not crying under the unripe fig, or sorrowful among the scarlet poppies pressing to the sympathetic earth the head asked to accept and understand something too all-embracing for its trembling frame.

O Earth (like the seductions of my soothing mother lullabies – peace peace and the green growing around the rocking cradle, the entrancing beauty of growth, O perishable growth). On your breast I seek also your soporifics, unutterably sweet, and also yielding salve for the finding of the key. Entering daily and nightly into the body of God, yet unable to do other than suggest –

And now – upwards to that staggering vision. Will I have the courage to raise my eyes? Can I face the things I laboriously flee? The hot day breathes a sigh.

(The going down is always the easy way – but then there is no prize.)

I am crouching behind a boulder. The sun soaks into me from within and from without. The cold stones below caress my behind and the dazzling Mediterranean lies like still silk lapping the plain, around the misty hills and the too bright sky – testing with a terrible perfection my desperate endurance. The leaves, the bushes, the young plants, even thyme, confront me with their hardy inexhaustion. The trivial flies. The gay industrial birds of the trees. But the vision, too blinding to behold, is there waiting and my heart throbs and aches, and half halting like an old machine forced too far.

Yet the rocks tower above. Yet there are elements unfaced. My death to dare before I reach those green top trees, I attain the world, to drink in forever my overflowing metaphors.

The Tree on the Ledge

Now I understand terror a little. Now do I want to embrace those empty skies? And my desires so large? Below sheer drop of rock, and almost pin point, the far road I toiled up. Ledges, thin and leading perhaps nowhere are to left and right and utter unbroken cliffs. I curl my legs about this tree and shake, face to face with terror. I cling to the tree. Yet all I need is to know no fear. I shall sit calm and in a strong desperation attempt the feat.

Yet how otherwise can the spirit find an instrument for that mysterious force but by the bashing of the sleepy body, whose only desire is to sink coiled into a soft and flowery sleep, and with the earth to dissolve, without having sent *its* essence, as even each tree must?

On the way up I saw two rare orchids, one white and one magenta, both solitary. Great spidery ants are crawling on this tree.

Yet – if there were, by the crashing against these uncompromising rocks, by a slip of the foot, of my quaking body, my last words – what could I write? Nothing – Nothing – even knowing that – for now I am not inspired – I am nearer the earth than ever, the natural mother sending every power to help me cling to the rocks.

Yet I still desire the sky, and though I shake I am glad.

May 15: Cassis

There was a tree weighted with unripe fruit. I was that tree.

Excitingly the boughs bent, about to burst forth into redness. But all the cherries were pulled off green, hard, unluscious in their fall, and when I awoke in the morning it was a great stone waste, and the sky was dark. 'There shall be no more morning,' said God's voice with a pointing finger. And I was dead and there was not one comfort. 'He who binds to himself a joy,' said my abashed soul. Will even the fields of clover join now in this great conspiracy?

III

OTTAWA AND NEW YORK
August, 1938–October, 1939

In August, 1938, Smart returned to Canada and spent the rest of the summer and September in Kingsmere. On December 12, she began working for The Ottawa Journal, *writing for the social pages and contributing interviews and articles. She lived at home during this time in an effort to save money, although her mother felt it was not necessary for her to work and discouraged her from it. She stayed with the paper until July; on July 10, 1939, she left Ottawa for New York to begin what she called her 'independent life.' In New York she stayed with her sister Helen, who was now living there, and looked for work. She was soon joined by Jean Varda, who came for an exhibition of his work.*

There are three notebooks for this period, with some overlapping. The early notebook contains the poems on which she has been working; the second one contains the drafts of the articles she wrote for The Ottawa Journal; *and the third is the account of her stay in New York.*

September 23[1]
'What do you think of the war scare
Bill, my good man?'
(I like to get the opinion of the people when I can)
'Looks pretty bad. But I guess I'd do the same again,'
Says Bill offhand
(His imagination shutting like a trap
All true news banned)
'Honour above life' says the complacent wife 3000 miles from
    death
'I say it now and shall continue to say it till my last breath.'
And the gaunt dreamers in their disturbed garrets
Disaster-provoking eyes
Seeing really, as they have so often in mind

Bombs hurling from the skies?
They rise trembling, they foretold him here
The nerve-straining wait done
They are relieved their role of prophet is over
And doom at last begun.

November 6

It's not an easy thing to write poetry. The blue walls are cold. My bills, my deceits, my incapacity crowd in upon me. O the whole world's deceit! How have I done wrong? Should I have roused myself, unglued life's lips and said Stoic I will be! and written a book that sold? Or given concerts in the provincial towns? Or, lying that I loved him, married an impotent peer? (There was some tenderness of spirit but a log of wood knows more about the body's joys than he knew.) Life that was so rich, why are the plains so flat now? My lies O my shallow, unpetty lies crowd back. My unseeing eyes! (And all the time he wanted me out of the house. Married or making money. A worldly success!) How I have floundered! And my long debts grow! They increase! And my fatal steps! No one loves you said the angry keeper. My face will grow hard and jealous. My spirits sour. They fall like lifeless limbs. Even Paris a waste of streets!

December 12

I JOINED THE JOURNAL

(Between December 1938 and July 1939, the journals contain drafts of articles Smart writes for The Ottawa Journal.*)*

July 10

Left Ottawa Thursday, July 6, left Montreal July 7, and arrived NY that night at 9:30. Went to Locust Valley for weekend next day – so real New York began on Monday July 10 – or, really, as I was late getting back, on Tuesday July 11.

My America

All Whitman prophesied. History of film. History of records. Jitterbug. Policeman pally. 'I like your dress,' the girl seller said.

The vast towers – the life, gaiety – here now colossal life. England dead in a winding sheet. Canada not even conceived.

The people – the strength and beauty, staggering beauty – the life – the becoming, the IS, the now. The fun: pick-up gangsters who motored me thirty miles. The Negro girl in the Women's room. Policeman 'makes a nice change.' Not hard pavements. Shoes. Beauty. Friendliness. Art. Music. Films. Records. Theatre. Grand Central Park. The Cuban man where we bought shirts. Jitterbugs. The Fair. Everybody's pal – the drugstore man hearing troubles and tries to help. The people *own* it – interest in politics – Coca-cola case.

'New York is dangerous and difficult. The streets are hard, the conductors are rude, the taximen are gangsters, if you don't shove you get shoved, even brilliant people starve in garrets. It is glittering and cruel. You could never stand it.'

Thus the elders wag their heads and point their fingers and cluck-cluck, and little ambitious girls in home towns decide, after all, they had better marry the pimply persevering suitor from over the way.

Even Mr Leaf in, 'Listen Little Girl before you come to NY,' now gives good advice in case you go against his cautions, but thinks on the whole it would be better if you just stayed quietly and smelt the flowers.

But even gangsters must have moments when they are only dewey-eyed apprentices – everyone must begin somehow. The cake and ale are there for those who can get them – why shouldn't it be *you*?

'It will be me,' I decided after walking the snoozing streets of my home town for months and gazing with glazed eyes at the same 'wholesome' hats in the same shop windows. 'I won't listen Mr Leaf! I'm off to New York! I'm going into the great world. With a hey nonny nonny and a hotch-cha!'

I gave Mr Leaf to the oldest inhabitant and stepped onto a bus. It was easy!

October 6

The ghoulish aboriginal rites over the air of Hitler's 'Peace or Destruction' speech. The clapping and foot stamping like a tom tom's beat, gathering hysteria. All in the six o'clock grey dawn. Helen crouched over it, and the elevator roared past, flashing lights, like a long drawn out terror. I lay on the sofa (my bed), my head at the radio, towards the window's pale path.

An American announcer translates with strident note and urgency in his voice, and an imitation English one, very very precise like the girl in *Pygmalion* – no mistakes, but obviously a foreigner, 'too correct.'

To the photographic agency (Powers).[2] A dark man let me come into his office. 'Listen honey, we can't tell anything without photographs. You can't just walk in like that. It takes months to become a model. And don't come out with your hair like that it looks as if you had been out in a storm.'

'O dear – I'm going to cry.'

'Well, go and cry somewhere else!'

But he said I had an interesting head. I went and cried in the ladies' room. I couldn't find it at first and got locked out and cried and stood against it.

I lunched with JB Neumann; he said I looked as if I wanted to get back to my mother's womb. He took me to Johnny O'Toole's to see about a job. We waited in the phoney marble halls and then left.

At home I waited for John MacGillivray[3] who arrived but refused to come up. He rang. I rang. He rang. At last the porter came up, upset, and said there was a gentleman. I said he must come up. 'That's what I kept telling him,' the porter said.

An hour passed. John phoned.

'What's the idea?'

'What's your idea. It's very rude,' etc.

But he came up, and we took a taxi and drove aimlessly to Grand Central Station and finally, wandering around underground, found a big deserted stately dining room and had tea, muffins, and fresh pastry.

The ins and outs of this are too boring and complicated. Yanko's warm shoulder shone like a haven to a desperate traveller.

'Artifice.' 'That's all rubbish.' 'If you could say what you meant for once.' 'You never say what you mean.'

'If you could be honest and humble for half an hour you might begin to do something,' I said.

'Alright. I'm honest and humble now. What do I do?'

We taxied back and he dumped me.

O the weary world.

Helen was sweet and concerned for my depressed tiredness and lent me her new red dress and did my hair a new way with a flower on top. When her Averill[4] with the avaricious eyes came I was perky. Chit – chat, chit – chat. My tail flipped like a contrary cat.

'Nowadays people aren't buying pictures.' 'My dear let me tell you there are people who have been selling pictures for ten or twelve years, and if they can't sell any how can you hope to?'

I ate scalloped corn, and cracked the dish on the stove. Helen rescued me. We laughed and laughed at my inefficiency.

Yanko was late but he was balm. I adored him. We walked hand in hand all the way to the station, ate on the way and life sparkled and I was invulnerable. Pop-Eye the Sailor munched at a nearby table and his jaw worked frantically and we laughed hysterically.

The Orly taxis at Locust Valley delivered everyone. Through the dark highways and byways, Yanko and I in front. I held his hand tight but he was enervated by so much driving after his long day on the bus.

'Really didn't find this at all pleasant.' 'You should have told us.' I tried to soothe.

But when we got home and he saw we had not gone so far afield as he had been afraid, he complimented the driver and took it all back.

The playful night. The hug's arrow. I see love is the second most searched for after the first cruel thrusting forth. I can only live, in its warm envelope, expanding, breathing, like a live, blind thing, more blessed than the embryo for it *knows* its own bliss. Be my surrounding cloak.

October 7

Day lived in the warm state. Gathering driftwood along the beach in the Indian Summer sun, and what the shipwrecks cast up to make furniture for my new loft.

Yanko sawed and hammered, and at night I painted them a strawberry pink, flip flop, flip flop, the rich edible colour, the fat brush, squatting on the floor under the big blue bulb. A table, a

tête à tête sofa, and a high grandfather's chair. I read Donne. Yanko
went to the village on his bicycle. I cleared the kitchen and tidied
and changed my dress.

We fell asleep at once.

October 8

They came while I was still getting dressed – Francis Lee, Bill
Simmons, Mac M. . . . , Holbe Baker and Helen, Ethel and Jilda.

Romeo and Juliet of Tchaikovsky – and the love, the youth, the
overflowing love of Holbe and Helen. Her dark curly halo of hair,
her lovely eyes, her scarred mouth, her pretty slender bare legs, her
green velveteen skirt, plaid blouse and red bobby socks.

Gathering mussels. The overcast sea. Two ducks. The buzzing in
the shelly rock crevices of flies. Photographing. Goldenrod.

Wild dancing. The strange sailors' and lovers' dance of Holbe and
Helen. Picking inch-round tomatoes with Francis in the garden. His
bright darting eyes.

I cried with laughter at Bill's impersonation of Sarah Bernhardt
in the movies. He is full of grace.

Why was I sad? 'You are never open with me,' Yanko said. He
is so generous, so loving for my every wish – But my wish is only
that he love me and want me so much willy nilly that he can do
nothing else. He *must* devour me. Minute by minute pouncing on it
ravenously. Not for my sake – because he loves me so much he wants
me to be happy – For his own – *Only* because he is compelled.

His eyes chase away after *things*.

Ah, but if he didn't do the practical planning who would?

But in the dance too his eyes seek the idea in his mind. So
urgently, that my tentative idea, poised for a *pas de deux*, has to
pirouette alone.

Ah, but that is the force, the flow that drives him through the
tempests and safely with his barge (his booty, his gaiety) on the
happiest shores.

You see, these young lovers make me sad. But sadder, loving and
being loved so much too, to have a measuring eye and longing for a
quick trembling response.

When I have in my heart and in my hands so big a thing as his
heart surrounding me like a womb.

But oh, I had to leave, when my head longed to be hid on the comforting shoulder, and I came up to town with them all in the station wagon, beside Lee. They sang, and he played a mandolin. Holbe drove and Helen sat beside him, kissing his shoulder.

The flat was dark but no shadows lurked and I made hot tea.

Think, *Trouble* to arrange the threads, *Dare* to be honest.
                    Scribere Ande.

October 9

There was the October park, fading like an English park on a hot sunny day. The water and the languorous boaters and ducks in private rows. Duncan Miller with his pale face and hot dogs at the round iron table by the stone steps. And the lattice place with exciting shade, stillness, opening the mind.

His intentness – I grow loquacious – I pour my past rolled in fantastic dough. A meadow spot in New York's steel symphony. Why don't I always lunch in the park?

Saligmann and JB Neumann before lunch. His nose waits like a hawk to prey, and his glistening eyes are the clever boys of the class. But from their two pairs of eyes flow the most buoyant doves into the huge empty stadium of my ego.

I walked to Radio City. I was afraid I was too red. My dress, my hat, my purse, all red red red. Bicycle boys cried out 'O the lady in Red' and the tune stayed teasing me.

Jacques Bieler of the saucer eyes, and spiral voice via the nasal. Carmen from an orchestra lacking the lip-smacking attack that compensates for the toil. But a miraculous row of chorus girl legs, beautiful, easeful, and as exact as machines only with the lovely possibility of precariousness.

An exciting girl, Ingrid Bergman, in the movie *Intermezzo* with Leslie Howard and Edna Best. Inspiringly beautiful, with no makeup, simple but becoming clothes, a radiance, and a real laugh, real smiling eyes, and soft natural hair.

The dark streets to walk. The hats the eye corrects or rejects, the dresses, the towers lit up.

The cocktails at King Gordon's with Pegi Nichol, Marian Scott,[5] Mark Saxton, Jacques Bieler, Kathleen ----? and Mary Anderson.

Marian's innocent excited shining eyes, and great daring nose, that sees too and is excited and lusts after beautiful pictures and life in shapes and colours.

At Leopoldis' Viennese place a tipply happiness so great my feet longed to do a hurling dance. At all tables all possibilities – All flavours brought to an intoxicating moment. The dark-eyed couple reading papers. The funny hat man who sang and joked about his bad English. (He kissed the ground when he landed in America, a refugee.) The dark girl who sang.

See what may come! Home in dark cafes! The warm tingling creeping all over! The desire of other people! The rich curiosity. What can be done to outlet it? make it into a world? For 'it could beget a world of light.'

Pegi in a red coat and red-banded hat, gnomelike, open, generous, sweet. Mark Saxton poised on the El as I got out. 'Could I interest you in a beer?' and jumped off as the train jerked. He had a whisky here with Helen. But sleep's hand was too heavy.

I wrote at last to Mummy and mailed it in the night box.

She had phoned and was hysterical. If I were going to marry Yanko she might just as well commit suicide. I would have killed her etc. Also Jane had brought up again the subject of marrying D'Arcy, and she had a cold, and the war was getting her down.

I am glad I was out. But way below I am afraid she may catch me and drill her fierce bitter will into my escaping life, and I am troubled by her and for her.

Yanko says she is a flagellist, a passionate woman who never got her share of fun in bed.

October 31: All Hallow's Eve

I have lost my polarity. Since about a year I have been dizzily revolving, jaggedly, convulsively, or being stuck stagnant in some miscellaneous pocket.

The hectic *Journal* life kept the issue at bay, and I fed occasionally on a loosening breeze or a bracing sky. But now that no obvious chains bind me and I am indeed floating in the great ocean alone, the who, why, what and where are lost. Shall I be submerged?

The one stable thing my eye can pin its giddy focus to is Yanko, spiritually the most intangible creature. For that desperation, the tragedy I saw in his face the night I first saw him is still undiscovered.

It is not a definite thing, like having loved a woman and lost her, or having been an unrecognized artist for years and years – it is a deeper, more mystical thing and has to do with the very laws of life and the eternal verities.

For I say to my friends, O you should meet Yanko. There is a man that knows how to live – who can greet each day as a new day, who loves, who gives, who can receive. He is gay and happy as a child, he enters every fun, he fills other people with gaiety and happiness, *YET* the tragedy grows on his face.

Is the hiddenness – the impossible-to-be-disclosed hiddenness – the tragedy? That even he cannot know, cannot, will not, could not bear to tell himself, and so it is written on his face?

This is the wall. And though the wall's softness, the tender gesture, comfort the weary head, the spirit weeps. I cannot uncork my wine into the unknown bowl.

Those very moons rising over the pond – sometimes I heard his voice break through the wind with a geometry set, measuring the mystery, charting even its unchartability.

The butterfly escapes. A whisper disperses life's pollen. He says this. But it is a word too much. The thing said calms the wonder, but, unattended, the mystery grows.

You see why I wept under the birch trees?

I am not honest enough. I am too fond of the veiling metaphor. I cringe. I acquiesce; I am a coward to hurt people's feelings. I haven't the dignity to speak out, to dare to be myself even if it offends. But I don't want to offend. But I can't call *anyone* fool.

I must find a solution.

IV

FOR THE LITTLE CASSIS BOOK

When I sat down at the window waiting for them to come, I thought they never would come. I did not believe anything could ever happen to me, except what I laboriously pulled out of myself, by dry pain, alone. I was dressed in black, sober and ugly. For the death of my past? Or, as Ruth[2] liked to say, 'mourning for a future?' I don't know. I sat on the window sill poised. My past was finished and discarded. What if they should never come and I should have no future? Could I sit on my window sill, the narrow ledge of the present, eating apples forever? For I believed they *could* not come. Like gas, I thought life would not 'take' with me.

But the miracle happened. Hours late, but it happened. And the miracle contained miracles. Ruth was one of these. There she was, sitting in Roland's car, radiant, alive like a bird about to take off, just charged with electricity, heading for the sky. Ruth was one of these miracles because she was the woman in London I most wanted to know. I met her at that party where I met them all. And she smiled. I mean really. Not 'You are a woman and therefore my rival,' but 'Perhaps we may be friends.' And later I saw her at Spender's play, with her alighted look, and her hair contacting the air. I thought, 'There is a woman born for poets to love.' And in the May Day Parade, walking quickly by, she paused, and smiled.

I got into the back of Julian and Ursula's[3] car, beside Varda, as I called him then. He hated my death's head black. I hated it too. But it was the coffin I still was in. All Varda's travelling kit was in a small tin biscuit box. I had a huge valise, inaccessible and heavy as lead. Why? I felt bound. When I was small I used to sleep without pillows or sheets, to be free, in case I should ever be wrecked on a desert island, or too poor to own them. I suffered to be weighted down now. I squirmed in my coffin.

How shall I describe what Varda was to me then? He terrified me and yet I knew he was good. He was like an element. He was a wild manly gale. He smelt of wet brown earth and grass. But he had satyr's eyes. I knew no conventions would restrain him. Virginity to him was a fruit to be eaten, to be taken in his chaotic stride. But I believed still nothing could happen to me – the power of the cold eye, the biting tongue. I was going to France to work. All these people were my stimulating friends. Women and men.

On the channel boat something happened. There were psychological clouds. I wanted most of all for everything to be harmonious. I loved them all. But I could feel an uneasiness among the women, putting leashes on their men. How wrong they were! I was alone. I would always be alone. I looked at the sea. Dark and foaming. There was a chill wind and large cold moon. I only wanted to love them all. They misunderstood. The exciting, chastening moon! But I cried to be so misinterpreted. At the end of the boat, standing gazing at the moon and the sea till I grew stiff and blue with cold, I suddenly turned and there were Varda and Simonette, close by the sheltered funnels. They smiled but I hurried away. I was interrupting. I was outside. I was left out.

In the morning Varda said curtly, 'You will go in Michael and Tanya's[4] car and Simonette[5] will come with me.' Shall I cry another tear? No. I am contrary and unconcerned. I shall be flippant not hurt. I shall observe. I only want to *Work*.

It was lovely in the back of the open car. The resuscitating wind – the caressing sun. Alone I can feel and see, I thought, and saw the countryside and fields, emerging spring colours.

But meals were quiet, slightly awkward. There was a constriction. Like animals peering out suspiciously before acting, before going about naturally unconcerned. No one wanted to take the first, compromising step. No statements. I was displeased with myself for this. Somehow I thought I could have done something about it. It is painful to have no flow.

But how, I thought, watching the others too, shall physical discomforts such as cold or tiredness, late hours, food, sudden fresh air, govern us all! I was glad it was not only my own weakness, but all the time at the time I kept thinking it was only me and despairing, and blaming my death. But when I looked around it was not only the contrariness of my own always reacting words, but the steadier ones, yes the calm and calculating sat silent at the table, nibbling a piece of bread, squashing it into a pellet, staring staring at their inward unaliveness.

In Paris Varda accused me of being a 'vamp.' At a party he backed me against a wall and said, 'Take Care! Take Care! I am Oriental. I will not be played with!' It was like a sudden thunderstorm. His wild insistent pressing, his tears, his emotion. I was afraid. He said I had been flirting all evening with Roland and Ruth was getting distressed. But I wasn't flirting I was only talking. I wanted to know Roland. Even more I wanted to know Ruth. I could have 'flirted' with Ruth but at a party men are for women. If I didn't want to know people I would be demoralized, dead.

He accused me because I refused him my body. It is true that when the heart expands the hand reached out to follow: the gesture towards wants an outward sign as well. I want to flow towards everyone. But if I give my body as the natural accompaniment to my flow towards, what is to prevent me from giving my body to every sympathetic man I meet? And nearly every man I meet is sympathetic. I cannot think that would be right.

The days in Paris were full of new worlds – sympathy, emotion and an intoxicating excitement of the brain. Varda changing shapes and colours moved in and out like a tune on the radio which fades and grows sometimes disturbingly loud. The fadings and increasings seemed for no reason, and the images were endless.

One day we walked in the Dome on tip-toe, and through a flower market hand in hand. It flashed into me like a vision. 'We will be walking in many flower markets hand in hand years and years later.' But it was a daring vision. I couldn't believe this was the Man.

We met Paalen and his radiantly beautiful wife Alice. We went to his studio. He was trembling when we looked at his pictures, and drinking coffee, the excitement of communication through laboured and unknown words, rose to a pitch. But running in the words he grew colder and softer. And for me going home coldness and cramps shut out the flow.

Varda faded that evening. I was alone again. A low loop ended the day. But in my tragic dream he walked by sadly in the distance in the midst of my tears and despair. I woke up in the middle of the night and I was horrified and trembling. It was pitch dark. I was alone. It was a strange country. Everything was unknown. I was a baby bewilderingly out of the womb left on a windy plain. My feather mattress was on the floor. I drew it up and around to be the ultimate comforter.

I have not spoken of Julian and Ursula but they were the guides and the tone, and always affecting my moods. Julian was very tall and generous, and had a camel's graciousness – I mean he wished well to the world and found trouble getting it across – but he did, bumpily. Ursula was generous too, quiet, storing what she saw. At a negro place where we went to dance she danced with a negro who asked her, and that involved him with endless glamour for me. Her gentleness, her eyes that measured and stored. She wore little magenta ribbons and magenta lipstick. She loved cats and her face had slanting eyes, and a cat's half-smile, a secretive beauty which you couldn't at first see.

Tanya had a baby's face and smooth round forehead. She looked adorable in peasant headshawls. When she put her head back her mouth turned into a rose. She giggled and hung on Michael's arm, or rested on his shoulder. Michael peed beside the car and she giggled.

'Don't pretend you've never seen a gentleman make water before,' he said, and went on.

In my violent dreams Michael was something between Varda and me.

Roland and Ruth were aloof in their car. Its back was piled high with luggage.

At Avignon, Varda and Simonette and I had to share a bedroom. Varda asked Simonette to lend him her toothbrush. She did. She stood by the small wooden table taking off her false braid. When she wasn't there Varda pinned me to the bed. But I escaped and walked through the streets in a rage. I will NOT be taken like Abyssinia. I will not be taken like Abyssinia. I clenched my fists. Varda came out and walked behind me in a sulk. Julian said, 'Pay no attention. He'll be alright soon.' We walked down the narrow streets – there were brothels and women and gypsies with sore eyes, and dirt.

We sat in a ring drinking coffee. I tried to be gay to assert my right to be independent. But undertones obstructed.

Simonette made me sleep on the outside of the bed. But Varda was far on the other side of his. He spoke no word and got up early before I awoke.

At *Notre Dame de la Charité* there was a sweet small hotel on the edge of a river, and swampy land. When we drove up Tanya and Michael, both nude, were framed in a small round window in the side of the house.

The day was fair. We saw red poppies under the olive trees, blobs of spring green willow, yellow in the late sun, and red filigree against the blue green heaviness of pine. There were medicinals or alchemy. In Julian's car with Varda we sang and were happy.

After dinner I ran out into the night across the bridge. There were too many things converging and unwieldy seas. Varda ran after me. But while we were talking Tanya walked quickly by on the other side and wouldn't say hello. 'She's having a little scene with Michael,' Varda said. 'He will follow her and there will be a wonderful reunion. She often has little scenes because the reconciliation is so passionate. She can't live without drama.'

The pools of mica in the waste place, lying priceless and ephemeral among the desolate weeds, and by night the warbling of the nightingales in the islands of bush, pale but slantingly lit by the sidling moon. I never heard nightingales before.

Down on this bank let us lie. Down on the bank the moon disappears behind my head. The mounds, a paucity of cropped grass take away from what might be a desert's richness. We lean against the mounds. From far below, beneath the mountainous clothes I wear, great coats like continents weighing me down, I hear the tickling song of the nightingales – not sad. Do they sing for me? Do I think they sing for me? I waver. But now. Let us go home. The hour and its enchanted instruments all point one way but bared (the unassailable) I cannot feel. I know the radiant night with pangs.

But as we crossed back over the bridge, with the moon shining on the patches of mica, Varda whispered:

'On the thirteenth you will be mine.'

I tried to know the others, to feel what they felt – there is so much to feel and know. If mine was like this what was theirs? But can I presume to speak of more than myself? Each one entered, but Varda was my personal drama. Shall I leave out the dates. Do I speak too freely of a private circumstance? Gradually the others will emerge. Skip this for the pictures if you will. It is not the ocean of my self that I desire to flow over the others – but how can I measure

but by the latitude and longitude of my own eye and heart? The
other men were strong too, but eyes watched them. And the women
were preoccupied. Varda pushed and entered that personal arena.
Therefore I write as I do.

Cassis – coming over the desert from Marseilles, along the winding
dangerous road, I held Varda's hand, trying to understand all he had
known and felt here, all the women he had loved and suffered for
here, all he must be feeling – so many years of accumulated emotions
– turning a corner, the blue sea – the sea – my head burst, my heart
burst, I had too much to understand.

Yes this is the house. Up this stony path? But it's a brick house
not far from the road – it's not wild, but the rocky hills are near.
I shall climb those hills at once. The path has been trod so often!

A lion tamer in an embroidered cap, and a young negro came
running down. Varda darted off in greeting. I turned over the
stones of the path with my toe. But the landscape has no colour,
I thought.

In Paris, Yanko made a plan of his house. 'This is the captain's
room,' he said. 'It is like a ship. I would like you to have this room
next to mine. It has a lock on it.'

We saw the house, in layers level with the rising grades of ground.
His room above the kitchen up the stony steps, his large bed where
so many women. . . . Next to it a large well-lit room. For me. But
isolated from the rest of the house. 'This one or if you would rather
the one next to the kitchen.'

I went down. That one was two by four, with no light, and there
was a passage from the kitchen to the studio. I wanted to write.
How could I write there? Shall I go home? I went up to my room.
The lock was on the outside of the door. Rage. Rage. Rage. Shall
I go home? O Julian, Ursula – help! help! help! What's Spain if a
woman can't be independent.

Simonette installed herself in a little room off the studio. When I
found her and it she had hung up all her things. Change with me?
But no, it was too late. She liked that one. She was ensconsed.

Fear began to dog me. Julian! Ursula! Will you stand by and see
a woman taken like Abyssinia?

Varda, the first day alone, attacked me in my room. I bit and
fought like a wild animal and we scuffled around on the dusty floor.
The nightmares that night! The cold shuddering fears!

Face fear. I faced fear. Ah well. Flowers must fruit.

'Come for a walk,' he said that night.

We walked up the road, up the hill, up a path to the haunted house, up to a stone altar among the pines. The nightingales warbled, the moon shone – the mountains of rock were bulwarks. We sat on the cold stone of the altar, all the time the nightingales trilled around.

PART FOUR

1939–1941

I

MEXICO
November–December, 1939

Disillusioned with New York, Elizabeth Smart decided to visit Alice and Wolfgang Paalen, artists she had met in Paris, but who were now living near San Angel outside Mexico City. She arranged to meet Varda in either Mexico or California. During her stay with the Paalens, Smart was attracted to the beauty and the poetry of Alice Paalen. However, the oblique reference to George Barker is the first indication that she is already interested in him. When Smart had been in Ottawa working on The Ottawa Journal, *she had been sending poems to the little magazines for publication. She had sent some to Lawrence Durrell in Paris, who had started a magazine,* Booster, *and they had begun a correspondence. Smart had told Durrell that she admired George Barker's poetry. Durrell gave her Barker's address, suggesting that if she had some money, Barker might be willing to sell her a manuscript because he needed money. With some money her mother had given her ($25.00), Smart bought her first Barker manuscript, a poem, 'O Who will Speak from a Womb or a Cloud?' thus beginning the Elizabeth Smart and George Barker liaison.*

There are numerous small notebooks kept between 1939 and 1941 and the chronology is often difficult to follow. The Mexico notebooks are full of Alice Paalen's poems and Smart's translations of them, as well as lists of French vocabulary. There is a further move away from an external focus; the external natural world is now internalized and becomes a part of the internal landscape.

To Mexico On *The Siboney*
Leaving New York Behind

November 24: Nighttime
   This is no time for contemplation, but there is going to be no time for contemplation, or rather no place. No bed yet – a weird new world. Soup that smells of a cross cook's hands and the kitchen sink

– and no room to sit down in. I skulked up to first class and sat unobtrusively in the jiggling corner of the lounge. The odd lounger lounges vacantly.

The paper towers floated on the evilly rich waters and made the moon strong and trusty as a pole to loop my life on. Unbelievable long combs lit up, floating – huge penises – agog in their rape of heaven.

Was it there? – it was there. They choke. They go black. Their lights go out. Old papers whirl about the cold streets.

And up the hundred stories of those faery palaces are those offices where the So Whats sit, and the Ladies' Rooms where you cry after the insulting No. That's all. No tinsel even. No illusion. (Would I rape heaven do they say? NO. They compete against their children – whose stone virility they ape – lost in the shadows – jealous most of all.)

I speak in parables so that the mystery may remain. The towers blowable at a puff floated insubstantially and the moon, pale and mighty, was the real rock, the pillar of faith (O swear not by the moon).

They might say 'In that glitter one moves' – the glamour seen now – most unfocusable when the heels wear down their sides.

But most of all at that magic moment I cried out loud with joy. TO BE ALONE For I can listen! I can listen! to the movement, the things around, and *not* only hear the loud tinkling of the man's psyche beside me.

With him I only hear *him*.

Now I hear the world, its ideas, its meaning shifting, teasing, about my head – adorable, exciting pursuit.

I am alone. I am alive. At last, at last I can think. I can pray. I am filled with that spirit. Or, if you will, god, that individual who loves and dwells with me – eking each power to gather its evasive gold.

All those muddled months crystallize too and love's warmth is warmer, and the whole meaning of life (the corpse and the upright penis that all avoid – the two secret symbols – but who dares hold them in his hand?).

The skyscrapers they say are virility, but the New Yorkers do not have that so frantically, and push all down to get love's warm

advance. They twinkle and glitter at the eye – and rebuff by cold
and inflexibility the arms' invitation, a mystery that glides as the
strange fantastic island shrinks.

I am dying, I said, that paper island is the mirage of life – now
back to the cold, deep, terrible horizon of reality.

(Ah! I can feel again – cold but desiring.)

Lynn's drama.[1] Her ropey face like a parched and battered thing
too long exposed. Alone – to leave all – to make the brave break.

Robin grew chillier and chillier standing alone and blue on the
dock below among the screeching people. I felt the drama, but it
was for a people's magazine.

9 PM [2]

Here I was taking the vomiting body of humanity to my bosom,
living their greed over the last tutti-frutti cake, their fear, their imaginary ills, lulled in the very rough arms of father neptune himself.

I said smiling when I had to lie on the canvas cot, and they
vomited on all sides so that it splashed right onto my face, and the
stench was everywhere. O I am in the thick of it. I love love love
this my humanity, my people, themselves. It was so good – I was
so escaped I smiled all over and said not one man am I expanded
to, but all men and all women come what may, if they should do
this or that forbidden thing I can but yield, I am all open and can
offer no resistance – can only love.

Smiling, smiling, rocking on the rough sea on my rough bed –
through the foreign language the friendliness the backnotes better
than through words – and most of all the adventure.

Then as I slept as after love, 'Betty Betty,' a knocking on the porthole
one after one the fourteen adorable women waking and speaking. The
Betty from mouth to mouth tossed and I too from my warm dream
sat up and the dark-eyed face at the window through signs led me
to be discovered. Cables – first class cabin – Up up the night air.

O I am discovered in my lair. Can I refuse though when it is
thus done? Was it Helen, though, or Avery through her, or Daddy
through her?

The creature comforts! How men hug them as if they were life!

When I was in my loving bed below I thought what things do

we most fear to lose, what are most important? And I thought after virginity is lost the world can be your lover. Before so much is clutched because so much is unknown and the vague intimations startle and alarm. Some eyed the cake. The old lady, plump and battered, fingered each one as if it were really life. Others their flirtation's success, or that they be a man in the eyes of men.

How they loved the advancing of the *mal de mer* heralded gloomingly and gloatingly its approach groaned and retched with what full relish!

At dinner (at two long wooden tables in a sort of cement cell below on wooden benches) I thought, though, they are possessors of tradition which otherwise only the few attain, the middlemen miss all thanks to their miserable padding from the rough real kisses of truth, and are not aware enough to be taught by the gentler teachers, or the aware ones that tried to tell.

Now – can I sustain my great adventure in this familiar comfortable isolation? Cherished and guarded my work is double – to break through the misty clouds that lull and ease, and to translate when I get there.

But could I refuse?

November 25: The Morning

The beautiful before.

The cosy lapping pink pyjamas, silk inside and downy wool outside. Breakfast in bed by large amicable scrubbed stewardess. The changing blue sky, the all-embracing sun.

An officer came and said, 'Miss would you like your breakfast,' and the stewardess said, 'Here's the sick lady!' 'I'm not sick. I'm only lazy. I'm never sick,' I said.

O the beautiful beginning. I could live here tasting it cherished by these tender pyjamas (like love's cosy accessories, even) tasting the brilliant, happy, free day which is entirely mine, of which I can make what I will, and which has all possibilities.

For not one evil binding thing is in me. My insides fly like air, I can do anything. I am happy, light, gay. Full of love and should a burly sour one get in my way, I should laugh as if he were an angry kitten with his eyes just open, laugh and love his ridiculousness. Richer and richer only can be any approaching event.

November 26: On the Siboney

Lynn's palliative and lugubrious scales and arpeggios break through my sleep, and the grey white porthole's discouraging eye.

'There is always work,' she said.

And so the yards and yards of unnecessary steady gymnastics, like soporifics, magic repetitions to soothe and lull her pain. For the same results, a better technique could be attained by so much less effort, a few notes over and over, but with *attack*. Not this long, even melancholy necklace. But it has the same note that poor drunken broken Bob Devlin's saxophone had across the water at Kingsmere in the misty dawn. Its sadness always reached my heart like a stab. How dared Philoctetes[3] on his lonely isle complain.

Had he not the sea and the sky to return his love.

And do the seeds of man compare with rain?

These grey days all sky and sea are wild with innuendo and submerged life. The green, blues, whites, half greys, large embryonic clouds floating, the unformed bigness of potentiality. The whitecaps' foam, the gulls' flight – the strong warm wet air – like the spring message wind it goes through everything, through every pore, the brain, the sex, the mouth, the hair; it ravishes, exhilarates, possesses, cannot weary – O to leap only into the sea – to *be* sea – to be sky – to be air. I will be there. I will by willing *be*.

The sea's rhythm is love enveloping, surrounding, adoring and expanding. The sky's melting meeting.

You knew love – you thought of it as warm. Now you know these are its origins. The back box from which all emerges.

Thou piece!

(Let me be a piece, a harmonious piece of this. Love was that – but momentary – a spasmodic bit – a spot in discordancy.)

Before love I knew this. But thought its premonition told of love to come – specific love.

Now love has come. But by it I only take this world more slowly, more specifically. Love loosened each several part to love this whole more willingly.

Sea – Sky – Wind – O God.

Who would cling to a match-stick polarity?

Note

I want my book to be about love. But love is so large and formless. (But so full of new worlds.)

Durrell's book[4] was all love and joy though it was about 'the decay of English civilization.' But not formless – concentrated. At the end I felt – OO – I have been well loved.

December 4: San Angel[5]

These violent dreams! This confusion! When will the water be clear? I cry Yanko! Or I cry for a hermit's rod, and I clothe myself in buffer mists. For all social life (people, world, contact, things in the limelight, markets) Yanko is my buffer, and to fulfil the alas too urgent geranium's wish. The night is lying down on a hard board to let those fearful dreams possess me – not the soft nest, rose clouds that remade the unravelled day.

Yesterday I entered my face in a rose. Be a rose, woman, I said, and fall to plotting ways.

And do you know, the rose never was his? Dew and rain wait on her so dutifully. She breathes luxuriantly. (Woman, did you hear?) (Perfume to make the senses rock.)

December 5: San Angel

Under the feathery-leaved tree, with mountain on all sides, the pale dried maize field rustling all around, the cactus sands in rows between, clouds billowing, the valley in a haze, I begin to feel the *earth* of Mexico. I begin to mingle. The small yellow butterfly or the escaping lizard have the same rhythm – I am at last again a continuation of the ground I walk on – the dust even and my feet have a union of harmony, and the rocks I jump from hug, render in passing their essence.

Yanko's letter: – I looked out into the garden sadly, and Alice put her arm around me. When he is alone he begins to weep for the war, the used, to feel shame for his happiness and success, his inability to help. He becomes frantic with anxiety and sorrow. He saw poverty and filth on his trip, and fourteen-year-old prostitutes hanging on his arm, and his great sympathy, his fierce sense of injustice, makes him want to leap into the bloodstreams too. But I, I insist on shutting my imagination, and when I am with him his too. I insist on looking the other way, like the last pregnant woman in a desolated world. It is the vital thing to keep your eyes on the sun, to grow calm, to hang to that hope, to cherish with every ounce of love to be squeezed from the universe, the *seed*, the frail seed.

But he infects me again. I only tremble. We are slipping slipping too.

But I will obey my mother-nature's laws. Her laws denied bring death. Love the flower by your side. Live, she commands. Suns come out and dazzle, maize rustles, birds sing, mysterious night signs arrive to solve the universe. Here is the clue – can its worth ever be less?

If I feel swamping pity too, we shall both be submerged. But I am at all times her (nature's) instrument. I shall continue to look the other way. I shall dazzle his eyes with the sun. Fill his heart with love. Bind him to the earth with life, and if he still weeps, turn his tears to a personal pool, where he will not drown but lose himself in swimming.

Yes. But maybe he is just MAN? *Your* man. *The* man? He is MAN, *my* man, *the man* – why say just? Would any other do? Or would an IDEA be warmer in the night? (scorn). *He* is life, not you. (Tread the bitter road, send questions into the powdery grey dust. But he is after all that brown field, the cradle of the seed.)

Remember those three terrible visions at Ste Sixte, with the evil yellow moon leering? The falling, the trampling, the ropeless abyss? The earth gets smaller, the barbarian swarm and overrun the delicate fields. (Shall I snatch a gay green garment to pose?) Will they at last find you too in your lair? (From the front, the mossy cave, the high spiked fence, the mountain.) All things the young mind knew, the destruction, the desolation, the persecution, the terrible final capture, the mountain bursting into flame, all the green grass trampled into cement, the treacherous lake flooding, deceit even in the sky. It spreads, it spreads, can *anyone* escape?

(Cradle the seed, cradle the seed, even in the volcano's mouth.)

Mexico City

Your beautiful palace, Alice, I could walk into it wide-eyed and innocent and betray no one. Bringing too the most far and secret boxes of my heart and my distrustful soul. Clothed in not one image – tenderness springing only from its spontaneous font.

But not *his*[6] palaces without a crowd of betrayals. Why? Not his could I walk in but starting with fear, bound in shames, ropes

attended by ghosts, and premature regret. And there would be no
wells springing heart to heart, no soul with her Pandora Box. A
quilt, a game, a cringing. Forgive me this? Shame. And yet some
argue not to enter is a betrayal too.

Why are these mysteries?

December 6

Dreams pouring overwhelmingly emotional. Sitting for hours and
hours with Yanko and Geraldine Fitzgerald while neither addressed
a word to me or looked at me.

Finally I dashed away, my coat half off. The streets were wet,
railway tracks, cement structures, buildings, wet puddles. He dashed
after me, scolded me. I packed some things, some red crêpe paper.
Then everyone gathered sitting on a highly polished floor, a scene
like school, only the head mistress (Mrs Birch) teacher's house, also
half the governor-general and diplomatique. Some teachers asked
me a question and I looked to answer, but I had on a hat with a
veil pulled so tightly that all my features were squashed together. I
tried to pull it off but it was too well tied. Then children on a bus,
sweet, on my knee, Lynn in a seat nearby, and I before I saw her
was recommending her to the mothers of the children who wanted
someone to cut their hair. The bus went along by the Chaudière
Falls,[7] which were terribly swollen, and all the people from the
diplomatique school gathering were swimming there, especially two
young people with red hair. But as we passed the stiller water to the
terrible falls I cried out No! No! not there! not there! I can't bear
it! But we passed and the swollen waters were in wild frothy foam,
furious and overflowing. At the edge a hypocrite was smiling and
saying, 'See this board – it is shallow, there is absolutely no danger
for our clients.' The water in such force gave me terrible pain and
emotion. I sobbed and sobbed. Then I awoke.

And Yanko writes: 'I can't tell you what joy that you shook off the
New York lethargy and now only I can tell you how much I suffered
of it at the time. Mexico will be an ideal place for you to come again
in contact with the soil.'

Yes. I am nature's instrument. A key that fits no other lock, a plant
that can only be fed from one source. And yet, sometimes, I forget.
I wander under this terrible black misery, saying, with my myopic,

measuring brain, Is it this? Is it that? gathering irrelevancies, small stumbling blocks, that earth's sea of joy would submerge.

But alas! it is something I can't combat. There is no substitute. What may not happen when I starve in a desert, not alone in those revengeful clouds but with someone 'suffering of it,' thinking it is I that walk there, rather than my parched corpse from which the elusive wayward soul has flown? It is no use upbraiding the dead, living, thing, only put its lips to the source again, and it will grow wings and a thousand angels return to attend it.

Drapery. What of drapery? I mean the oblique camouflaged form of putting the truth in a work of art. A Poem, a note, a diary. These are the raw moments, the raw thoughts. I do not want, I am irritated with the devious method and hidden indirectness of the novel, for instance, or even the short story, or a play. Poems, notes, diaries, letters, or prose such as *The House of Incest*,[8] in *The Black Book*, only meet my need.

Yet would I not be happy to make a book like *Green Mansions*,[9] or *Wuthering Heights*, *The Waves*, or *Tess of the D'Urbervilles*? Well, yes. But when I think of the things I want to say, I cannot think *that* way of saying them. The fierce impart things, drawn over this huge irrelevant skeleton. But what form? Infinite pains for a poem. But I need a new form even for a poem. I have used up my ones. Tricks begin to slouch about. Each word must rip virgin ground. No past effort must ease the new birth. Rather than that, the haphazard note, the unborn child, the bottled embryo.

In the bath I thought so much of life is *waiting*. But then on the sofa the moment flowered and flooded me with life. I had Bach, Picasso, and Alice's poems[10] (an exciting day-by-day entrance into a strange all-possible language and its literature). Such riches, that only tears could tell. This is the full vibrating life, and such a lovely sea of silence surrounding it that its essence could be savoured, it could be a conscious moment. And every article in the whole room blossomed led to new world, contained the universe's seed. O what happiness! What a mountain after what bogs!

LIFE BEGINS HERE.

December 8

 Music – the harmonizer, the suggester, the absolver, the resolver, the bringer of tears, and whipper of the blood. For that lost liquid would a recompense of steel. And from that prison imposed, the gradual speaking of the adjacent earth, slow, slow growth, a sudden light breath on the neck as the chain break into flower, and the walls' dreams slow their motion in the clearer, listening air.

Yes. There is a form beneath. There is a symbol for the time. A seeking, and a struggle to know the enemy-faced god of love. But for the vision a long long price of silence and waiting, of opening the heart and sifting sifting the mind.

Diego Rivera's[11] birthday and the mandolin and native songs and the little Indian girl on my knee smiling and Diego large, benevolent, and full of his work thoughts. His home all layers, cubbyholes outside, stairs over and above, lovely old Mexican sculptures, huge images of cardboard with friends all over, a portrait of a little dark girl in white dress with a skeleton and luminous tree, and one of a copper-mother-of-pearl girl, all bare, on her knees. Lovely model and mistress Navia, lovely second wife, Lupe Maria, horrid girl Maitza, and many middle-aged women.

 A smiling sunny morning. We walked across a field, Alice in her beige-ribbed velvet dressing gown. An iron gate opened by body-guards, and tall forms of soldiers, the house bright blue and pink.

 Rivera, large, friendly and smiling, a man of immense work and irrepressible gusto. Kind though, and sauve. But steady steady steady on his own earth.

 We ate a paw paw.

December 10: The Music and Sappho's Girl[12]

 The trembling on the thresholds. Were all thresholds trembling? Two outwards eyes watching. A death chorus of the world's super-stitions. A mask face. The legend of Narcissus. Outward tangible gestures are never born with my secretive heart. My heart is a bouncing gazelle. Nothing is more contrary. It listens, it waits, hidden in its nearby bushes. It trembles too.

'Ozozco!' he scoffed, 'Ronsardt,' he scoffed, 'Rabelais, Corneille, Racine,' he scoffed, 'Christians,' he scoffed. Scoff! Scoff! (O love I am kneeling at the door. For God's sake let me in).

December 11: Alice in bed all day

A bad seed sprouted. It grew and grew. Fanatically. I began to despise and hate him for despising and hating. What he calls 'discipline' – his lack of wonder and joy, his belittling of almost everything, his doughy, unlined baby face, immaturity, untouchedness. I chewed on these things and began to look madly for any escape. Then in the morning I saw my bumpy face and small eyes and I remembered – Emily is near! Do nothing! Think nothing till nature is let loose!

But we were to go to Lupe Rivera's party – but Paalen had irritating work all day and Alice was tired, so we played tiddly-winks instead. A day without joy at all – though I smelt a rose, and went to town, and read *Moby Dick* and ate 'maplecream' candy. Eva[13] was sweet, but to him she cringes and agrees, and is afraid of life's wild seas that cleanse and straighten.

George Barker's approach[14] is in my mind always, and Jane's marriage.

II

MEXICO AND ACAPULCO
December, 1939–January, 1940

While at 'Los Cedros y Begonias' with the Paalens, Smart became involved
with Alice Paalen when they went to Acapulco together. Not only was Alice
Paalen a poet and a beautiful woman, but she was also unconventional and
exotic to Smart; she lived in a ménage à trois and her background and past
experiences had been vastly different from Smart's own. Smart also began to
dislike Wolfgang Paalen, who was abusive to his wife, and who, despite his art,
she felt had no sensitivity to life. During the time Smart was with the Paalens,
she was working on what she called 'The Mother Book,' what would become
her novella, 'Let Us Dig A Grave and Bury Our Mother,' a fictional work
based on her relationship with Alice Paalen.[1]

December 11

'O Love – I am knocking on the door for God's sake let me in.'

I mean – don't let my eyes get narrow – don't let me pick and
pick in secret into the nursery wall. Let my chase have a beast in
view. Not to scoff just to scoff – to help explain timeless miseries. 'I
don't approve of tolerance at all,' he said, knocking down everything
around so that even the flowers in his own garden wouldn't flower.
Christianity was the reason for all that Rabelais did. The English
have done nothing. Those people are worth nothing.

Nothing worth nothing for a painter? His mind pursued so inde-
fatigably his irritation with Cesar[2] that he hadn't the eyes or the
repose or the love to see a yellow tree, or a sky, or a beggar's blue
necktie. 'These people! How they persecute one and destroy one's
peace!' To shut out more and more of the world from his island
dictatorship of infallibility.

But Alice carries her beautiful hanging gardens with her wherever
she goes, and smiles, and watches when the light changes, and leaps
for joy when a housefly, even, makes a joke.

Her fingers caress life's pulse. Life flies by him and he grumbles because he feels a draught.

This makes me guilty. The small-eyed look. But to me the only stupidity is not to be alive, not to enjoy, love, and wonder. Surrealism, say their pamphlets, is the marvellous; anything that is marvellous is beautiful. Has he marvelled *once* these last ten days? Laughed like Rowlandson at other's quirks, rather than been annoyed? Loved the *flavour* rather than despised the *measurements* of the persons he was forced to consort with?

I thought before, he was a delicate sensitive instrument, pale with what he received, whom thought poured over. But no. He is bound in swaddling bands of pedantic dogma, and thinks truth can be laid out flat on a map.

I am most pleased when Yanko calls me his 'harmonious one.' For to me the goal of every single soul is to achieve harmony with every surrounding it *has* to have, with every person it *has* to be with. Harmony is the key into heaven. If you carry it with you, who can come with bombs?

The earth's harmony floods you. Harmony with *one* can easily be attained. New York has a rhythm I cannot reach (so I left) and a group of people confuse me, or a didactic one. But to reach that harmony means an opening of all the little sensitive notes, and so if suddenly a rough word comes, a sharp tone, the terrible shock disproportionately can unlock the whole world's tears.

(As mine when he said: 'You are not interesting,' when I ate a small piece of lettuce with lemon on it after he had told me not to.)

December 12

Winter of Artifice by Anaïs Nin. Djuna – Lilith – and the voice.

Like being loved, everything grows exciting – the buildings, the trees, the maids – a lust for love, life, to unite, to be, to luxuriate, to discipline. ALL ALL ALL And a WOMAN, a real woman, only by or from a woman, ALL. It fertilizes. It empowers.

December 13

When I woke up I thought what is causing that rich warm under-tone? Coffee? Mail? Alice? the Sun? No. It was Anaïs Nin. She has poured things into the world.

His face is doughy. I want to sere it with hot lava of pain, seas of tears, whips of rebuff, hunger, desolation; I want to *weather* it and *seam* it. The little dictator in his satin-lined tower, curling his lip over spawning life below. A telescope to see the stars, after all (that meticulous instrument of science) is only an elongated pair of blinkers like a horse wears so he won't see too much.

We are sitting in an office waiting for a man who is signing papers. Eva's feet huddle together and her hands cross dutifully by the packages on her knee. She is the attentive, humble one, waiting for orders, service, rebuff. The man who signs papers is scratching like a hen but with less passion or meaning, giving curt orders to those who bob in and out. And a huge poster of the Rockefeller centre hangs on the wall – all those millions of holes where people scratch and scratch and no one lives – a strange escape! Bureaucracy and business. Not, 'I a man straddling down the avenues!' But, 'I ensnared by dotted lines and paper, empowered to annoy and prohibit, strike lest I be struck.'

Fake! Phoney! Bogus! Prostitute! O I could cry, wail, gnash my teeth, beat my hands bloody. The American tourists' show at the phoney Mexican antique shop – the gullible tasteless condescending stupidity of the American tourists. The Mexican dancers were neither Mexican nor dancers. No one smiled. No one even enjoyed movement. They played Alexander's Ragtime Band and Beer Barrel Polka. Afterwards American cocktails were served in small pottery mugs (for local colour).

The cheap terrible trash sold to them! The phoney jewellery openly manufactured, the vile varnished 'curios.' Even the gardenias were dried and the 'genial' Americans around with glinting greedy slit eyes, to lure you to buy buy buy. Foul, underhand, deceit.

Shit. All SHIT. But lapped up by the Americans who prefer shit anyway.

December 14

George Barker grows into a long dangerous image and is woven among the undertones. ('He had a tired English voice,' 'those exhausted limbs,' 'my tired lips received that morning their first kiss,' 'a very honest and painful person.')[3]

But O the excitement is in for instance: 'Wondering one, wandering on.' 'I penetrate the valleys bringing correct direction.'[4] It is the complete juicy *sound* that runs bubbles over, that intoxicates till I can

hardly follow (and the recurring lines in 'Daedalus;' 'the moist palm
of my hand like handled fear like fear cramping my hand.'⁵ OO the
a – a – a!)

December 18

Why have I not spoken of Mexico? Because it has not made love
to me. Not one blandishment. Not once pulled by the hand. Can
you kiss dust or mingle with it until you become anyone? Smells
seduce you to become one with their source. But if there are no
smells what thread? What to lead you to the lair where you will be
captive with love, and bound inextricably in the soil, the essence,
of a place. 'Abstract,' Alice says – nothing breathes ('no land, no
water, no love') you cannot mingle with the sprouting life as you
walk along the streets because it does not sprout.

'When I look in the mirror I wonder who it is,' said Alice. 'It's
like being drunk. You look and look and say Who's that? and you
move from side to side and it moves from side to side, so you say
Well, I suppose it must be me. I have got so old since I came here.
I never lost that sense of brutality I had when we came from Los
Angeles in the airplane – the frightful noise, at the vast altitude, at
so many miles an hour, above the clouds, and arriving here in the
evening suddenly, without knowing anything. Of course Diego and
Frieda⁶ met us and brought us to San Angel and of course there was
the disillusionment over Frieda. I loved her very much and admired
her. I still like her and admire her, but I see what kind of woman she
is. She seems to me now a photograph of herself – a walking picture,
a phantom, not the warm human creature I loved so much in Paris.
And she must be worshipped, a kind of little idol. I can't do that. I
had counted so much on her – her sympathy – her understanding –
but what can you do?

'There is no love in Mexico. In all these months I have only seen
two couples walking in the moonlight, holding hands, or with their
arms around each others' waists, looking or speaking with tenderness.
I could as soon make love to these shoes, or the table, or the bed,
as to the people I have met here. Cold, absolutely cold. And the
flowers have no smell. The cold kills the sweet smells but the bad
ones remain. Mr Hill stinks, but the roses in the garden are odourless.
India was so different. The man leading these huge oxen in the street,
the trees, the flowers, the music, everything breathed love. I had a

great flirt with the man who carried my chair on the expedition with
Valentine. Such sympathy. Such equality between men and women.
He was one of that noble race who rather than love their liberty or
become merchants whom they despised choose to become coolies. I
was really in love with him during the two days that he carried me.
And the tenderness then. I had several little adventures and they
were all lovely. So sympathetic. I had more contact with one whom
I could not even speak with, just by their looks, their understanding
eyes, than I have with hours of talking to Mr Boal, for instance, or
any of the people I have met here, like the man I gave a lot of matches
to and who said "Backsheesh?" with humour and gentle irony. I feel if
you dig down under the earth here several feet you might find love,
a corpse, some underground thing. But there is no love in the air.'

'Couldn't we escape to the sea?'

'Paalen needs me.'

'He has Eva!'

'That's not enough. He needs someone to consult and advise him
about what he is doing and thinking, to help him with his work.'

'It might be good for him to be left alone. He could have some of
that discipline he's so fond of.'

'He doesn't like discipline. That's why he talks so much about
it.'

(Remember his scorn that any woman be so sentimental as to think
she could help *any* man. He has *two*, like a pair of crutches, and even
then life harasses him, and flows over him too rudely. And his pearl
watery and unborn.)

'I don't want to be an egoist. I hate people who are always irritated
and dissatisfied with their surroundings. Usually the slightest thing
gives me great joy. I can become happy over nothing. But all these
months of travelling and adjustment. It confused me. You adjusted
your eyes to something very far away, and suddenly some other one
very near was put in front of you. But the people in India knew,
they understood that love is the most important thing in the world,
that you think about it, live for it. There was a sumptuousness, a
sensuality in the air. Your skin was quickened, breathing, alive. Here
I feel cold, dead, hard.'

'How did Mexico ever get its reputation as the colourful exciting
alive place, where things came out in you that you didn't know you
had in you, where you lived, loved, radiated?'

'I don't know. Probably the Americans, who don't know, who have no sensibilities anyway. It seemed exotic to them, like those horrible cheap pictures of native costumes they gave *you* at that tourist place. To them that was probably terribly local colour – exotic – foreign. O – I don't know. Perhaps it is only the climate that doesn't agree with me. I am not myself. I thought you wouldn't know me. I thought you might think I was my sister or cousin. I don't feel alive to sensation. It's abstract, the country. You can't become part of it. You are forced to turn into yourself for nourishment. That is why it might possibly make you write or paint in the end. All the sources of nourishment are cut off, so you have to turn in on yourself. I am dissatisfied and discontent so I have begun doing those little pictures. It's a sort of manual, automatic work. I would never do them if I were happy.'

Her beautiful face that usually dazzles and radiates in a miraculous way, was drooped and colourless, her voice sad and tired, but with the urgency of its message, her Buddha hands wandering, wilted flower pleading, feeling its sadness, afraid to ask life for itself, lest it be a complainer or egoist without life's elegance.

The evening

Ah but in the hour of my need I go out baying at the moon with a greater want than ever. And the withered moon in a great circle of greenish light and two desultory stars unwink, unrespond – the breathless dust no other life whispering. Undine! Rima![7] One melted back to the sea weeping. One fell into a sea of flames crying her lover's name in vain. I am caged – caged – caged. They fear – what? They people my blackness with their own soul's images. I am in that blackness (that dazzling light) and I fear them.

To strike down brutally the delicate upward urge, tender timid tentative flowering unfolding to heaven in a rhythm. He struck that down! O Yanko where is your shoulder of refuge? The moon's pale effort no single alchemy sends. I remembered that other night – I by the dark water-lapped wharf sitting and later across the fields running, stumbling, crying – for then it was the shoulder that I had doubted – and there was nowhere to turn.

It is my mountain I run towards when I run – my woods and my rocks – but here – how can I reach them, fenced, bound, wearing my warning, dissembling heels. Saying, after all, this soft strange painful thing I must know – take outward clothes like his, listen, be hurt but say nothing, wait, with much love, all will be revealed.

Can I have no avenging whip? See injustice done? No words tell? Silent showing by implication only is the only way – and even then – tears for the fact that endures are the only relief.

Alice smells of white of egg and has a tender dry sympathy. I can feel the struggle (can't you see?) I long to help too. She soothes. She will be the world's lover-mother. She is all tenderness. She could not hurt.

Paalen bought me *Undine*.[8] Paalen was tenderly humble and contrite. But I am never angry when I cry. I cry then for the world's accumulated sorrow – I cry for my unhappiness – that's all – for his sorrows as well as mine – I just cry. There is no focal point – he ceases to be the cause. By mistake he turned the tap and the sea flooded through.

December 19

We were standing on the front of the boat with that voluptuous wind blowing and the sun setting somewhere beyond that land. 'Nietzsche,' Lynn said, and I – 'O yes but I have always considered him as a poet rather than a philosopher.' But his philosophy is none the less true for that, because poets always speak the truth (my globular orange). How can one word – a flat, straight thing, encompass the globe of truth – even a long long string of words only wraps round the circumference so each can only picture one facet – each must be true. Paalen ordered a set of Nietzsche and they arrived the day we walked to Villa Obregon Post Office. There is a note of apology in his praise. The Nazis allowed Nietzsche at first but then one less stupid read him, pointed out his danger, and he was prohibited in Germany. But haven't I heard arguers lay the blame on him?

Less and less I am able to speak, to tell, even to know what is in my mind. Yes, it's breaking down the multiple images. But I do not feel a great desire even for such a one as The Voice to pour things out to. I only want the covering, the merging. It's afraid too of not being able to *receive* by having any too definite thing in the mind, and feelings. My machine, sensitive and open, receives and receives and never reacts.

But mustn't things be sharp and vivid, mustn't I *care* definitely

one way or another. I see this side, that side, but with which side
do I side?

But fair fights are only with mutual weapons. If there weren't a
deficit to be made up, a want, I might be able to speak.

Anaïs Nin exposes me. She sees so clearly, and she dares to speak,
she rouses herself to examine, not flops into the moment. She knows,
she puts it all gathered and whole and true. All right to dissemble,
but know why and watch.

But supposing you feel nothing, nothing at all, lying a livid
registering instrument, otherwise paralysed. Would a lashing at
last bring livelier results? Would stimulation generate the seeds
of a true feeling? And the cold, frightened, repulsive image of
unresponsiveness!

Must not love though, be fed on images? Or specially lit views, or
unknown, magnified facets? The long solitary walks in the woods,
breeding those accompanying atmospheres for the similar equation
of a single human being – the long firelit hours with doleful musical
background – alone – always alone – building a background –
attendant angels – or even in streets, teeming pubs – the lusty
images, the elegant gestures, the romance Proust gave snobbery
and artificiality – and for the spendthrift prodigal generous one,
the life giver, Pan's stance.

Perhaps these are their true elements, their source, rather than
manufactured backdrops. But they must be resurrected, searched
out by the lonely compelling.

What then of lashing when no images arise? What when the
imagination petrifies and the heart stands still?

Does my unrecognizing spring from fear, bound to me with the
spikes of my mother's wounding words? Or my fear of fearing? Of
not greeting graciously the throbbing supplicant minute?

I don't know why but that desert where we three walked comes
back and back and is the scene of all my imaginary scenes and sees
my unborn passions *act*.

She leans over me as into a pool, tender, her hair falling, her eyes
eternally smiling, but like jewels smiling, their smile cut out eternally
and unchangeable, her mouth too stretched and smiling the eternal
smile, a woman taking pleasure in a dream. And her whole smiling

face, with its dark falling hair is like a reflection in a pool – her glance smiles on, only the water makes it waver and tremble. The smiling gaze penetrates, is unceasing.

Love's twilight, pictures, the hold I do not know. I never could return an eye's gaze. I know the lonely image-building, I know the escaping to be followed, the hand holding but the head's opposite ways, the undeclared communion and of course the night; all love that loses itself melts or heaves passionately, or has become one.

But the savouring, the lingering – the articulation like Sappho with her girls in the flowery grottos. 'To me, Sappho, you are like the lotus unfolding.' My eyes are wild animals – they have never seen any of the race of men. They dare not see love. Their terror makes them dash madly in escape, freezes them stock-still.

I am a blunderer here, heavy-handed, an American tourist in the Buddhist temple. 'Well say now, isn't that the cutest idea?' I hate my inexperienced tread, my brusque inadequacy. Can I not melt too in tenderness or is my home always to be a tree? Can I not become an image gazing at a pool's image, and not the distant analytical one eyeing the proceedings, saying what next? Will the evening fall when our two mouths come unglued?

Tentative, tentative, the tendrils creeping from the frozen plant onto this unknown ground. Creeping, too, in the light of day, consciously, without passion's impetus, without a forgetful cloak. It is a dance, and the watching eyes are pain.

December 20

I dreamt a long dream of Henry Miller and his friends and of escaping and indoor swimming pools and then my mother and a flock of sexual babies and Neumann – my mother had liked the preliminaries, not knowing or suspecting where they led, but when she came back from Neumann's she was terrified, terrified. Neumann had tried to put his hand under her dress. She said. Look! and she lifted her skirt and showed me how she had sewn her underskirt together into a kind of below-the-knees bloomers, with great untidy stitches in sailor's strong thread. She was defiant, but I touched her face and it was as hard as stone, petrified with fear. All over she was hard lumps. I was filled with compassion for her terror arisen from

ignorance so I sat her down sprawled in a chair and told her to relax
– 'Now your toes,' I said, and she relaxed her toes – and I went all
the way up, being careful, I remember, not to mention any delicate
parts (don't say 'thighs,' I remember I said to myself – change it to
'top of your leg'). Gradually she thawed out and I went away to a
cafeteria to get something to eat.

Yanko loves artifice, said Alice. Catharine[9] always got him with
her exclamations over the beauty of other men, how other men
pleased her, etc., or her mysterious airs, fine one day, indifferent
the next. 'What's the matter? What's the matter?' Yanko would
say, and she would sigh, turn away her head, surround herself in
mystery.

Then must I too always be cloaked in tricks? Never my bare
body, my bare soul meeting and merging in true peace? O my
God! I thought of our bed at E 60th St., his disinterestedness. How
I could have had tricks – and followed my instinct to dash out into
the raining night – perhaps disappear for a couple of days – let him
be in anguish!

But I could not bear his anguish. How could I love him and
want him to suffer like that, knowing, too, his terrible capacity for
suffering? I want to be good for him, to him. And for myself, too. I
want to be good.

At Cassis, to begin with, all the men were hovering around me,
all the women were fearful – and I enjoyed the men, for only like
that can you love and feel the flavours, taste the real essence of the
men – but I hated the unease of the women. I couldn't bear them to
be jealous – I hated the lack of harmony, the distrust. So I turned
my eyes ON THE GROUND, did not look with light at one of the men,
and fed on myself.

And all was well.

But would Yanko prefer storms? Should I disregard the distress of
the woman I love, make wild with jealousy the man I love? For what?
To be more excitingly loved? To be brutally loved like a wayward
courtesan?

The pain that shakes me now is not so much jealousy, as love.
I love all the more for Yanko's love of her – and because she
was physically and femalely that perfection I can never be, I
love her more. I love her too much. I despair. I am frustrated.
For no matter how I long, how I strive, I can only be me.

'That unattainable image cuts a great wound in my breast.' (Ah
my *breast!*)

My jealousy would never turn upon her, or the other women he has
loved, only it turns in on me, it *cuts* and *cuts* and *cuts*. O my God!

But do you know what reaction happened? Still trembling, feeling
my *heaviness*, my inadequacy, I began to flirt, to assert my womanly
powers. (O well, if *that's* what you want, it's easy to seduce and
enslave.) Alice and Eva went to town and I had tea with Paalen and
he talked from his heart and the light grew darker and the words
deeper. But I said, after a while – 'I made a promise.' He called
that Christian and bourgeois! I hung over the balcony thinking of
Tristan and Isolde, but dared not mention them. I wanted to say
at tea – O how I love *man*, and I love woman too. I love *love*. How
I wanted to melt and was partly dissolved. For he opened his heart
sweetly – that time in Paris he was sick after I left: now when he
is cross he is jealous because he has a *tel enise* of me. But his strict
and cabalistical principles insist on his following every feeling, every
desire, as saved (ah, but he *reasons* too much). He said also he wanted
to have women come to him now, not chase them, he had reached
that age, and he didn't want to take them brutally. I said didn't he
know women wanted to be taken brutally? He said of course – but
he wanted to dominate in that subtle way – that they were drawn
irresistibly, because they couldn't help themselves, to him.

He asked about Yanko and said his always siding with facility
was dangerous – that he always avoided anything 'spiritually,' that
he never understood surrealism, that he attacked the things that he,
Paalen, admired. He only said all this after saying how he liked
Yanko, how he was his friend, and would he, should he, could
he speak frankly, man to man, knowing how I felt about him? I
pressed him to. He said if I wanted a pleasant happy life, Yanko
would be fine – But if I wanted to accomplish something, the facility
was dangerous – I must be unhappy to create. He spoke about his
ménage – said he couldn't bear to have the intimacy of two and with
three he could be alone in a crowd, and that was better.

But there were complications – sometimes he didn't know – life
was so difficult to understand. But he had a vision in him of what he
wanted to do, really. The turn of an animal's head in the trees, something *précise*, just, exact, perfect – but that perfection was dangerous
– a bit this way a bit that. He said that he was ahead, shifting from

surrealism, that as soon as he finished the exhibition he would break with them. This would give him pain on account of André Breton whom he loved as a man, as a friend, as a brother as well as he admired him as a great artist. But the break would have to come. But this was a secret, not to be mentioned.

December 21, 22, 23

We went for a walk. Also saw Riviera, Teotihuacán[10] and the pyramids, but mostly the tenseness, the hard knot in the stomach from their sadness and irritation – the flaming sky in tiers; religion from dust; squares in nature pointed corners so unnatural; a desert's breath, at last Mexico a beautiful backdrop – pink earth, houses, red and green trees with translucent intimate bunches of falling fruit, dismembered antiquities; smiling children, a row of soldiers at a gala day with a speech; the Pyramid of the sun, neat and geometrical, but squatting on the ground, satisfying the comfortable longings – 'let us have no wild fling here' – a reaffirmation of solidity – a deep well and six faces peering in like a perianth; Popocatèpetl's[11] fierce white gleam when everything else grows grey; pools of water and a strange sea-like mist which descended till I strained to join it, slipping back to water, slipping and swimming and escaping; or the fearful purple mountains, batting back balls, whose horizon has a greenish tinge; (it was a vain endeavour? No – I leapt too in fiery tiers).

But with all these under I wonder more why he – (he came then – then after he left – I sat – suddenly the distant train steel shrieked like a trapped woman and afterwards the masculine pursuing whistle, low, predatory and sure) why he binds, blinds himself with protesting hate, and cramping irritation – half on his seat – the gold day riotous outside – '*il faut demander*' – OO the lumps of swelling vexation bump and batter me too – and Alice's hysteria and fatigue – her face turned to a sad-coloured stone, her mouth set – opened as I am to her. I cannot escape the breaths she exudes – my stomach turned hard and hurt me – when I saw my mouth in the glass it was sullenly drooped. A gay pink and blue house flashed by, patches of yellow worn thin, trees of paddle-cactus in voluptuous frozen rhythms – I leapt up – then I leapt back guiltily. The desert, the faded yellow desert, the grass stiff with sterility, the dust swirling into the seeking nose – the pink-tipped porous brittle volcanic stones – American tourists (why is it always *that* sort of people who get the time and the money

to travel?) Paalen seeking possessions, Paalen condemning – Alice
cynically sad, resigned, tired, lifeless. Eva the faithful toiling servant.
I melted outside the window, into the multitudinous, strange, vivid
clouds, or the pools, or the trees, or the hills to harmonize, to loop my
life on, to be able to say, Love this one willy-nilly, pity the weakness,
not condemn – all all are *all*. No too scrutinous eye can merge with
that ditchpool's water. They speak of Undine, but can they *know* if
that shimmer has no power at all?

('Let it BE sea,' 'melting and merging with the fragrant bed.')

Why does he hit so against religion? (flippantly speaking, he is
its greatest argument in favour) gloat at a blasphemy? curse the
dust that engenders it? ('Ugh! *ces chrétiens!*') All men must worship.
(Russia's state – substituting even blood sacrifices for its faith –
Hawaiian harmony.) He is a last adolescent, fretting in the nursery
he has smashed. He believes it's wrong to deny sex – yet the equally
urgent urge he represses, denies, and pines away for. I would not be
thus always *reasoning* against him if he were not the dictator, whose
absolute opinions and reactions and momentary moods are forced on
three others, who *suffer*. To see one you love suffer thereby makes it
harder to forgive, and have compassion on the one that caused it.

'To give back electricity to the moon.'

My hand in the moonlight criss-crossed with a dead tree's shadow.
A hand, seen for the first time. So strange I trembled.

The moon draws me like a magnet – my head up hung to it, my
legs and arms dangling like marionettes.

Or it charges me and I leap like a shorn sheep. The moon forced
my mouth open and my teeth and entered me as I lay shaking
on the brittle beige grass. Like a baby forcing the womb open
its electric globe forced open my mouth. It was in me. Then
I noticed how each single star in that enormous wideness had
pinned me here and there ('my blood gathered in points'). So
I was strung on a clothes-line sagging only where there were
no stars. One star moved in a tripping glide like a housefly
on the ceiling. The moon's pulse shakes more potently than the
roaring machines at the power plant. The glitter glues my eye
not dazzled but bewitched. Who has been my lover like the
moon or possessed my eye? One finger went numb; I drank the
creeping cold like a caress. But the moon riveted me. Barking

dogs, men's mumbles in adjacent courtyards, far booms, but only I spread out on the grass by the moon, taken entirely, made its element.

I can never realize the *strangeness* of the moon, the *potency*, the *gloriousness*. When I see it I want to shout, to leap – Why did nobody ever tell me? If anybody else has ever seen the moon why don't they go around talking, raving, being astonished about it? So exciting. So mysterious. So appallingly beautiful. It's a miracle, an inconceivable splendour? Why is not the whole world buzzing with wonder and consternation? How can they exclaim over a soup bowl – and miss the moon. MISS IT ENTIRELY because some poet made a whore of its name, but a platitude. But even then, the exclaimer over the soup bowl, and the platitudinous poet – can they not REMEMBER? A hundredth part of that wild incredible phenomenon should be like a double dose of intoxicant drugs. It is a power plant terribly charged – and too much moon could easily kill me with shock.

And they (who despise all religion), the surrealists seek the *marvellous*. Surrealism then is only a religion, a measly simpering substitute. And they've *used up* the moon (they think) so they get their marvels out of (e.g.) a melting watch.

(When I look at the moon not only my flesh, but my eyes, my hair, my bones melt melt melt into the reverberating rays.)

Get Paalen to define – religion, stupidity, tolerance, discipline, precision.

December 24

Today began with the knots in the stomach – Paalen's voice with the damning note in it for all who did not agree – dictating and damning. Alice tried to put forward a view but he called it not thinking clearly, childish, not seeing before her nose. She was only saying that she couldn't see that the Spanish priests with their havoc bloodshed and enslaving of the Mexicans were any worse than the thousands of slaves sacrified to Quetzalcoatl.[12] I wouldn't dare venture out to get that scathing rebuff, and she only ventured timidly. But he says it is thus and thus. All who do not agree are idiots. My toast I dared not eat because it went down in lumps and turned to stone in my stomach.

Lying on Alice's bed – the eye of the heater encouraging. Alice talked and wept. Her enormous sympathy for all suffering was something she couldn't help, she said, she had always felt it even as a child. She *felt* the people's pain and she felt always responsible – that somehow it was her fault. Why was she suffering? It wasn't anything to do with religion she just *felt* like that. (At breakfast she said she only knew what she *felt*. 'Abstract' is one of her words against.) André Breton was wrong when he spoke of the cries of pain and joy of women in childbirth. Once outside her window a woman was run over by a taxi, cut across her head and legs. Another time Alice heard a woman in childbirth and the cries of each were exactly the same. 'I assure you that woman in the maternity room was not crying for joy.'

The thing that drew her to a man, she said, was to be needed. Paalen was dictatorial, intolerant, never thinking of them – but on the other hand he was one of the most intelligent really intelligent men she had ever known (and she had known a lot) with a view of the world. He was one who should paint all day and write all night – he was not made for a normal pleasant life with other people – he hated most other people and was always terribly tense and full of new ideas. When he was young, his body had not developed so his brain had grown and grown and become the chief thing. But he made her believe he needed her – he was in despair when she got sick in the west, and they thought she was going mad. He said Don't die Don't die You must you must get well. And for a few weeks was much quieter and thoughtful of her.

But also, she said, he was really one of the most generous men she had ever known. If anybody, even someone he didn't care for, asked for money and he had it, he gave it. And when Dominguez in a drunken fit had thrown a glass and hit someone and knocked their eye out, Paalen was the only one who helped him. Dominguez wanted to kill himself he was in such despair but Paalen ran after him, gave him money, and encouraged him and told him it was not his fault, when all the other surrealists were condemning him and accusing him. Paalen really had a warm and generous heart and had written some remarkable and moving things.

She spoke of an older woman, Paalen's first mistress, very beautiful, who had a son now twenty, and how Paalen still loved the woman as well, wrote to her, wanted her in his life – all of them at once. He was like that.

She spoke of the lover she had before Paalen, a seductive toy who, though, always wanted scenes, which she hated and refused to have. He would tell her how he had been unfaithful to her with another woman, with frightful details, but she would only grow paler and silenter and say, 'That's all right if you want to do it but please don't tell me all the details – I don't want to know.' She would leave when it got too bad. But one morning they were lying in bed and he said, 'I don't want to know anything more about you,' and she lay still. Then she said, 'Alright – perhaps it's better if you don't want to know anything more about me. I shall go.' So she left. In two days he came to the place she worked all pale and distraught and begged her to come back. So they had dinner together. And he was gay and cocky because he thought all was well and they would go on as before. But then he saw her to the metro. She was riding alone – and she suddenly knew it was ended. She couldn't stand one minute more of him. It was the end. More and more stations passed. She thought I love him I love him but still she knew it was the end so she got out and took a taxi to the Dome – because she had a presentiment he would be there – and he was sitting nicely talking to a friend. She said, 'I don't want to disturb you but there's something I forgot to tell you. Could you come outside for a minute?' Then she told him it was the end and she didn't want to see him again for any reason whatever and she knew he was nice and would not try to see her because it was absolutely over. And he turned ashen grey and she could see his terrible suffering.

(Then Eva opened the door.)

Alice jumped up wiping the tears from her eyes and went out onto the balcony. Eva handed me airplane paper she bought me yesterday.

Alice gave me a dress and spent all morning fixing it for me. I dressed up as a pagan queen and we took pictures. They of me and I of Alice. Then we laughed and were gay. (Alice said this other man had told her how much he needed her. He would wake her up in the night crying and sobbing and say how he needed her that she must never never leave him and she would say – No – No – Cheri. But then a few days later he would say and do horrible things, trying to make scenes.)

The morning got so gay that I thought all would be well. But

Paalen gathered us and the presents to give Carmen (the maid) and her children for Christmas – and he spoke another harsh autocratic word to Alice. I didn't hear it but I noticed the unkind hush. Then I saw a round tear slowly going down Alice's cheek – Paalen got mad at this – my tortillas stuck in my throat, grew stony and corpse-like on the plate. Later Paalen got up, went across to her chair and put his arm around her. 'It's nothing Cheri, don't trouble, it'll be over in a minute,' she said. So he went back to his chair. But her tears slowly followed one another. Everyone's eyes were fastened to the table. Every swallow could be heard. Paalen got up and got the morning papers and read. After a mouthful of dessert Alice went upstairs. 'I don't know what's the matter with Alice you can't open your mouth now without her getting into a mood.'

Eva and I went for a walk in San Angel and Villa Obregon looking for a studio for Yanko. I bought my curious pink flannel. We walked and walked.

Cutting the voluptuous paw paw for the salad – the drowning juice – the velvet resistance.

At tea Paalen said he thought he would send Alice to the beach and if I still had a desire to go – he was sheepish, you see, this being my victory, as three days ago I suggested it to him. We asked him if we could go to Acapulco as he was busy now and didn't need us and Alice needed the sea. But then Eva objected we wouldn't get hotel rooms at this season and Paalen objected Alice wouldn't benefit from such a sudden change of climate at this time of year. 'What's the real reason, do you suppose?' I said. 'Oh, egotism,' said Alice in a flat voice. 'Eva doesn't want to be left alone. She's jealous to think I'd be having a good time while she had to stay here and drive the car and look after the house and Paalen's egotistic – he wants me to be here – he doesn't like to think we want to leave him – he likes to consult me.'

But Alice with dishevelled hair and sad colourless face was quiet and sober. She always answers graciously and takes an interest if spoken to, but her eyes were on the ground. She lay on my sofa with her eyes closed while I cut the paw paw. She asked me to do it – she was so tired.

I am now the watcher cut and bled to watch impotently another's pain – a resolving tragedy. Paalen must have an unhappy life, Alice said, and as her life belonged to his, why should she not have an unhappy life too. It was hard and lonely, to have cast off all belief and safe holds as Paalen had – it was not easy – it made him unstable – it was terrible to live with – but she flattered herself she could help him.

Ah but sometimes the towers crumble and where was she then? She became sick. She wanted to die. She had no confidence in herself – he encouraged her to write poetry – he criticized it for her – told her when it was good – when it was only poetry and a waste of time.

But ah – but when her towers crumbled she didn't care to decorate her hair or make up her face – the bottom dropped out of the world – she hadn't the heart to live – she went about grey and listless – like these last two days.

(You see, you *see* her true goodness – her always humble always questioning soul? She needs to be needed – and Paalen called me adolescent when I said I wanted to help Yanko!)

December 25

Ah, well, quiet sweetness at last. Last night they gave me presents – Alice her poems with a special illustration and dedication, Alice and Eva with two big taffeta poinsettias, Paalen a little box with three ancient Indian things. So last night I made two little books of my poems for them, and at breakfast there was a serenity.

No mail – no news. No word from Yanko or from home. But Alice and Eva translated my poems and I did French, had a bath, talked English all through lunch with Paalen – Eva read Anaïs Nin's book – we went into the garden. At night we dressed – Alice in barbaric red with bone tooth necklace. Eva in the red sweater I gave her and blue-flowered skirt – I in yellow velvet. We played tiddly winks.

Was this all? But to say this is to say nothing. Why record the fact if they signify nothing but flowed over like atmosphere in an equable climate?

Well – you see, well – you see, the present has too wild a heart beat, is too near, its truth trembles.

I am hiding something. Did you know? Why am I hiding it? It

is not shame, nor even a sacred secretness. It is something only the body's language can say, oiled by the strange tides of mysterious passion.

OIL. OIL. OIL. The mind's measurements, surveys, calculations never know anything.

You can say, the water did not rise, but that is no conclusion the water will never rise. Suddenly the face flames. What can you know from peeping in at the door with an analytical eye? Am I being dishonest? What happened? It was nothing and yet it was a new world's real contact. Softly you step into things but the world gives them harsh names. Tenderness sends its hand, that's all, it wants a finite gesture.

But the world of sensation has an experimenter's enquiry. Does this do this? (O yes my back neck bitten made my right thigh quiver with a gulping shock.)

And then, without the purple floods, the stylized gesture grows dry, the eye comes back, the reaction's contrary tongue.

There was a moon as bright as daylight tonight. I could see my face in the brimming garden pool – and the lines on my palm. Tonight, though, its electricity did not bite.

It is hard to join the heart and mind that overflow with sympathy to passion. I can never so well love, understand, and sympathize if I become involved myself. And passion is *the* involver. My blood once mixed grows only contrary, fighting, and wooing the seas. Passion pays for itself. But passion is not to be played with. It is a force with but a single thought.

But what colouring powers it has! See with those flooded eyes, and later again with no flood. The world falls flat. You turn away sick from your spread out deeds – your flower-decked shrine.

At night, before bed, not overflowing insistence, but really only the tender gesture. 'Alright if you don't want to kiss me. But I am always the one to kiss you.' Ah yes. O well. Eyes, glance, tongue, come to my rescue, say the lubricative and the harmonious termination continues. Don't you SEE my naked mind watching? Bury it O bury it with those fiery-coloured robes.

Not that it condemns. But it knows too much, holds back the loving arm to measure its radius.

But this afternoon *oil* brought back the placid flush to my cheeks and I ran upstairs to change happily suffused and clasped Paalen and bit his arm on the way – it lubricates – right then I could have taken the whole world in my bed – and the flesh flowering the only act of living. *Life* – the name then is a caress, a warm bath, a flower garden vainly breathing after the sun's insistence. I want to *act*! I want to be *used*!

Today, thinking over what Alice said of Paalen and the necessity for unhappiness in bringing forth art, I was thinking if it *is* really necessary to renounce living to bring forth compensating art. *Living* – that quickening and glow, the lovely instruments of love, dancing, laughing, talking, loving, swimming, lying in the sun expanded – But art – only the realization, capture and condensation of the MOMENT, any MOMENT, in any time or place (a lady's head like a bird bent, a oneness with a stone, Eva's feet like whipped but faithful dogs). Or pulling strange substitutes out of your own dark depths in lonely cells, in isolated towers.

December 26

The blue forest on the way to the Desertio del limas. The spectacular clouds.

Then the disrupting effect of letters. Why is it that I should want so much to be at Jane's wedding? I never know what she *feels*, what she's going through unless I'm there to see. And she is important. And she could never tell.

Tears. Anyway it's the eve of the beginning of middle age (my birthday is tomorrow).

Paalen has begun to measure the stars – big mathematical books and books on time and space with Nietzsche for lighter moments. I think I heard him say that some of the more fascinating scientific calculations made art seem infantile.

This I could refute in one thousand pages. The temperament of a dandelion or cosmic preservation. Where does wonder begin?

December 27 (*'Perennial Day of Tears'*)

By the Devil's Pit facing the White Sleeping Woman and Popocatè-petl among the rustling deadness of the desert – with my small gnawing grievance to be dissolved – resolved.

But it is so beautiful, so still. I think of George Barker leaping to his death[13] (as it would be so easy to do here on the edge of this precipitate cliff) and falling falling – only to wake up at the bottom, not dead, bruised and battered, but not dead.

The lower mountains are bathed in gentleness, pastel vapours rise from them from the harsh white snow on the two great ones, and their attendant strange opaque white clouds.

The air is riotous with birds dashing in all directions and insects. There is a patch of fire red 'Oswego Bee Balm' and flowers – scarlet and trumpet-like, but like so many things in the desert, thorny. Why is the desert thorny? Because with scarcity, rare life needs more defence? (Do thorny people cover a paucity? John MacGillivray dwelt on purpose in a desert and mostly only shot forth thorns.)

I ran up here because Alice insisted on finding in my desire to be at Jane's wedding something bourgeois, lover of engraved invitations, receptions at the Chateau, wedding dresses.[14] She insisted on being disappointed – in seeing a 'different' side of me – or me in a different light. But there are two points in this that I gnaw against (besides being gloom-coloured in the pall her withdrawn disapproval brings). First – it is *not* the social trimmings I hanker for (of course) – but Jane – *Jane* what she must be suffering and feeling to be put through all these paces – if I am not there I shall never know – and I love Jane – it is a lot to miss this revelation. And second – *festivals*. Why do they hate festivals so violently? They curse and deride them and want to sweep them all away. But festivals are the rhythm of daily life – the periods that make the dance. A straight monotonous life can never be a rhythm. Surely an artist should know that? And then these occasions of abnormal and heightened loving, of excitement, bring out unknown sides, reveal things – even parties are indispensable mirrors. Since the first man and the first woman the need for rhythmic stops and gala days has been felt by human nature.

Well – she insists on misunderstanding – and as I walked up the dry path the purple mountains were so brilliant I was soothed with the shock. When has that medicinal failed? Any rubbish you throw to nature she can soften and metamorphose into a bearable shape.

Paalen reads books – begins to measure space – is the proud

extoller of science – I listen – I *become* space – but I am 'infantile' to be pushed out of the way when the real wonders pass by.

A minute hummingbird sat in a bush nearby. He had a dazzling jade-green back, pale yellow and pink breast, whiter near the tail, black on his tail and long black down-curved beak. After a long rest he visited the red trumpet-flowers for a drink, his invisible wings buzzing like electric fans with a low tone. His tail wobbles up and down when he drinks. He poises, darts – drinks with his head thrust forward and all his body quivering. He is incredibly small, but voluptuous with the body of an acrobatic dancer. When he stops still he loses his brilliance. His body is a roly-poly shape. When he drinks at the scarlet flowers his scale-like jewelled greenness makes a rich round eyeful.

I often thought of this pit since we visited it first. It is a focus. It magnetizes the imagination. Its incurving cliffs – its strange weeds sprouting out – its bowl-like bottom full of tumbled rocks. Its fearful depths. It is stored in all its hugeness in my mind, and is used for troubling dreams, for finite things, climaxes, something ever present, menacing but rich.

It is not so deep. It is the suddenness. And its tangledness – and full-grown paddle-cactus trees. Are there thrown bodies' bones there on its indeterminate floor? The stone wall, convex, has layers defined in its cement-coloured side.

Mexico City slouches in its plain, tufted with pubic trees.

This is an animal's world. I can feel their sanctuary. You can sink into it if you sit motionless, and the little bushes begin their otherwise unheard singing – the drone of graves always alone – and birds' cries are signals – secret when too many steps tread. Even houseflies have a musical hum, stretched to interpret the 'desert that has been a desert from of old and will continue a desert forever.'

Now I am under the cedars in the shade. How wonderful to be alone! The expansion! Even the love of man is only a remedy for man. A crutch that will be easily forgotten in space.

The top of the hill! Pines and a row of singing trees! Fields sloping down and all around more mountains! Now I am happy happy really happy. The wind! Impossible not to yield to joy!

A letter from Yanko – full of news and a news clipping full of laughs. If I could only squeeze the week I must wait into a pancake with my impatience! OO that balmy shoulder to bandage my wounds – that electricity to dispel my gnawing gloom!

December 31 (The last day of the year)

Something Wednesday evening gay and happy and the next day. The small tortoise, Dr Frances MacMillan and her ideas about men with 'no nonsense about sex.' Women were better, they could be trusted. Never trust a man. And if you want to marry a man never have an affair with him first. If you don't want to marry him alright. Have your little affair! But don't expect him to marry you! Men were untrustworthy! On Saturday she brought out her two men-with-no-nonsense. They were the worse sort of snob-homosexuals. An elderly fat retired stockbroker with small hard greedy eyes and acquisitive snobbery and execrable French accent, and a weedy young man with obscene mustache, greasy face, and rat eyes. I was hysterical with objective delight.

Afterwards, suddenly something happened to my heart – the almost-going-to-faint feeling in the head. Frail instruments bodies – such an exhausted feeling from purely physical causes brought death the physical fact too close. I saw my heart beating in its wire bag in the mirror that day – my heart had left me – I was without a heart – what beat my blood then? How could I stand?

Discovered Peter Neagroe's[15] charming stories of Romanian peasants – full of quiet joy like new milk. And pastoral lyricism. Healthy, lightly moving the heart, pleasant.

Finished *Moby Dick* and Henry Miller's *Tropic of Cancer*. The whale swam in and out of my dreams, but 675 pages is too much for even the most lyrical jokes. Miller at times moved me unbearably *sensually*, and then with pity for his great hungry mouth roaming the deserted streets, his heart always receiving receiving – but – he *protects*. It did not have the complete whole-worldness of Lawrence Durrell's *Black Book* – nor the feeling of naked, terribly condensed and understated truth of Anaïs Nin – her feeling of every moment being bursting

to capacity with *awareness* of itself. Miller left a great *pity* – love
for the *man*, his *force*, his greatness. But *Tropic of Cancer* is not the
gold nugget the other two are – and would not go on my fingered
shelf of one hundred percent books. He made me feel sexy as a cat,
but did not, as the other two do, show the glory, the meaning, the
great image of it.

Sunday the Boals and César Moro, the bony-headed small
Peruvian surrealist homosexual came to lunch. Jolly, but his professional *niceness* bores.

The white flower inside my window is withered. *Il pend comme
une membre mortre.* The moon too has done that and tonight is
not up yet.

At five tomorrow morning we get up to get ready to fly to Acapulco
and a balmy Pacific.

Eva's face is like a skull and her shoulders huddle and she always
thinks of things to be done, and sees about them, and does the dirty
work, and worries. When she sees a careless driver she cries, '*Aha!
couchon – vraiment c'etait un cretin!*' with her whole soul in it.

Paalen is buried in his smooth, doughlike face. His lower lip shoots
out like a knee in a tenser adjusted. He came down to say goodbye
– hoped I would have a good time, hoped I still had a drop of
sympathy for him, said his character was rather unstable and not
very nice, kissed me, reminded me of Graham, called me a Siren,
said I had beautiful eyes, beautiful hands, hands of a woman, the
rest of me *jeune fille*, but my hands real woman, kissed me again,
looked at me speculatively, fumbles, laughs sheepishly, leaves. Ah!
he is in his cradle.

I read an old 1934 notebook of mine. So I see youth's fierce
meticulousness. I feared maturity's wisdom might be degenera-
tion. Is it?

But it is like talking French. At first each word was an excitement
intense, forged into raw virgin brain, an adventure, a new never tried
direction – now the thrill has gone, but without doubt I talk better
French. The straining pain has gone – but that is because now the
words don't have to be forged. They come unhunted.

Yet perhaps, if only I could keep that explorer's wild-eyed hunting
face even from this comfortable foothold, what heights might I not
attain? Say the whole dictionary's fabulous wealth!

Perhaps – if – only –

But I don't weep for my placider maturity – I love – I listen –
I record. If circumstance wants to whip me to a different shape, it
may, I only yield. (Blows? I can bear them.)

In a minute the new year dawns.

January 1, 1940: To Acapulco

Years have gone by since this morning. Life at 'Los Cedus y
Begonias' is far in the past. An hour after arrival Alice and I had
blossomed. We had never seen each other more beautiful. We were
bursting with happiness. Eva's shape came towards me in the dark.
Her very shape, dressed, getting larger and larger. *Alice est dans la
salle de bain mais elle serait finis dans dix minutes.* Five o'clock! Cats
howling outside the window. I looked out. A white one, strong, taut,
just below.

The sky in spots is wildly streaked with pink, then, along the edge
of the black and purple mountains that fierce rich Mexican yellow.
Yellow all the way – pink tiers floating above. The pools among the
pueblo roads in the flat fields reflecting the rose, the stimulant flush
on the highest mountains as the sun touched them. Lone Mexicans
huddled in their blankets along the road, waiting for the bus. Activity
beginning to issue from the untidy geometrical adobe houses.

We went miles out of our way, as there was no sign to the airport.
It was cold. Your breath could almost be seen. Alice had blankets
over her coat. Paalen sat on the edge of his seat, saying ask here!
ask there!

Ah! the little airplane. Barely room for the pilot and five passengers. The cold waiting room. A journalist with a hat slouched over
his eyes tapping a typewriter with one finger, not giving a damn
for anyone. Paalen tender. Eva sweet. Coffee in a little counter-bar.
Americans waiting for various planes. They kissed us, admonished
us, waved tenderly. They ran smiling after us as we took off. We
kept looking at each other, bursting with smiles.

Will it stay up? Can it stay up? The precarious pulley feeling.
Touch a button and the elevator hurtles down. Oh! Oh! – Abandon
the body – say all is over – it's the same to me – powerless, suc-
cumb – and see the marvellous pattern. Mexico City's miraculous
surrounding fields, woven with a basket's precision, some dotted
with symmetrical haystacks along their stripes. I abandon the body
with precariousness – I enjoy the patterns below – the hills, sharply

shadowed – buff the predominant colour, sometimes pink, the far hills purple, the fields of earth dark, but dusted over, as if they had been sprinkled with cinnamon.

But it is a *mineral* country. You can never kiss the earth. The best you can be is covered with dust. The ground will not receive you. It flies up dryly at your approach.

We headed for the hills. The loud noise drowned all attempts to talk. An elderly round-eyed sympathetic man and a Mexican behind. In front a chic American boy who looked more Spanish.

Hills. Deserts. Untouched deserts – slightly green trees volcanic bowls dipping in on top, sometimes green, and made into culti-vated fields.

As we descended and it got warmer more vibrant green – a road cut like a sore, violent rust-coloured, narrow. Rust gashes – boulders untidily. Then heat at last – a lake – the Pacific.

Alice wrote a poem.

The day, the long wide pale beaches, the warmth. We thought we would dash into the bushes but we landed safely. The town, expanding warmth, the market, the tropical smell, the flowers, the palms. We rode in a taxi, through the town up a hill where we found Las Palmas and a kind elderly American who keeps it – very pensive – full of Americans with a private bay to swim in. We swam – etc., etc., etc.

January 2: Acapulco

O the well-being, the well-being, the freedom. Sun Sea Sand Foam. Waves that break that really break. That *joy*. The enormous sea's rhythm quivers like a jelly – and men within themselves have a rhythmic sea that never finds its moment of foam – Oh the boiling over, the curdling cuddle of the sea's burst! No wonder the men with their shoreless seas that have no outlet find release in that.

Be sea. Be foam. Be seaweed. Be sand. Be the sun's mistress, let the wind's hand and hair be your hands and hair. Inside and out. Keep no single resistance back. Urge the rhythm to their rhythms beat in tune, and a sustainable tune, though so wildly happy!

January 5: Acapulco

Monday night peering peering into womanhood – grasping new worlds, pliable like seaweed stretched and floated ('That was the first

time I ever tasted woman,' said Anaïs Nin. 'I didn't like it much. It
tasted like seashells.') Gooey ropes connect us. I stare upward, trying
to keep my image focused.

The next night lying under the innumerable stars on the beach
my thigh two lovers' cushion. A Mexican boy with a lantern came
and tortured two seashells. Hurling them to the sand or putting them
on top of each other to fight. He squatted in his ring of light, intense
on his sadistic operations, smiling, saying nothing.

The boring American man, trying to do as his neighbour did, not
because he felt the urge, but so as to miss nothing that was going –
and his sordid, usual story – wife of fifteen years whom he doesn't
love – their mean relationship, he going his way, she hers, his one
desire in life security – his fun hunting (duck, partridge, deer, fish).
The stockmarket crash only made him want security. So he built his
house in the woods.

At night lying alone – suddenly a cock crew like a woman's
shriek – but another answered and another. When Alice came in
she brought a black and white cat with her, and bent over me smiling
and kissed me.

The Wednesday – O – at night – she talked for many hours, telling
me her story – her early years in the east, her second accident, the
baby she had at seventeen who died at nine months – working – many
things – from other abortions and her other life in Paris, her lovers.
'What impression does it make on you to know I have had a baby?'
'How do you mean?' 'Does it not disgust you?' 'On the contrary, it
makes me think how much of life I have missed not to have had a
baby too at seventeen.'

Then her smiling face bending over me with the falling hair. (I
listening, listening, waiting, gathering this rare essence, waiting
for the full revelation.) Her eyes – though – she was all woman
– womanhood – her eyes then were worn, tired, sad, deceived, full of
bitter knowledge, love, all the wonderful and terrible things that ever
came to woman – her eyes like this, naked – eyes my mother had after
her long scenes of hysterics and crying – but all the time her smiling
dream mouth, smiling, smiling. 'Have you ever been with another
woman as you have been with me?' 'No.' 'Never?' 'Never.' 'And it
seems natural to you to be like this with me?' 'Yes.' 'Most women like
men, some women like women, but it's rare to like both.' 'I like *being*,'
I said. In the night she entered the enormous caves. We are in the

caves, warm, damp, fold upon fold, the caves bigger than the mind can hold, they hug the mind, enveloping, sinking it back, burying it in rocking softness. Or with my mouth I swallow myself and her.

Then the day of enervation with the decent pension Americans who so badly lack good manners and sensibilities. This was Jane's wedding day. Through pages of Blake, whose top pages give off a chalky blue onto the fingers, but no Epithalamion, I kept thinking what a lovely blowy day for a wedding. But of course there are miles of storms and weathers of roughness between her and me.

Yesterday when we got letters, mine disgruntled me, and Alice's made her almost remorseful. But then she talked. As I listened I held my breath fearfully; it was so precious. I was afraid the least movement might stop her and I lose forever those invaluable revelations I so desired. They come at me – like drops of water in a rush from some fountain of perpetual youth where pilgrims glue their eyes dryly throughout the ages, waiting patiently for the miracle – but when it comes the patience has got used to itself, has got a stiff neck, and they stand petrified, watching the water trickle irretrievably into the ground.

And last night enduring drinks in the confusedly lit bedroom of the doctor with the bony, jealous wife. Claustrophobia. Aching with boredom.

Today Calete Beach – American boys in numbers. But Alice with her wet hair flat behind swimming interminably her crawl. Refusing to come alive – after lunch we went to get her – her face and lips were blue, her skin and eyes red – but she still refused. She looked deathly – I pulled her but she got angry. 'I am neither mad nor drunk and I shall stay in the water as long as I want to.' So I left her. But the nervous apprehensions and fear for her pulled my face down into the gloomy, brooding pit. Can I think of buying blue-checked cotton when I have such dark forebodings for Alice? I skipped from door to door. But it was not so gay, like at the family rows where mother left the table in tears, and you, laughing, nervously try to enjoy the special ice cream which she had bought for a great treat, and now is lumpy and tasteless in the general tense unhappiness. And when I saw a man dressed as a skeleton with a scythe walking the streets, my heart kicked my ribs with a thump of ice. We went to the beach, but she had got a lift back – when we drew up she was there in her long beige cape, and she stuck out her tongue at us and walked away.

Then Alice standing at the bathroom door, quite naked, with her hair rolled up on top, reciting two poems by Baudelaire. A poised moment, and I said to myself could anything be richer? For it couldn't be planned. She was having a shower and I asked her a question about a poem by Baudelaire and she came to the door to answer me, and began it, and then went on, carried by it, standing like a dancer, her hands too, poised in the poem, and I lay, immovable electricity, watching.

(And don't forget that while we were dashing along in the car to rescue Alice, I admired my new sunburned reflection in the glass windows of the car.)

January 7

These smugly mediocre Americans. I thought again how they have turned their penises to stone – in braggadocio enlarged them in a sky-raping gesture – but petrified them – monuments to their impotence. America is still-born. These leftovers are the swarming maggots. ('But we have our skyscrapers.' 'Do not dare to mention those beautiful but shamefully revealing tombstones to your death.') 'Too late the stirring of the stone heart in the passionate red fever of the blood.'

I want to work at some definite work so that I can measure my accomplishment. But since mother forgave me, and I could feel some tenderness again, I am no longer possessed by her and my dissipated forces embrace wind. Fiercely free the concentration till and willy-nilly pearl is born. *Think.*

III

HOLLYWOOD
January–July, 1940

On her return from Acapulco, Smart met Varda in Hollywood, where they lived together. He was preparing work for an upcoming exhibition; she was writing and sitting in on philosophy classes at UCLA. Although she was initially happy to be with Varda, again, George Barker was on her mind. She received a frantic request from Barker to rescue him and his wife, Jessica (the first Smart had heard Barker was married), from Japan, where the British Council had sent him as a professor in the autumn of 1939. Smart tried to raise the money to bring the Barkers back. In the meantime, tension had developed between Smart and Varda. At the end of May, they left Hollywood with a few other friends and artists and moved to Anderson Creek on the Big Sur to live and work.

The early 1940 notebooks contain poems, philosophy notes, and French vocabulary.

January 13

Above Mexico flying to Los Angeles. The cold starry before-dawn, but then the sparkling sun. The dark mountains breathing cold air. The dry mud-coloured plateau formed in the ruts and flat heights of March road ruts in Canada. All is buff-coloured except for the dusty green tree-growths you would expect to find on such a dull brown body and fields like the marks savages cut in their faces. Geometric huts, fences, fields. Pools of aquamarine blue water, rich jewels in the long moonstone of colourlessness. Bumps, jagged crevices in the earth which has always the air of being used up, and yet newly-formed (quite different from Canada's earth, which has the air of being newly-born, and yet age-old). The haphazard pools are muddy pools when you are directly over them, like water drying after rain in the back yard. The little brown Mexican people with their chins buried in their blankets, their slightly bowed legs, sombreros, sandals, baggy pyjamas.

The sweet women in their cavelike houses who embrace you tenderly.

Can you imagine a desert newly formed from some worn out earth god scraped up from what was left over when he had finished everything else? The stony crevices cut the wavy ground, dry now, raw routes. Yesterday flying from Acapulco I saw a road making a ring – I thought that magic circle saves lives – see its significance from here is its pea-size round white ring – it's a clever contrivance of man and averts, wards off with its wizard's eye, tragedies.

A very fat Mexican and I share the plane. He offers me chewing gum and cotton for my ears and keeps looking at me. I am not afraid, though frighteningly vulnerable and unaidable. I say the pencil is more fearful than the pistol, and I muse upon my Mexico unconcernedly. 'Him I mourn from morn to morning.'[1] A whole, brand new day to travel to Yanko through the blue sky above continents. Mexico is made out of dust and mud, and to understand it, and its people you must become dust and mud. Nature has no smell here – only the rich breathing life smells that rise from the adobe cave houses, where the pigs, spotted and grunting, often share the family life, and flies add flavour to the food. Sometimes the earth's pink-tinged, or a once fertile field shows some darkly-yielding green patch in the long subdued beige. The dryness sometimes reaches a yellow tone, squeezed yellow with no juice. The villages are neatly divided from the fields, for their courtyards make a definite ridge, like a nicely healing scab. A pale mist tinged with watery blood rests on the mountains. Yesterday the White Woman lay in it, as in a passionate dream.

Eva told me something that helped explain her and the character of the Swiss as we drove along in the darkness before dawn to the airport. She and all Swiss children have to get up at six every morning to go to school. I saw the fortitude that can endure to go through an unbearable routine, that can remember the minute particles of the most intricate watch but has no juice left. Who could have juice left? Every effort spends itself on the meaningless exhausting foundation.

Now (after our first stop) the real desert lies below, flat, far spreading as a sea. The wide wide world.

Parched Mexico's tumbled mountains.

The sea-bed – the desert more confused by tracks, wavering, maze winding in a wilderness of desert.

Over the grey-pink mountains, bare, grooved like an armadillo's back, faintly green-tinged pink bursting intimately forth from gashes – pink and green the mottled floor – no trees, but patches, like the sores on a horse's leg. Bumps, sudden drops. The fear the slackening engine engenders. Then Torreon (lunch).

Real calm at last. The mountains, pink, light and gay, speckled with green tufts – pink and white and green earth and yellow merging and mingling gently spotted with seagreen tufts. Some more of that coalblack mass with the factory around it and a well laid out town light pastel and squarely and widely spaced. The pink blowing and refined and what is now a river winding languorous curves over soft sand. At last some life sprouting, and in the steeper, barer, sharplier defined mountains, more of the strangeness (*terriblement étrange*). Mexico is so proverbially supposed to possess. Here, there seems more graciousness in the laying out of the fields, not exactly a wild abandon of luxuriousness, but a ladylike liberality, and the pinks and greens so endless and varied, traced with finesse like so many Klees. Beyond, the mountains take a soft rich blue. Two houseflies walk up my leg. The pattern below at last *feeds* my eye.

Mountains with dignity. Exquisite pink and yellow hills, daintily speckled. Smouldering grey. An alive yellow bursting through, faintly mustard. Miles and miles of wavy land like the bottom of the ocean, and wetness in the crevices as when the sea recedes.

Chihuahua – two hundred and eighty miles by car to Jaurez and El Paso – to Los Angeles.

January 15: Hollywood

Why is it so hard to write, now that I have benevolent peace? There was that beginning, that shock of seeing a cherished image incorporated after the airy liberties the imagination takes – always a bumpy landing. His face is always more cunning than I expected, for it is always his soft melting shoulder, his gentle generous flesh that I remember. If I see him suddenly in a vision he is bounding like a deer. I see his small tight thighs that he swings from side to side. I see his intent look concentrating on something but it is the look alone, without face or features. (And in my images he never wears clothes.) In my mind he is like his hand in my hand, felt comfortably, but the faces turned away, sure of the warm mutual seas.

January 16

'And I thought then we weren't like fishes at all in the night when we swam in and out of each other and were all mixed up, it was just an illusion I had then, this illusion of harmony, this perfumed sleep.' No. We were like fishes. We were like fishes. With all my soul I will bring the fishes back, feed them, keep them, believe in them till they become as large as whales and as substantial.

But oh these resilient sunny mornings! The lemon trees, the tall poinsettias and hibiscus and residential palms! He gives me back my love of the world, my medicinal, alchemical love that can convert everything into food for the soul and senses. I am happy. I go to him at lunchtime with two lettuces and a basket of strawberries under my arm. I see the tall palms with fat trunks, the dark untidy garden and the little hut that is his studio. Such underground tunes singing in my head! And the things said and unsaid hardly have a difference so little do they burst or break the surface in issuing forth. The sun through the high window over the door, the pots of paint, the mosaics over the floor, half done, the size, the cement. And, too, as I walk up the street, absolutely free in body and soul, I feel I can summon any spirit I desire. The things to be written are waterdrops only to be collected, or just to lie savouring is enough life. IS ENOUGH ('Distil in some inviolate casket the yellow sun.') I am so happy, so lovingly open to the world. The timidest breath of a joke can shake me with laughter like a hurricane, and I roll with it in the wildest glee on the inexhaustible flowery grass.

But it is another instrument I want to play upon. My rich brain had abundant words, gorged, while my body waited. Waited anguished but patient, extolling the hands' obedient work. But now – those rich folds fall between the page and me and when I sit down to write the rich evening sensations I say, what are words? What is a poem? and I am as at sea, as ignorant and mystified, as the first day I ever saw algebra. I cannot write poems now. Other things are rumbling pregnantly in my brain but cannot emerge yet, want *rumination*, and encourage the mouth to cover the earth with a kiss.

This is TODAY, this is where all words strive to lead, all feet to attain. If I write one page, part of its radiance might slip by me untasted – I must stay aware, awake, adoring it, like Yanko said the angels did, singing the praises of the Lord.

And the book about Mummy – I say I must rend the Now, the Now is only important – I can't reconstruct the past, and if I could I'm afraid of missing the present. The important juice-drops are small, but worth a million of the garrulous chaff that the will forces out when it says do this or that. I cannot write a novel – the form needs padding, the form needs to be filled up with air – for no nugget of truth can last so long or be so boringly consistent. I want each word to be essence, irreplaceably and authentically the only only note. Mummy can only be a book about now, with Mummy as a recurring note slowly revealing its source. More (NOW) would be drudgery or cheating.

And I am too happy (praising the lord) for that. My island of harmony!

Is all this for me? All? And this too? And everything? What have I done to deserve it to be so overloaded with riches and harmony. As if suddenly all your indifferent friends should decide you had been too long neglected and come with fabulous presents, the things you most longed for, in profusion, and praise you and love you and call you hero, genius, unique one, and tell you you and you alone had made their lives this and that. The thick pines dropping globular cones! And the feathery palms saying this is a far land anything strange and beautiful may happen! And the new moon attended by two enormous stars! And the sunny day fading with a glow to a fresh exhilarating evening! And I walking freely to him in his hut where the huge bulbs shine onto his absorbing work. 'You are more shiny than all the glass here,' he said. 'What have you done to be so beautiful? Tell me, tell me what you have done. Are you going to die? You are so beautiful you make me afraid.' Not death no but life after taunting me above my head so long has come to rest in me. I love love love: the day, the night, the trees, America's easy voice, the fruits in riotous profusion and the vegetables in the market, the boarding house people with their macabre Thurber remarks, and the old lady with the staring resentful face, who, her daughter said, woke

up one morning and refused to talk or walk. The daughter said this
as if it were a charming caprice of the old lady. Now she just sits
and thinks and thinks. 'What are you thinking about?' they ask her.
'You're an old sphinx not to tell us what you're thinking about.' The
other day I opened the door of the bathroom and the old lady was
sitting on the toilet with her skirt up and her grey bloomers down.
'O excuse me!' I said. 'Oh, come right in, Momma doesn't mind,'
said the daughter. And the next day Yanko came back hysterical
with laughter because he had walked in on her too, the showpiece of
the family, like a Buddha on her throne. 'I really think they oughtn't
to let her be exposed like that,' he said.

'After taunting me so long' – yes – how I skulked lustfully through
the gloaming aching after it, hoping to pass by unnoticed in my
drab black dress and lopsided shoes with heels, hoping, thus surreptitiously, to come upon it. But I was afraid. You see my divine
delivery? Walking in my open sandals, in my bought cotton dress,
hatless and happy, singing, loving, knowing no small boys will throw
stones or shoot peas, because I love them too, and know how to
speak to them so that they understand, or even give them a look.
And, would I walk to him without my mother's terror freezing my
flesh, or my own doubts, or, as with John, praying fervently, filled
with apprehension, that the evening might have some successful
harmony.

I am a piece of the earth, one of its waves flooding and leaping.
I am the same tune now as the trees, humming birds ('It's a fish!'
he said, watching it quivering before the red trumpets), sky, fruits,
vegetables. Do you need some joy or love? Handfuls and handfuls
for you to spare.

Make them up into bed socks, tea cosies, wrappers, cushions, for
their electricity can contaminate everything, build at one blow a new
and adorable world.

January 25

Why don't I write the terrible, heavy blanks. I open the book, I
stare. I say, there is nothing to write. But there is the important,
powerful, evil blankness to write. Catch the disease, and dissect
it to find the cure. Put *facts* if necessary, and minutely the bleak-
eyed look.

Why did I not stay in Mexico for the show?[2] It is always with me as if I waited lovingly eight months for my child, knitting, sewing, eating salads and drinking milk, living quietly and contently, and then at eight and a half months couldn't wait any longer, killed myself, killed my unborn child, escaped to begin with.

I told myself at the time, 'If you regret, say it would have been impossible to wait those five days, you would have been *on edge*, anxious, straining towards Yanko like a bloodhound on the leash, and no matter what happened your eyes and ears and receiving mind would have been elsewhere.' And when I had those five days I said, 'Can anyone be so happy! Is this ALL for me? Bursting with happiness I could have squandered the world for.'

But now the waiting minutes begin – the inaction – an inconspicuous oiled wheel, and I say – O why did I miss the Exhibition and O those first five days would have been first five days five days later! The wisdom old people get because they cannot remember the passion.

And Alice's tearful articulate love frightens me, rather, and I don't know where to put my eyes. I bury them with Yanko in his shoulder and our eyes never meet. But my mind whines, asks why, carps. Is the avoiding elegant? I ask, for Yanko must think it is. I cannot experiment with such gossamer, the precarious image. To be that image is worth its world price – but how sure of the image can you be? A mirage darts about the desert unaccountably and is caprice itself. I ask Yanko intangibles and he dashes along some concrete road. 'Yes. But that is not what I meant.' At cross purposes, and what I only saw poised for a moment like a humming bird, I cannot pin down – I cannot catch and stuff till I have taught his eye with its preconceptions to see. Is your pattern for the world so set? Unchangeable? Algebraic? 'O yes of course. That often happens with girls. It is dangerous to have it in the mind.' All reduces to a too tangible scene, one woman doing this or that, a worn path that any watcher knows.

When he tries to preserve the mysteries, encourages them, and fantasy and mystery – that is where my *doubt* of them begins. For if they were as *real* to him as they are to me, he would not be *encouraging* them, they would *BE* too all present. I know and believe, and try not too much to acknowledge them because they too much possess me as they are. He is the grownup pretending to be scared, for the fun of the game, for his amusement and entertainment. But I am the child, and my terror is terrible.

February 27

Yanko has just left.[3] The emptiness. The listlessness that begins to form on everything everywhere I look like dust in a deserted house. The tearing asunder – my warm warm arms.

Even today, before he left, I could say, 'We must part, it is time we parted.' He grabs at life, he talks with his mouth full, he rushes, full of only his own purpose, hither and thither, my threadlike life is smothered. He never hears anything. But Oh the minute he left – I could have thrown all my belongings and ambitions away and rushed after him not to have to face the empty room and the terrible empty bed where he will never come again, and the whole of big empty Los Angeles which I have to face, which I shall look at for the first time with my own eyes not his. Till now, it was he only I saw and heard and explored.

Apathy – an inward sinking descends – I say – Is it only a *lover* I need? To be fertilized with life by another's gusts. For I lean over and look into the mirror and say Tonight I am beautiful. But O for whom? Why be beautiful tonight? These my poetical lovers lay lilies at the feet and catch the subtle glow – but looking around who can I see that would make me glow? Not one. Not one. I see a chain of days, and diligent and assiduous gathering of 'friends,' dancing lessons, fatigue, striving to write, listening to Bach's sea-urge.

Lunching with Tony – or saying Well then goodbye goodbye, turning and going home along the wet streets. Staring around my room, thick with inaction like one too long unloved, I see the formula a love bright look to 'draw out' the dull squirrel cage antics.

Nature cushions my sharp sorrow with listlessness – sleep sleep she comforts – and I do not feel, but sink inward unseeing and uncaring saying sometime I shall understand these things.

March 1

My world begins to be all dancing. The gathering of the energy in goblets for the concentrated moment of its release. But this my book I carry everywhere, and its blank unwritten pages and shabby cover – its menial use for dancing notes, addresses, and accounts deglamourize it. I must not forget IT is my heavenly key – my work – my purpose. Dancing only my prayer. (Those sacred rites of Greece – man and earth in a love kiss).

But what was it I wanted to say? I have been listening to Yanko with a soft receptive ear. An organ tuned only to him.

One thing that deflates me here is the impossibility of *communication* with anyone. No language, no look of the eye to see your meaning is caught.

I know I have been sealed up, silent, unrevealed and inarticulate – I let Yanko do the work – But my own work is such a different kind (my contacts differently made) they do not mix together.

And the chasing after that studio flat – the rejected feeling, like job-hunting.

But the healing balm of dancing – and my gramophone with Bach and the Californian sun.

If George Barker should appear now I would eat him up with eagerness. I can feel the flushed glow of minds functioning in divine understanding and communication.

March 4

Anything that interferes with the poetry is to be 'ejected' Yanko says. Rightly.

The mountains. They were the poetry's symbol, as it has no outward (physical) form. But now I look up and say Nice – But I do not need the mountains – They are in my dancing.

I dance but I am strong now and full of love when it is finished.

What shall I write? Where is the poetry?

Students – the expectant excitement – bubbling – aware too much is happening – *will* happen to them – the bold flushed embarrassed bumptious and apologetic look of adolescence.[4] The talk all in a rush – it comes tumbling bursting out – so *important*, so exciting. Its eagerness to come out dams it up till it stutters and splutters and spills skewgee.

Sun-oozing pines are an aphrodisiac – but not any love-urge but my original – the wild wooded hills – that absolute force benign on the lonely breathing places that knows each single atom's want and fulfils its most hidden, most half-imagined wish. I will escape there, I say, when the sun shines, and wind is warmer. Pavements grow hard, shoes prisons, belts harnesses.

The sad night at the ballet alone, I outcast, ignored, said I want that wilderness again, refueling and commingling with what responds to love. But the next night, after a day with the sweet friendly Prendergasts, jokes, and drives, and old bookshops, and their Santa Monica house, all painted sunny yellow, and a great yellow bell flower that fell from the vine, big as a hat, smelling sweet and fruity, and soft expensive kid, and the tall student who picked me up so amusingly in my top storey galley, and asked me out – I thought leaning over the rails to watch *Chronica* – to leave all this rich excitement? The pearls of combined civilizations? The rare mind's new discoveries? The centres where only the special knowers are to be found? Lovely lovely artificial gestes, the sumptuous gown, the superficial wit, intrigue, *flavour*? And its attractions grew too great to renounce.

But walking along the half wild flower bordered paths of the university, after Bertrand Russell, I smelt that sudden pine in the sun, and the grass growing green, and a far breath of the Hermit's Orchard: seduced and seduced and I said bare feet or I die!

In the Refectory, eating lunch I thought the wilderness! And in all this I am to, I *can* gather all that is the poetry and the dancing, the essence and its physical aspect. Each gesture of the waiters pouring chocolate malts, the student sucking straws, and the whole (WHOLE), with the nugget, the poem. O my luck to be free of the irrelevant facts, the journalist's chronicle, the frenzy of slipping time. I have all time to distill, and have only to gather and be aware, and wait, listening and loving. And the coffee surged through me and while the waiters complained of the heat, and the mob of noisy students, I adored the sweat, the medley, melange – I'll come, why not? to some of the other English lectures, for the luxury of at last gathering only my own honey with alert ears, and ruminating mind. I am rich rich. RICH. None other so rich.

March 19

All my life I fight the glazed eye, the lethargy. I insist I am independent. I *will* the sitting down at the blank page to write. I say I have no need of the people; I can pull out the vital thing myself if I am strong and moral enough. But I go flatfootedly up the hills, blearily eyed searching for my vision with a dead heart, just so much dead weight to cart along – Yes – I find in my physical exertion,

in the climbing of my physical mountain a relief, an exhilaration. But
it is the dance I have invoked and not the poetry.

It seems it must tumble involuntarily in the midst of the jazz of
the life and the only discipline is to catch the drops when it bursts.
These mile-long desert rays of uninterrupted calm grow only a scum
on my looking-glass pool.

'Write the blanks,' I said before. This evil, this sin, so monstrous
in its descent – its jellyfish anatomy so known, so stale. It is just the
flight of all delight, mystery and love – unambiguous bones left but
invoking less than any earthly skeleton or a lead grey day. A pall,
a drugged relapse into the state of nonexistence – no pain except
the fatal knowledge that life is embracing me and I cannot feel
her touch.

Other men appear, stoop over me, breathe into my ear with insistence. Their very approach to the holy passion I long for makes me
repulse them harder. Their poor imitation of my sweet soft happy
love repels and saddens with a world of insufficiency.

If I had my wilderness, nature could be my lover. What can I do
in the paved streets for my thirsty roots? I waste time. I encourage
fools. I slip the vital hours into penny slot machines – to pass time,
to start my stuck wheels only love can oil.

April 12

I knew love would never be enough. But then, there was no sweet
exchange. Who looked into whose eyes?

Did I offer myself? No, I did not. Neither fully nor freely. But was
I *asked* to give? Was it *my self* that was demanded? No. I saw I was
not wanted. '*I*,' I said, with my antennae sensitive in their ambush
– 'I will see, and give, if I can, only what he wants.'

But – my genus, my species. I am an artist first. *Pan*, not man,
my lover. My wires' messages do not contact his. Nor the nights'
messages breathe the same. O yes all outward signs of him, all intimations I could love. But a tree and I more freely shared each other,
letting our essences mix. Now he says, 'Choose between dancing and
me!' But I had chosen – and not him. For I never chose him. I only
loved him because he was so obviously good, so to-be-loved, worthy
and worth. But I knew he was not for me.

My mind can love more the bumpy face, the grandmother's flabby flesh – probing deeper into the mysteries. He desires images – the outward pagan show – beauty – with bursting apple flesh, not the struggling spirit straining through. He has his images all made, his standards and desires. I *must* only look and try to understand – and love, all the same. I knew with him if I became deformed his love would cease – not cease altogether perhaps – but cause only pain never pleasure again. My youth would have scorned that. Though I realized and I learnt what the sweet manifestations of physical things can be – I embraced and understood them and in many things became free as I never could have been before. But I was right in the beginning. The flesh is sweet, but only the spirit can deliver the ecstasy.

It is as easy to close the eyes of communication in the bed of love, as in the cement streets, with no desire to meet. The spirit has devious ways – and the flesh tries to combat, and though they can help each other, their desire is to *hinder*. I must choose. Well, nightingale, strike that hollow thorn.

April 13

Heat and hay fever and that stern closed face of morning its fierce dementia.

A tentative arm but there was no melting within me. Or in *it*? Did I feel a gentleness tinged with experimentation?

All day and all night I wrangle ways to rescue Barker from Japan.[5] One by one my begging letters are refused or worse ignored. The promise I blithely made him (and WILL keep) begins to be a centre of radiating apprehension sending shivers from the bottom of my spine.

And the stern face – It is my fault he can't work here?[6] He creates the disorder I am too tired to dispel. He said, 'I become just the valet. Doing errands. The room is a suntrap full of stagnant heat like an oven.' He says the light comes down too low and he can't draw. But his materials make much of the room's litter. I don't mind at all, really, the litter – only the reproaches.

I always swore housework would never become an issue with me – an obsession substituted for living. Even is it better to live in filth than empty resignation of hours preparing preparing for a *something* that never arrives. (Because its place has been usurped by the preparing – a usual historical situation.)

April 18: Las Vegas

The hot sleepy-breathed afternoon. Mourning doves and questing pigs. Birds chirp, hens scratch. But we lie down in our pink-glowing cabin side by side and he sleeps, heavily falling and rising with deep breath. I hate his sleep. I am mortified by the spurning it implies – the wonderful unexplored region of the mind he never woos. Will it know how to wake when *one* does? For it is that cerebral exploration I so ardently desire – and though the physical floods can always die down its unquiet flame – the desire only buried in pleasure's seas, lives on and on and on. It will one day be a volcano erupting terrible and pitiless and uncontrollable. And the frustration breeds a kind of inaction, a numbness to do, because it sees no image of success, a desolate coma, very despairing, a tasteless white-of-egg around the dwindling dwindling but jealously guarded yolk. I want growth. But I cannot have your litmus-paper presence here, to colour all my feelings, sights, and reactions, unless something better is conceived thereby. It paralyses without begetting.

(He snores. The birds chirp. I lie alone. I am eaten with the unclasped hours going by.)

April 29

No poem. I am engaged as a maid with Mrs Kennedy.[7] All for George Barker. But I am gleeful. Durrell scolds me vaguely. I search. I say, well, a cell will do. The painful white face straining upward. Writing and lonely in my 'little room.' But more than a nun's glee.

May 2

I stopped being a maid.[8]

May 27: Anderson Creek

He preaches what he takes away. The mysticisms when he has turned me into a sucking mouth. Didn't he take green and turn it to the mist glowing rosiest pink?

But leave him. Be ready to receive again yellow mustard, intercourse with grass. The stream is always rushing. It forces me to listen but says nothing.

Prose, please, prose for a while, straighten out the rushing-water excuses – say, This is my only whole duty. Don't take refuge in the automatic poem-formula. It increases the falseness – know that the only important thing is to extract the essence, the miracle – God. Well, you knew that better sulking among the oak leaves and bracken on Kingsmere mountain, escaping Mummy's nagging to take more interest in the house. Know it *now* – but know it *better*. Sit and brood till it arrives and don't compromise and don't sit waiting for another to fertilize you.

What disturbs me, though, is that the ecstacy in nature doesn't arrive. It used to be heady rapturous identity in a moment.

Heine said, 'You do the same as I do – identify yourself with nature. But it's bad to. It makes you hate people!' And he does hate people. But he keeps the ecstacy, shouting like a drunkard on the edge of the ridge. I crawl sympathetically into the earth holes where people suffer and I say I must understand not condemn. Like Daddy, I begin to say, Perhaps I have been too lenient and my tolerance has been my laziness.

Barker's new poems arrived[9] and I say O how ashamed I am to have thought *mine* were poetry, for he alone says *exactly* what I wanted to say, and even the very word sounds I was wanting to utter and the same elastic bounding back. That is my maddening injury. His are all true. Mine limp and labour.

But when I opened the book my excitement made me too impotent to read. My head ached with too much greed. My eyes were glazed with wanting too much at once.

June 2

The sense of guilt because of the sense of selfishness by shutting the girls out,[10] hardening my heart and forbidding my curiosity leeway. But it is my present preoccupation in Yanko that breeds this bare rejection and shutting-out of them.

But how can I love anything, I say, as I look small-eyed at the landscape, if I will not pity their gentle and suffering humanity, and let my sympathy be a soothing river because unfair circumstances and unhappy chance has made them what they are? I have had everything, and I should be only generous. I give them plates, candles, food, cotton, wool. I give them all I have, but I despise myself because it was only *myself* they needed and I pretended not to know. It takes no more time to give them myself than the shameful sunblind hardness uncommunicativeness. I am frozen and it is not only Yanko's fault. I am guilty guilty guilty and the sin is the worst sin.

Last night in the starry sky there was a terrifying long black rainbow,[11] tubular and snakelike in the clear sky. I thought I could hear it roaring, and I was terribly conscious of my baseness towards the girls. I can't open my heart to beauty, I can't open my heart at all, if there is anything I still so reject. Melt me, God. Show me how to atone in a flood of *true* generosity.

July 4

Last night I dreamt about the Barkers – it was all very awkward; it was Kingsmere, and Mummy was there, and not enough beds unless I slept with Yanko which was impossible. And the McLaines were there and the woods were a refuge. I took the Barkers but especially Jessie who was small and sweet and rather silent up to a great cliff to see Anderson Creek. It was several miles above and very steep. She said, 'This way down?' and I said, 'Yes but be careful,' and she smiled and leapt down. How could she? She didn't seem to know she would be killed. At the bottom she was bloody and smashed. George was on a camp bed bent over. I tried to take his hand. He said, 'Leave me alone.' I wept. He was softened. I found a little fat man, elderly; he said 'I don't want them to see me cut her throat.' I ran to Jessie. She was still limply warm and alive. There was a horrible blue-bloody line around her throat. I said to the man, 'You're only a dentist. Wait and I'll go and get a surgeon.' I ran out into the road. It was paved and bordered with cedar trees. Some people went by in a Rolls-Royce dressed for guests to a wedding. They were disgusted at my torn clothes and bare legs. I was afraid to ask them. But I did. They didn't understand. I went distractedly along, under the cedar bushes, I ran back. I told the dentist he had better operate, everybody was going along to the wedding. They all had harassed faces and said it was an outrage my being allowed onto the highway. George was always in the background, tender, grave, sympathetic, tall and thin with a smooth pale face. Jessie must have recovered for later there were flowers in the sun.

But in the first part Mummy was predominant, and George and Jessie I had to keep in the woods. When I was on the Kingsmere veranda, I said why didn't I remember his face when I saw it?

IV

ANDERSON CREEK, NEW YORK, OTTAWA, VANCOUVER, PENDER HARBOUR

July, 1940–July, 1941

On July 19, 1940, Smart drove to Monterey to pick up George and Jessica Barker, who had sailed from Japan to California. By August, Smart and Barker were lovers: the relationship with Varda ended. In the early autumn, Barker, Smart, and Jessica Barker drove to Los Angeles to find Jessica Barker a place to live. Smart and Barker set off by car for New York. However, they were arrested at the Arizona border, suspected of being spies. Smart was arrested for illegal entry into the US because she had not had her passport stamped on entry. Barker, on the other hand, had his papers in order and was let go. Smart was released into the custody of Mrs Witchner and her son, Milton (who becomes Mr Wurtle in By Grand Central Station I Sat Down and Wept*). Barker, in the meantime, returned to Jessica Barker in California. When Smart was released from custody, he returned for her and they set off again, for New York. They spent two weeks in New York, after which time Barker stayed in New York to prepare his* Selected Poems *(Macmillan, 1941) and Smart returned to Ottawa. They made frequent trips between the two cities, and they spent New Year's Eve together in Ottawa. During this time she began to see that Barker was still involved with Jessica Barker, although he told her differently. Smart was also pregnant.*

Entries in the final notebooks are sporadic, with a fair amount of overlapping. The final notebooks contain poems by both Smart and George Barker. The last notebooks, kept when she was in Pender Harbour, are full of recipes and the beginning drafts of By Grand Central Station I Sat Down and Wept. *The hyperbolic and metaphoric writing in the final notebooks characterizes the style of* By Grand Central Station I Sat Down and Wept.

> 'and tell me, who will be born
> and who will drown from so much blood?'

September 21

God, come down out of the eucalyptus tree and tell me who will drown in so much blood. I saw her face coming out of the mist by the dying geraniums.

It was angular with the tears that should have blurred with liquid her unendurable torture. Her body was bent like a broken bow waiting for the wound which swung in perpetual suspension above her. But her eyes Oh my god pierced all the protecting veils that covered my imagination. Bleed me too in this terrible pool of birth.

Is there no other channel of deliverance? At first my reporter eyes gave no communication. By severing all the wires I functioned severally. But who could be proof against that future ghost holding pity like a time bomb in its look of agony? What gangsters of forgetfulness of justification can nature find, or you, god, engage, to quiet these thieves of endurance?

On her mangledness I am spreading my amorous sheets, but who will have any pride in the wedding red, seeping up between the colossus thighs whose issue is only the cold semen of grief?

Not god but two bats and the spider of guilt keep the rendezvous and shame copulates with every September housefly. My room echoes with the screams she never uttered and under my floor the vines of remorse get ready to push up through the damp. The cricket drips remembrance into my ear lest I mislay any item of cruelty's fiendish itinerary. The trap is springing and I am in the trap.

But it is not easing or escape I crave when I pray god to understand my corrupt language and step down for a moment to sit on my broken bench. Will there be a birth from all this blood or is death only pouring out his fatal prime? Is an infant struggling in the triangular womb? I am blind but blood not love has blinded my eye. Love lifted the weapon and guided my crime, locked my limbs when the anguish rose out of the sea to cry Help and now over that piercing mask superimposes the cloudy mouth of desire.

I have locked my door but terror is ambushed outside. The eucalyptus batters the window and all smitten Europe wails from the stream below. The ghosts will appear at the black squares unabashed by the pale crosses of the sash, for Jesus Christ walks the waters of another planet bleeding history from his old wounds. All lives are lost in the confusion. The coughing of the sheep in the lost hills of Dorset, of the gassed soldiers, of the two-year-old child with croup roll into one Avalanche of calamity with the insensitive stamp that broke the heart of the harlot. America with Californian claws clutches at the Pacific, masses her voice for frantic appeal. They roar like Niagara. They shake the synthetic hills. The sand of catastrophe is loosened and every breast is marked with doom. But the cheating cicada arrives first to lie all's well in god's ear which measures time so generously, and the woodlice are rocking their babies under the log. Anxiety lies still while his eye makes its vast convolutions.

Standing a thousand feet above the sea, how does my adoring shadow look with the fishes of death swimming through its hair? Pearls float up from Mozart's oyster for a prettier noose, ring-a-rosing the ghouling vision. When we meet and I clasp the deceiver in my arms our liquidation will poison the sea. But not tonight. There is no moon. Threateners of life are horrible enough and she my penalty lies gasping on the land. Shuddering like a coward I dare not grasp either life or death from the gruesome palm that offers them.

Cut, the rocks breathe their accumulated gases and the greedy castor tree casts them up and down the canyon that is so in love with tragedy.

Under the redwood tree my grave was laid and I beguiled my only lover to lie down. The stream of our kiss put a bridge around the world where love like a refugee sailed in the last ship. My hair made my inglorious shroud and kept the coyotes at bay while we wrote our hieroglyphics with anatomy's futile tools. The silver seeds spilt on the ground had grown giant fangs when we opened our eyes. The wind boomed triumph sounding the heaviest note on our vulnerable spines. A smile like a cobweb was fastened across the mouth of the cave of fate.

Fear will be a terrible fox at my vitals under my tunic of behaviour. Oh canary sing out in the thunderstorm, prove your yellow pride. But there is no tangible knock on the door of my sanity, nor decipherer for the code of the eucalyptus thumping on my roof. I am unnerved by the opponents of god and out of earshot. I must spin ghosts out of my hope to oppose the hordes at my window. If those who look in see me descend to barricade the door, they will know too much and crowd in to overcome me. The parchment philosopher has no traffic with the night and our conception of the price of love. With smoky circles of thought he combats the fog and with anagrams defeats anatomy. I posture with his weapons, balmed with nicotine herbs.

Moon, moon, rise in the sky to be a reminder of comfort and the hours when I was brave.

But the gentle flowers able to die unceremoniously remind me of her grief that drowns all ghosts, and though I swing in torture from the windiest hill, more angels weep for her whose love runs in blood into all the oceans of the world.

What did she hold in protection when the ship pursued the storm and she fought the cancer her lost child gnawed within? I have broken her heart like a robin's egg. Its wreck reaches her finite horizon.

What was your price Gabriel, Michael of the ministering wing? What pulley from headlong man pulled you up in the nick of time, till you gushed vegetable laughter and fed only off the sun?

The texts are meaningless; they are the enemy's deception. My foot danced by mistake over the helpless and bled no solace for my butchery. Tell me how to atone for the dove in the eucalyptus who speaks with thunder of the future's revenge. My heart is its own destructive just to beat out the truth.

Tell me this gush ushers in my wonder.

A wet wing brushes away the trembling night and morning breathes cold analyses into my spectre-waiting mind. The vines assume their social air, ingratiating green with children's fingers.

The impotent eucalyptus stands gaunt as dawn. But faint as a dream and definite as death my possible phoenix is a graph totemed in the sky breathing like a workman setting out on a job.

September 28

But how to go through the daily motions when the intense fusion makes all molten? The inward flood drenches all my outward implements of trivial intercourse. My eyes spill the fiery fluid rich as the gold furnaces at the mint, but stare incomprehension at the simplest question. How many fathoms deep. How liquid I am to besiege your every orifice. More single-purposed than the new bird all mouth with his one want, I close my eyes and tremble, soliciting the sky for you.

O water, water of love melted from the very pasture of the definite eye, love's food. Your hand's precise geometry dissolves me by gazing and itself flows away on this sea sprung from liquid combustion. All flows like the Mississippi over a devastated but grateful earth which drinks unsurfeited, which raises a praise to deafen all doubters forever, to burst their shameful inadequate eardrums with the roar of proof, louder than bombs, screams, or the sobbing of remorse, and stronger even than the spilt blood's poisonous tides.

October 25: Ottawa
'Look Homeward Angel Now and Melt with Ruth'

Passion and reason produced these children and reason was the tenderer. But now my father has three prodigal daughters perennially and periodically supplicating for the fatted calf. But there are none of them left, and the slaughter-blood has added no red to my parents' cheeks whose eyes are harassed by what they see from the window or what they fear they see like premature ghosts straggling homeward over the plain. Parents' imaginations build a fountain out of their hopes and regrets into which children seldom grow, but contrary as a tree, lean sideways out of the architecture, blown by a fatal wind their parents never envisaged.

Approaching November kills me with the passion of the dying year, as come from a California which is oblivious of regret. Autumn air has a finality in its nip as ruthless and as straight for the inevitable as death itself.

But the faces are kind and I see that the porter carrying my bags has extracted a spiritual lesson from his hardship. Gentleness and modesty grow great just by their acceptance of their minor roll. But from this cradle of Canada, after the greedy death already hardening into stone the American face, I think surely a life will grow. For its mediocrity is tender and solicitous of the better, wistful to be told of the gladiator brains of the elder vanquished world.

Did you notice, too, how in Toronto, they sat on the ground with conviction, and held about them also reminiscences of the pioneer's passion and the determination of the early hopes of statesmen, who were mild but individual and able to allude to Shakespeare while discussing politics under the elm tree? No great neon face has been superimposed over the faded wooden houses of a minor but true history. Nor has the early settlers' blood spilt in feuds been bottled by a Coca Cola firm and sold as a cheap tradition for the ego. Unnoticed, lesser Canada has therefore escaped cheapening, and cherishing memories may therefore retain traces of their past, which otherwise the curious might destroy in their greed, desiring to acquire aging by synthetic process.

The faces, the air, and the old gold of the October trees, make omens to this prodigal. Surely I see a stirring?

(*In George Barker's hand:*
dear Elizabeth do not permit your reminiscence to disremember me too easily or I shall sit by myself in Central Park with a pigeon in my left hand to console me and four roses in my throat to disremember you. I give you back, for five days, your eyebrows and eyelashes. G)

My father has three prodigal daughters, perennially and periodically supplicating for the fatted calf. Passion, which was my mother, and reason, which was my father, produced these children, and hurled them defiantly out of Canada to strut equally with the rest of the greater world, if they could. They noticed the tea-parties, policemen like nannies, and the cautious impotence inarticulately garrulous on Parliament Hill. School friends lacked even the ingenuity of rabbits, and kept the comeback of their schoolgirl days, or with bridge-party housewifing, cling well away from growth. They desired no other, so conversation ceased, and soon in Honey Dew cafés, a little censor gave them something to talk about, which my father's daughters in no way discouraged, soon willing even to be bombed out of their fear of shrivelling under three thousand miles of snow. And some who mildly saw the passion that tore out the entrails of England's greatest poets wrote imitations mildly including the indigenous bloodwort, and thus they were crowned with phoney laurels, imported from America's Greece, but cluttered the passage of birth for Canada's first words.

This the three noticed and yelled their discontent.

In London's traffic, or Geneva's confusion, much revealed itself but never content; and on the splashy continent were tricks learned and a way to feather the nest. Nevertheless one by one they kept returning after departure, and though they included triumph in their ignominy, my father's fatted calves were always killed in vain.

Itinerant prodigals we were, or I should say we are, myself returning through the fall morning to another home of my parents' mourning. Asking no one's forgiveness for sins I refuse to recognize, why do I cry so for having my face again in Canada? The cedar trees and the chilly gullies with their red willow whips seduce me beyond control and envelope me too like an indisputable mother, saying Whether or No, Whether or No, my darling.

Five million refugees and America cannot drown out her voice, or make ineffective her beauty, as she forces me to confess it after my fading denials.

Note

I say to you (ES) *keep* that vision. Remember that the faces *are* kind and have reserve, and that the birds gather in groups to migrate and prove a foretaste of death. When your eyes shrivel aggrievedly because you notice the jealousy of those that stay at home, hurt that others prefer the greater world, remember this first smell of the air and the deserted pastures and the lavish autumn. Here is no underlining of an accidental picturesqueness, but a waiting, unselfconscious as the unborn, for future history to be performed upon it.

I know this initial intoxication will disappear, therefore I wish urgently to articulate it. Make a list, write down. '*This* in that hour moved me to tears and made a gaze through the dining-car window a plenitude not to be borne.'

December 1: New York

Now I have got my four walls, my bed, and my table, and my blank book, and my indelible pencil, and a compulsion of circumstance more formidable than all these. And also, with George, has come an ability to count out all the distracting faces in the street. Therefore and only to explore within, or build them again but better in the more becoming mind.

Gene[4] discomposes me with telling me that I should not want to be a poet because George is and I can never be so great a one as he; he insists also that there are no male and female poets but just the one word containing both. But though unable to articulate my protest I feel that the thing I want to say is the thing never said but always done, the saying invariably abandoned for the being. Which is, in truth, the simple fact of being a woman overpowered by voices of blood each time she rises to speak her piece. And love that gives, compels her to adore being devoured surrendering to a destruction that of course causes her to be born again, but obliterates all private ambition and blinds her eyes and her heart with images of unborn babies.

But I feel even in this room the beginning of that silence necessary for hearing my own voices, the voices of the thing I must capture. And all things that now distract me do so only to remind me of some important point.

December 17: Ottawa, magnanimous despair. Alone.

I see my crime is secretiveness. It is for that you barb and sling me. Thus by negation my implication is insult. I prefer *not* to open my heart to your jealous demand. Nor to stoop to a semblance of surrender. My demand is privacy and your prying makes me more adamant. It is true I am a changeling. I know my most private wish is nearer to a tree's than to your understanding. I always knew and therefore I suppose shut up soon and as a child was hated by and hated back the slighted Miss Tipples who bribed me so ignominiously with chocolates I scorned. So M thinks to shame me or make me jealous with news of wedding lingerie or praise of Nini's 'well-bred' look, or Audrey's flat where her presents are so well displayed, or with fear of being *declassée*? How could she ever even grasp my greatest hopes or meet my intimates who meet me by appointment between two mountains or in the rainy night in Dorset? So I say nothing and when I can no longer posture, writhe with her not so oblique hurts, or at risk of death, spin my soundproof cocoon.

Where does George stalk like a horse in pasture very far afield. I can't feel him and silence writes more terrible things than he can ever deny. Is there a suspicion the battle is lost? Certainly he killed me fourteen nights in succession. To rise again from such slaughter Messiah must indeed 'become a woman.'

He says it is the mere mechanics of the thing. But IT is not the same. He did the one sin love won't allow.* The FBI, Mummy, Witchie, the Montreal Police,[3] and Hull were powerless, but love has other laws and a slight trespass is punished without trail. George did sin here, and though he says it was in pity's name and that pity was only fighting a losing battle with love, he was useless to pity and in wavering injured love which was, after all what he staked all for, all he had, ungamblable.

    *(In George Barker's hand.) I did bloody well not. GB

December 22
    Caught. And no polestar. No inhibitions to restrain my despair. What can pull me back? Too many nights have built their explosive facts. And without the one fact these facts violate, the five hundred thousand refugees, the corpses that died of starvation, the blood and mangling, have absolutely no dam. 'Only Love can with a great gaze stop.' But where is love? Crucified over five hundred miles. Stretched out in the snow over the dilapidated country where only the birds are at home and they only for six months of the year. How can I put love up to my hopes so suicidal and wild-eyed when the matter is too simple and too plain: it is her tears he feels trickling over his breast each night. It is for her he feels the concern; and the *pity* after all (which he said was losing the battle with love) fills all his twenty-four hours.
    Perhaps I am his hope. But she is his present. And if then she is his present, I am not his present. Therefore I am not, and I wonder why no one has noticed I am dead and taken the trouble to bury me. My utter collapse can not even bother to do the clear deed of death but cringes glazed or weeps a tear of sheer weakness. The temptations are strange and new – besides simple death I could even consider a nunnery, nursing at the war, or simply sitting and staring until the blunder is relieved by nature.
    I can't read and all people seem criminally irrelevant. I ignore, or if cornered or interrupted in my decay, hate. Nature is only the irking weather and flowers crude reminders of stale states of being. I have not been in love but in despair these last ten days. And without love I am lost more fatally than he can have any idea of, who thinks nature revives me so resiliently. She has been good. But this is where it all led and for what she preserved me. So if it lacks totality, it all topples, it lacks all, and I am as dead as the parson's egg was bad.

I say sometimes, when I squeeze the pain from side to side in my caged head; well, if you are suffering think what Jessie suffered, one hundred times more and with no hope – and you had no pity but were dazzlingly happy on top of her most profound and excrutiating misery. And I say, Yes, what she had and is having is so much more there is no comparison. But my heart does not open and break for her, nor even flow in pity. I die again and again only for myself.

I can't take George as my love for comfort. It is as if they were both photographed together and I couldn't cut his picture out without getting hers. Neither can I get hers alone, though I love her still and have no feeling at all but compassion. But the fact: It is she he is with. He is with her. He is not with me because he is sleeping with her. That is the barrier to any abandonment to love. But dully I plod along with legal and financial solutions.

I don't bleed. The pin stuck in my flesh leaves only the hole that proves I am dead.

December 29

Why does he say minor martyrdoms? Didn't the crucifixion only last three days? Is it the shortness of the days of torture or the fact that hope still breathes that lets him say minor? How can anything so total not be major? He has martyred me but for no cause nor has he any idea of the size or consequence of my wounds. Perhaps he won't know for to say, You killed me daily and O most especially nightly, would imply blame. I don't imply blame, nor even say, You might have done this or this rather than that. Even I say, That you must do, you have to do it, it is the only thing to do, urging my own murder. But if a knife is stuck in the engine that pumps my blood, my blood stops, no matter how I reason with it. I shall say nothing but perhaps he will notice that my heart has ceased to beat. Or he may with one glance restore me and flood me with so much new love that every scar will have a satin covering and be new glitter to attack and sing. From this great distance of a night of separation more I cannot see. My imagination is snowed under the eternal unpunctuated hours. What should happen if there is no instantaneous resurrection I don't know. Blackness more than death's blackest premonitions or the oblivion of the prehistoric tribe. But of one thing I feel too sure, too deadly a foreboding. If ever again he lets those nights happen or dallies with remorse for past sin to others while sinning O most dangerously against me, I shall be unrevivable. I shall, whether I want to or not, be struck dead with the fact. And he may clothe it in all humanity's most melting colours, and call on love to be big and kind. And I too shall play let me be kind, but it will be no good. Only the fact has potency. And that fact will be fatal.

I read *Troilus and Cressida*, and other tales of love. But the very word I avoid. Until I have it in my very arms and I will have nothing nothing else, the world and all others are blank, and the days airless regions boggling even astronomers.

February 4: New York

That evening when my eyes floated around my room like two ships lost on the sea, I knew the measurements of my captivity. For neither could I escape by bashing my mind against that boxlike confine, nor summon into my company the significant shadows with visionary eyeballs. For clues to all calamity I had the painful lovemaking of alleycats, voiced with horror along the roofs outside my window, the deadly quarter hour chiming of a clock whose notes partly never struck, and the wheezing of the coils, cheerful and regular like crickets. The elevator clattered a promise of event never fulfilled and sometimes the plumbing shrieked remotely like the message of a falling comet.

I reviewed all I knew but could synthesize no meaning. When I dozed that fact woke me with a shudder like a cruel nurse. I saw it crouching inflexibly in a corner of the ceiling. It came down in geometrical diagonal, like lightning. It said, I remain, I am and shall never cease to be: only your memory shall grow a deathly glaze. Thus every quarter hour it put the taste of death in my mouth. It showed me, but not gently, how I went whoring after oblivion.

But all revolves back, as we tell ourselves unbelieving when the ship cracks in the typhoon. Not, of course, for the dinosaurs, for their legend is kept and they have lovers still whose passion transcends what many humans know. Perhaps not for us, either, though we shall also certainly have our archives full of archetypes, like those composite photographs of movie heroines. But the day will return when the joke at least sits basking in the sun, decorating her idle body with nameless red, once called blood. Philosophy like lichens takes centuries to grow and is always ignored. If you can't take it, Get Out.

I can't take it so I lie on the ground dissolving into chemicals whose adventures will surface.

February 18: Ottawa

What have I got to say? They are at war and I am peace. They are in hate and I am in love. They are annihilating and I am bringing forth.

O I know they make war because they want peace; they hate so that they may live; and they destroy the present to make the world safe for the future. When have they not done and said they did it for that?

Women also mouth the words, rise up in their chairs and shriek: 'Let's stone Hitler as he goes through the streets! Let's make them all walk naked and lash them with horse whips!' Who ever though admitted doing a deed for its obvious evil? (Sade is another question).

The weeping first row of the audience is composed of religious teachers whose words hopped out of their mouths and took arms against them. They trust men, cannot take their sayings to bed and remain forever unaware of their true meaning. But while the men sleep, whoring with the sayings misunderstood, they mystically joined to what they believe will in time awake them. Well, the weeping now trusts this, but they must trust or go out. They weep. They only hope because otherwise their eyes would have no guiding shine.

February (no date)

If the facts weren't so against me – I mean if my faith in the one fact were impregnable – that is if I had no doubts of you – why then I would cut off my hands and give them to her to comfort her for an hour. But all the facts attack my peace. They say, Look fool, can you deny this? Why did he say this if this? And if this why not that? O it brings enough clues for me to finish the conundrum with damnation for myself. O then I stiffen into paralysis and the five hundred miles stand like rocks between us. And I could rush to her in a thaw of remorse and shame to have killed her all for nothing.

Don't think I don't understand how we are all Lot's wife under our heroic loving faces. The only way not to betray another is to give the betrayal as they are.

Don't you see how the only way you can love me is to tell me how, for a whirlpool minute, you stopped loving me? The only way you can not betray me is to give me the moment, when you were that moment, that you most betrayed me? I live for that.

All day and all night, away from you and with you, everywhere and always that is my gravity and the apples fall only towards that.

(In George Barker's hand:

When I turn and investigate the hinterland of my mind then I stand in a fixation of fear and disgust at all corners, horrified at the possible onrush of what poltergeists, ambushing me in the mountains of my own amorousness: for these are the demi-gorgons of your O your unforgivable, unforgettable, all the frequently bestowed* infidelities*. Not that these, at the occasion of their occurrence, were anything more than afternoon frolics* of a bitch in the dust or the crepuscular dance: but now, when the consummation of all improbables, namely the unmentionable love, has devolved upon you, now these kisses in undergrowth* or maudlin manhandling* on the Mexican beaches, these amusements* these purely frivolous pastimes,* O they open their harmless arms and show their chests full of daggers and teeth that will turn even my [illegible] (but never, never, never my adoration) to tatters of lamentation: to tatters of degradation: to tatters of devastation.)

ES footnotes: *Lie *Lie *Lie *Error *I did not, ever, you Bum.

It is, alas, the unhappy circumstance of your own promiscuous past that allows your imagination to wallow in these gross injustices to and betrayals of me. All my life, and god knows, it is long enough, I had to fight like a lynx to preserve what I desired so vehemently and was so firmly determined to preserve. The protections I devised to fool the enemy have alas O too too alas fooled you, the one for whom I so painfully devised them, and to whom I only wish to offer them inadequate but never assaulted. It is sad if, after my superhuman achievement, you do not believe me. It is very very sad.

(*Barker's hand:*
          It is bloody sad, like Chatterton's fate. Bloody sad.)

          But, unlike Chatterton, not too late to amend.[4]
          Why Silence Please Wire Why Silence.

Well I have doubts. I am not convinced. O, of myself, yes. That is too clear, too unescapable. But of you. Why this and why that paralyses me when I would go out with the passionate welcome. I don't *want* something that belongs to someone else. I don't want to beg borrow or steal. I *want* too *much* for that. Taking less destroys all.

The simple fact I believe is that I love and you love – temporarily. Oh, you say, Do you think I could have done what I did if I didn't love you? But you didn't do it. I saw the beginning myself, but you have spent five months denying it in deeds and in words.

I never told you about the letter I saw by mistake when I was bringing your papers down to you when you were in jail in Montreal. It began 'Darling' in your handwriting and it had no envelope so I couldn't help seeing it. It was written in the train coming up to Canada to see me. But it was not to me. It was to her. And it said, 'My mind is quite made up. I want to go on living just as I have always lived – with you. It's all you, and forever.' Surely that is more than just soothing one whom you had hurt? If it wasn't true it was criminal. But O it was criminal anyway. On the same train, the same day, you wrote to me. 'What can I prize but your simple kiss?'

What I would have prized more would have been a true understanding. I would rather you had tried to make me understand your feelings towards her, your sudden reactions, if temporary, temporary, but in a constant undertone, oh, I would rather have known too.

I have suffered too much from smooth surfaces that conceal death in such deceit or withdrawal. I am more vulnerable than the princess from whom mattresses could not conceal the pea.

Don't think that reading that letter wasn't death and damnation for me. But when I got to Montreal you were in such trouble and you needed me, so that even that I overcame, though I noticed how you found the letter and removed it from your bag while I was in the bathroom.

O I loved you over that and over many other things too that made volcanoes in my stomach. And I know that she must have known and forgiven as much and more in so many years. But she wanted and was owed something different from what I want and am owed and if I do not get it – I mean if it is not that that you have to give, we are only sinning in the most deceitful and superficial and inexcusable way.

And since I have a horror of developing into an old cantankerous nagger with a grievance I prefer to say nothing at all – I can do nothing, being paralysed by doubt and I wait like an egg for the twenty-eighth day for you to arrive with all the west winds of irrefutable conviction.

All the things that happened in New York and many other facts especially concerning her only clawed off the safety covering I had laid over the past totem poles of danger and scars of your woundings. If you can't leave her then I don't ask you to. But if you can and must leave her, then you must, and not leave her dangling in the hope that you are coming back forever in six months. If you are coming back in six months then don't come at all. For though I could understand your feeling that *at the end* of six months, yet for you to be so sure of it *now* would cancel out everything. And anyway, then, why come? I despise such a desultory unnecessary action.

If I had the one surety I would have the faith that moves mountains and continents and worlds – but without it what have I but the prospect of a toad-in-the-hole existence, in exile, telling lies and plotting deceit.

It was best in the middle of the blood, when we really had to choose, and did. When also it was the only and the all and even if it involved the destruction of all else besides, the necessity.

You see how my mind is going to pieces and all my polestars become falling stars? You see how the most melodramatic conclusions of the morbid adolescent seem natural at such a time? But if I don't believe in love, if I don't believe I was made only for you, if I don't believe you are a poet, if I don't believe poetry is all there is, I don't believe anything.

Natural and elemental things will certainly soothe me and on sunny days and windy days I may seem happy. But O to have missed the entire point, the once-in-a-billion-years bull's-eye by a hairsbreadth.

The silence then is me holding my breath to see oh only to see if I have missed or not.

March 1: 'They've Severed all the Wires'[5]

The grass is already green in BC. My imagination seizes that fact like a hot water bottle and dopes itself and my heart and all my antennae and all my sources of life with it. My future is already planted there and my hope getting ready to sprout with the almond. He hovers around his murder. I can't call him. I can't say make the final kill. Neither can I say, revive her and stay with her forever, seemingly the only alternative.

He is not here. He is all gone. There is only this bloated glob. Nothing but the ring and the chain prove I am in bondage. My dead eye and blank days only prove I am dead, not why, not his existence.

I contemplate vaguely the instruments of love and say with cold wonder, was this the face that launched a thousand ships? The breast that once caught fire from far away lies colder, and less ignitable than Everest. I say can lips kiss and why do they want to?

This state is far from longing because it is far beyond it. It is the state beyond ecstasy or pain, the state where the unbearable suffers eclipse and becomes coma. It is so much in the dead unremembering purgatorial land that I have no belief in revival, no real belief in the return of spring, in love, in our joined mouths. Was it ever like that? Did we lie so close like irresistible currents driven together?

If I had wit to remember that my present numbness comes expressly from my too intense love, all would be proved. But logic is not love's pageboy and does not attend coma either. How headlessly I drift, how dangerously uninhabited.

Sometimes I glimpse an awakening – but the nightmare of knowledge, the too late volcanoes of my imagination bring back a thicker fog. Like a madman with his askew eyes fixed to a bead, I see that almond tree and the green grass and focus on it, and bend all in that direction. It will be achieved by the madman's articulateness. But tomorrow and tomorrow and tomorrow lie as locked and uncharted as the other face of the moon, and have far far fewer enquiries concerning them. I reach the tree and we all blossom. Or I reach the tree and we die. But I reach the tree. That is the entire plan and all the goal for my remaining forty years, if, as seems impossible, so many remain.

(*In George Barker's hand:* Dear Lamb: I write this from a dirty hotel bedroom in the lavatory of America, more or less akimbo on a friend of yours who at this moment caresses her right breast because my hand holds the pencil. (I said *pencil*.))

Dear Lamb: Please forgive my bawdy friend George Barker for bothering you with irrelevant details of my amatory pastimes. I trust you do not feel I have trespassed too far in promising you my friend in the midst of such pursuits. These latter, I may say, I have found to be life's chief balm, though often, like the rest of my undignified race, trying to disown them by rationalizing the superiority of things less inextricably woven with the undiluted flesh. Arguments that glisten with authority in the midst of formal ceremonial or forced chastity have less chance, I find, of surviving the sensual floods, than the stars have of outshining an equatorial noon. Do you, dear Lamb, not agree?

> (*In George Barker's hand:*
> Here, far from family and the friend*
> Whose head too often on my shoulder
> Found rest and temporary shelter
> From the red fret of love, here I stand
> Staring at windows with holly and ivy
> Gay as a circus, and as I look
> All sorrow in my throat like a rook
> Rises)

*Fuck this bleeding friend. Balls and shit to this friend and all my hate. ES

April 4

It is not possible that he will not return. I sit here on one elbow hourly expecting his tight peremptory tap on the door.[6] Each time the inefficient jangle of the elevator gets into motion, I start up. Will this monster stop at my floor and disgorge my miracle? I hurry back from a half-finished walk up the street. Are there any telegrams? Has there been a phone call? Is the red Buick parked a little way down the street? I see a car with a tall radio aerial – this is the grass of hope that grows indomitably over my eyes.

For to say he will not and never come is to throw myself into the whirlpool and to deliver my mind into madness and my dear my unborn child into a flood of blood and death. This I cannot do nor will my watchful protectors allow it. She sends me a thousand desperate instincts which make me hurry up and down streets, scrutinize magazines and become absorbed feverishly in the irrelevant price of gramophones.

I will not think of the things now. I have no time. When I have washed these stockings I will. When I have written these letters of thanks, or sewn on a button, I will. O – meticulousness showers me with the skill of Penelope to do small precise tasks I bungled before – buttonholes and frills for collars. For dear God, I must not think now for I cannot cry here. The walls are too thin.

I know that perhaps tonight his mouth like the centre of a rose closes over John's mouth burning with apologies of love like a baby at the breast.

Ten Days in Vancouver by ES

The wallpaper drips gloom and the walls press in like dread. This dark hotel room is the centre of the whirlpool where no one can any longer resist. There is the bed where love often liberates us and dissolves the walls, but where also the night shakes him by the collar like a dog till he spits out the rag ends of his fear, 'You're a cunt! You're nothing but a cunt!' 'You know you're only trying to bribe me.' 'No. No. No.'

There over there is the chair, less lucky in function, where he reads the newspaper or waits impersonally absorbed. It is my worst antagonist in the room for most often it wins him away. Though sometimes it opens benignly and I see him through his fingers beaming the paternal and possessive while I strut or antic.

The mirror is the best breeder. One night it turned him into an Assyrian girl casting his lashes down under a blossoming turban. Then we were two sisters and I the protective. He had no breasts, and this was nostalgic. O the glittering incest bird. But all so gracefully submissive who will put the hand over the heart? He removed his headdress and we were plain people ready for the night.

The typewriter typed holes in our foolproof games and made the gap that nearly broke us, as well as my fingernails. I see how alien love is to the clerical and why girls are so practical but never fulfilled.

It gnaws down the root which has never heard of a wish for a pink ruffled negligee or the leisure to concoct new ways to indulge the languorous and voluptuous five senses, so aware to hurry. It drills nerves and its sympathy is with the miser. It is not an instrument of love.

In cafés behind plush curtains sometimes it went well. I held my breath and poised my fork above the fishcakes when revelation came. In the mirror, here, too, I had less doubt of his indulgence. The curtains were drawn and for twenty-five cents each we had a full quota of luxury for two.

The pawnshop and Royal Bank had different moods like players subject to the revolving coloured lights. Mostly we had no money, but this account is superficial. If it had been why we who had no money those days wouldn't have disgruntled so.

Stanley Park was green and luxurious and served tea and crumpets at the lowest moments of our Saturdays. Once we sat at the root of a tree so dead that even nature would have had hard work to turn us into manure. That day also I wept as we sat in a wooden alcove near the Ladies' and Gents' rooms. That day everyone who passed urged suicide.

But back always to the room like cornered foxes. Not that I saw in it symbols as he did of wretchedness and no cash, or a land where there is no one to talk to and nothing ever happens. It is the wallpaper that is the cause of all our tragedies. If it had been less brutal perhaps he would have seen solutions in the writing on the wall. Who plans murder sitting in the sun? It is the pile of dust under the bed and the dirty sheets I never washed that precipitate fatal action.

Farewell sweet hell of all hotels.

April 14: Pender Harbour

I can write nothing for I have nothing to say. I am only waiting and waiting for my life to begin, which it never can until he comes back. Before I knew he was coming[7] I could write in a frenzy to forget, to record the death of so glorious a universe, to make a memorial that would also scorch and bleed the uncaring the inattentive world. But when the reprieve came, when he said, There is to be more life, there is the possibility of hope and continuance, then I sat staring or then I bustled about like a housewife, putting flowers in bowls, but mostly sitting with my hands folded and my skirt carefully laid out to be ready, O to be ready any moment he might arrive.

Though I know it is impossible for him to arrive before two weeks at least, at very least, and only on the days the boat arrives from Vancouver is even that possible, I sit ready at all times of the day or night, like a new bird waiting for the worm.

O the hurdles and trials still to be conquered. I see his return like the windup of a western film, with every horror pursuing him and touch and go whether he makes it in time. Mostly I fear his reckless driving, and his O so wickedly mistaken idea that his death would solve anything, or evolve anything but a most double-double tragedy. And I am powerless and have even no communication with him, nor any address where a messenger might reach him at an urgent urgent moment. I wish to hibernate, not think, not live. I was furious and disgruntled when those two young girls came knocking at my door and sat wasting my evening, interrupting my wait, and later their youths, whistling below, then knocking on the door too. The girls said Come in! Even though I scowled my aversion and went and sat in a corner morosely. They took possession of my room. O I know only out of curiosity, but they sat on the bed which was waiting for him and the table waiting for him; they looked at the pictures which were for his eyes; and they picked up the books for his hands and they smoked cigarettes, that also were his. They understood at last from my less and less hidden remarks that I wished to be alone, and the girls and boys left and have not, thank the lord, come back. At this moment I have no spare generosity to lavish on the spurious and shoddy world – it is all going to bring him safely back to build barriers against further calamity and find, from out of this wise basking room, even solutions. Not a second more will I waste on anything else. O Lord make haste to save us.

May 10

I am lonely.

I want the one I want. He is the one I picked out from the world. It was cold deliberation. But the passion was not cold. No it kindled me. I begat. This time last year it hung in strips. Now there may be sadness and sorrow and delay but no more precariousness. It is pinned down. It has confessed. This is the *one*. This is the one. And you try to fulfil a precious proposition of fate by being his. It is O a rare conjunction as a spark that settled into clarity.

I can feel the small hard head jutting out near my bladder. That's our child. That's why I drink milk and close my eyes to the shock of disaster. I read *The Prelude* and listen to Mozart. I gather rosebuds.

He ejects calm. But though he soothes he can not dispel my loneliness. To whom do I say Behold this mound! His time as an amorous bait is lost. Wait. Wait. Don't waste the ingredients today. When love comes be prodigal. Without, sit stiffly on the yellow chair so as not to crumple the spread. Don't wash. Go around in slacks. Save coal-oil and wood. Sleep while time passes. O waste of morn. Waste of lavish spring flowers and lilacs as I pass down the path. Stop all blandishments to spread them at his feet. But relentless spring goes on, dares to finish itself without him and I grow from one shape into another and the oblivious child leaps without waiting for a father.

Forty days in the wilderness and not one holy vision. Sights to dazzle the eye but I basked without one metaphor. Nature is using me. I am the seedbag. I have a different balance jumping down rocks and hills. I trip too easily, overloaded unusually in front. But I draw no parallels from patterns and throw off no silver sparkled words from my encounters.

May 24

No. I will not allow him to wreck my life or turn bitter and broken because, after all, he was only certain of loving me for perhaps three days or weeks. I will not say it was any less because now his incredible capacity for what is surely unnecessary deceit to both of us knocks everything from under me, entirely dissolves me so periodically. Of *course* he can love us both, but why be so to us both? We're both good people. We can understand. We might even both rise to hard demands made on us to love (the abstract I mean). Or must he be the all things to all things (both of us, who make the circle whole)? But I don't invalidate even the moments when I was most deceived. For they remain as good and I do as completely love; nor can I cease loving nor will there ever be another who was all the things I wanted so completely and the only one destined. But these things are true for her too, truer perhaps, who trusted better before the way, and therefore why does he have to lie to her? I can understand his stretching points for me who was to him the physical *minute*, apt to evaporate, proverbially finite, but why resurrect her so periodically and with such passionate avowals? For even if he intends wholly to return to her, he still turns from my tears with doubts and not willingly gives me up when he holds me in his arms – or does he? Or is it then all done but the final edging off of me? I could slit my throat from ear to ear better than know he stayed for melodramatic reasons concerning the world's favourite story of the too-well too-lightly loved and left with child. No one has done any wrong. It was all worth while. As for the child wasn't the first thing she wailed out when he told her he loved me, 'Oh why didn't you let me keep the child?'

The worst thing is the deceit. Even she who sees the offence itself so large (but then, to save herself from the total wreck she was able to make *me* the monster) minds the deceit most. 'My dearest love – you reign empress in my heart – you totally reign my mind.' 'Dearest Elizabeth I am all Elizabeth my head my heart my hand.'

(Quoted from a letter to Smart from George Barker.)

POSTSCRIPT

Barker did arrive for a visit at Pender Harbour, but he soon returned to New York. Smart began to draft and write the first hand-written extant version of By Grand Central Station I Sat Down and Wept *and dedicated it to Maximiliane von Urpani Southwell, a life-long friend she met in Pender Harbour. The novel was finished in August, two weeks before the birth of her first child, Georgina Barker, on August 28, 1941. Barker tried to return to Pender Harbour following the birth of Georgina, but he was not allowed into Canada on a charge of 'moral turpitude' laid against him by Mrs Smart. The family knew that Barker was married but they did not know about Georgina.*

In December, 1941, Smart left Georgina with Maximiliane Southwell and went east to Ottawa to visit her family. She then went on to Washington, where she stayed with her friends Eddie and Grisell Hastings while she looked for a job. She found a job as a filing clerk with the British Army Staff in Washington, and later was promoted to a better job as personal assistant to Harold Butler, a minister in charge of information at the British Embassy. In April she brought Georgina to Washington.

During this time, Smart and Barker visited between Washington and New York. Barker was still seeing his wife, although he told Smart differently. Smart decided to end the relationship by putting the Atlantic Ocean between them, and with great difficulty and string-pulling (relying on friends in External Affairs) she found a job in the Ministry of Information in London, England. In October, 1942, she travelled on a war convoy to England. However, she was pregnant again, and pregnant women were not supposed to travel on war convoys. By the time the papers had been arranged and during the three-week trip, the pregnancy became apparent, much to everyone's disapproval. During the trip, three of the ships in the convoy were sunk; the ship she was on was also hit but made it to England. Since her pregnancy was obvious, she did not have a job when she arrived in London. Although Smart had not given Barker any address, he found her three months later and their relationship resumed. Though they never married, Smart and Barker had three more children.

Smart raised the four children on her own, initially with the help of her family and friends, and later by writing advertising copy and editing fashion magazines. By Grand Central Station I Sat Down and Wept *was published in 1945.*

Elizabeth Smart eventually retired to a cottage in Suffolk, England, where she continued to write surrounded by the beauty of the English countryside and a spectacular garden she had created. She died March 4, 1986, while visiting in London, and while Necessary Secrets *was in production.*

END NOTES

Introduction

1. The work was published under the imprint *Editions Poetry London*, which was the property of the now defunct firm of Nicholson & Watson.

Part One/I

1. Sir William Traven Aitken (1904–1963), nephew of Lord Beaverbrook.

2. Mrs Barrington Ward, wife of the editor of *The Times* of London.

3. Smart, with the possible intentions of writing the examinations to get into Oxford, is studying with a tutor, Mrs Paynter, at Bendixon's tutoring establishment in London.

4. She could be referring to either a lesson with Mrs Paynter or a lesson with Katharine Goodson (1872–1958), the concert pianist under whom she is studying the piano. Goodson is married to Arthur Hinton, who also gave Smart lessons in theory, harmony, and composition. Goodson, who was busy at the time giving concert performances, had taken Elizabeth on as a special student. Later, she realized that, although talented, Smart was not serious about becoming a concert pianist; she sent her for lessons with a struggling pianist, Clifford Curzon.

5. Oliver Gatty, a friend who died on an expedition to the North Pole.

6. Susan Somerset, Smart's chaperone.

7. A statue in Hyde Park by Jack Epstein named after a character in a WH Hudson book.

8. A statue based on JM Barrie's character Peter Pan.

9. A statue of Queen Victoria, in Kensington Gardens.

10. Kensington Palace.

11. JM Barrie was one of Smart's favourite authors.

12. John Bowker, the son of a friend of Mrs Smart.

13. Leonard Maynard, a friend in the British Colonial Office in London.

14. She is referring to a statue of Prince Albert (the Albert Memorial) outside the Albert Hall that overlooks other statues of great men of history.

15. Mike Pearson (1897–1972), Lester Bowles Pearson, Liberal Prime Minister of Canada from 22 April 1963 to 20 April 1968. He is another friend working in the Colonial office.

16. Diana Cripps, daughter of Lady and Sir Stafford Cripps (1884-1952). Lady Cripps was Isobel Swithinbank, daughter of Lord Parmoor. Sir Stafford Cripps studied law at University College, London; he was the Solicitor General in 1930; British Ambassador to Moscow, 1940–42; Privy Councillor, 1941; member of the War Cabinet as Lord Privy Seal; leader of the House of Commons, 1942; and Chancellor of the Exchequer, 1947–50. He was also the author of numerous books. The Cripps became friends of the Smarts after Russel Smart met Sir Stafford in London on a Privy Council case. Although they often opposed each other on Privy cases, they became close friends. The Smarts visited the Cripps in Gloucestershire and the Cripps visited the Smarts in Kingsmere.

17. Marjorie Borden, a friend from Ottawa.

18. Suzette Bourinot, daughter of Canadian poet Arthur Bourinot. The Bourinots lived next to the Smarts at Kingsmere and were friends of the family.

19. Smart met Sir James Barrie (1860–1937) through a letter of introduction from a distinguished Canadian family friend, Bill Herridge (Major, Hon William Duncan). Herridge was one of RB Bennett's closest advisers, and the author of *Which Kind of Revolution* (1943).

20. Ralph Strauss, British journalist and novelist.

21. Sir Arthur Quiller-Couch, eminent literary critic and historian who taught for many years at Cambridge.

22. 'Swells,' slang for grand or posh persons.

23. JM Barrie, *Farewell Miss Julie Logan* (1932).

Part One/II

1. Ethel Jane, a London socialite friend of Mrs Smart and an expatriate Canadian.

2. Margaret Watt became a friend of the Smart family during their stay in London. Originally from British Columbia, Mrs Watt married Alfred Watt, a doctor, who committed suicide. They had two sons, Robin and Sholto. The elder son, Robin, was Art Master at Stowe School in England before he moved back to Montreal and became a painter. Doreen, his wife, was an assistant Art Mistress at Stowe. Sholto went to Oxford and became a sub-editor for *The Daily Telegraph*. Mrs Watt was one of the first women in Canada to receive an MA. By the time of this trip, she had successfully organized the Country Women's Institute in England. In 1933, in Sweden, there was an international conference of the Country Women's Organizations from around the world. At this conference they formed themselves into the

Associated Country Women of the World and voted Mrs Watt their president. She was re-elected in 1936.

3. *Precious Bane* (1924), a novel by Mary Webb.

4. Meredith Frampton (1894–1983), a painter, (RA 1942), Smart had met in London and with whom she was much infatuated. He was the son of the sculptor Sir George Frampton (RA) and the model for the statue of Peter Pan by Sir George in Kensington Gardens. He had a retrospective exhibition at the Tate Gallery in 1982.

5. Graham Spry (1900–1983), founder, with Alan Plaunt, of the Canadian Radio League in the 1930s, and also with Plaunt was instrumental in promoting the government policy decision in the 1930s to have network broadcasting in Canada declared a public responsibility, leading eventually to the creation of the Canadian Broadcasting Corporation. In 1933, Spry was a delegate to the founding convention of the Co-operative Commonwealth Federation (CCF), the forerunner of the New Democratic Party. In 1942, he was appointed personal assistant to British Cabinet Minister, Sir Stafford Cripps. With Plaunt, he also edited *The Weekly Sun* in Toronto, and in 1935 was the editor of *The Canadian Forum*. Elizabeth Smart had met Spry as a young girl through her family. He had taken an interest in her desire to write, recommended books for her to read, and assigned essay topics for her on which to write. He asked her to contribute an article on her trip to Sweden to *The Weekly Sun*.

6. The Allwards, a Canadian family living in London. Mr Allward was a sculptor and it was at the Allwards' that Smart met Meredith Frampton.

7. This journal is not in the National Archives. It documents a family trip by chauffeur to Scotland (Edinburgh, the Trossachs, the Isle of Skye), the west country of England, and Stratford-on-Avon.

8. Alan Plaunt (1904–1941), friend of Graham Spry, and with Spry started the Canadian Radio League in 1940, and edited *The Weekly Sun* in Toronto.

9. Kenneth Lindsay, a Scottish friend of the family and member of Parliament.

10. John Williams, a Canadian friend in the British Colonial Office in London.

11. The incident became the subject of an article that appeared in *The Weekly Sun*.

12. The quotation is from *Journal of Katherine Mansfield, 1888–1923*, ed. JM Murry (1927), journal entry May 16, 1915.

13. Friends from Ottawa and older sister, Helen Smart.

14. *Without My Cloak* (1931), a novel by Kate O'Brien.

15. Gilbert Ryle (1900–1976), famous Oxford philosopher, best known for his book, *The Concept of Mind* (1949), and a good friend of Graham Spry.

16. She is reading Virginia Woolf's *The Waves*.

17. *Wood Magic: A Fable* (1881) by Richard Jefferies.

18. Russel Smart (1921–), Elizabeth's younger brother.

19. Pegi Nichol McLeod (1904–1949), Canadian artist and family friend. She had taught Smart art at Elmwood School for Girls.

20. Norman Robertson (1845–1936), distinguished Canadian civil servant and author, who was a great friend of Smart's parents, and Harry Hodson, an economist and later editor of *The Sunday Times*. Smart had met Hodson in Ottawa when he had attended the Imperial Economic Conference of 1932.

21. 'The White Orchid' is possibly an allusion to a Marius Barbeau fable.

22. DH Lawrence's *Lady Chatterley's Lover* (1928), was initially banned in Canada and England upon publication.

23. Quoted from Lawrence's *Lady Chatterley's Lover*.

24. Possibly from a Barbeau fable, although I have been unable to trace it.

Part One/III

1. Toby Weaver, the adopted son of Sir Stafford and Lady Cripps.

2. A line from TS Eliot's 'The Love Song of J Alfred Prufrock.'

3. Delacour Beamish, a literary friend from Montreal.

4. Helen Smart, now married to Alan Swabey, a lawyer, and living in Montreal.

5. Esme and Sue, the young daughters of Arthur Bourinot.

6. John Swabey, eldest son of Helen Smart. He was killed in a car accident at the age of twenty-one.

7. Eugene Forsey (1904–   ), Canadian author of such books as *Freedom and Order* (1974) and *Trade Unions in Canada, 1812–1902* (1982). Hazel Hope is his aunt.

8. Smart's Great Aunt Harma Baldwin, Mrs Smart's mother's unmarried sister.

9. D'Arcy McGee, grandson of Canadian Confederation politician and poet, D'Arcy McGee, and an Ottawa suitor.

10. John Stevenson is *The Times'* correspondent in Canada. He will marry Mrs Smart following Russel Smart's death in 1944.

11. *Studio*, an English art magazine.

12. She is probably referring to Maurice Baring's translations of Indian and French legends titled *Translations, Ancient and Modern, With Originals* (1925).

13. Lord Duncannon, son of the Governor-General, the Earl of Bessborough.

14. Lord John Pentland (1907–1984), Henry John Sinclair, grandson of Lord and Lady Aberdeen of Aberdeenshire, friends of the Smarts, and a good friend of Bill Aitken.

15. Articles she is writing for *The Weekly Sun* about visiting Shropshire, the home of Mary Webb, immortalized in Webb's novels.

16. Ottawa debutantes presented to the Governor-General.

17. The people mentioned in this section are Ottawa friends of the family.

18. Confederation poet, Duncan Campbell Scott (1862–1947) worked for the Department of External Affairs and was a good friend of the family.

19. *Testament of Youth: An Autobiographical Study of the Years, 1900–1925* (1934) by Vera Mary Brittain.

20. Enrico Belcredi, an Italian friend from the Italian Embassy.

21. Sir Edward William Spencer Ford (1910–   ), Assistant Private Secretary to King George VI, 1946–52, and to Queen Elizabeth II, 1952–66. Sir Edward had given Smart private tutoring in Latin, in London. Chichester is the Earl of Chichester.

22. TS Eliot, 'Wordsworth and Coleridge,' in *The Use of Poetry and the Use of Criticism* (1933).

Part One/V

1. Archibald Richard Burton Haldane (1900–   ), son of Sir William Haldane, friend of Graham Spry, and author of numerous books on Scotland.

2. Mike and his wife, Maryon Pearson.

3. Bill Aitken is Pentland's friend and roommate.

4. A line from one of her own poems.

5. Tom Davies, one of a group of friends in the British Civil Service.

6. Gilbert Yates, also a friend in the British Civil Service.

7. 'H' is Helen Smart; the oblique reference may be to her interest in Charles Ritchie. He has been interested in Elizabeth Smart and they have become close friends. There was naturally a certain rivalry among the three Smart sisters; they were each attractive and close in age: Helen was born in 1910 and Jane in 1915.

8. The so-called 'lewd lines' are amusing, not lewd; titled 'Poetry-Vulgarity,' they read:

> Poetry's vulgarity
> Drives him to despairity
> Here he lies in dolourous dream
> Having missed life's violent cream
>
> The only fault of Mr Ritchie
> Is he makes the women bitchie

Part Two/I

1. Charles Ritchie (1906–   ), Canadian diplomat and diarist, was at this time in External Affairs in Ottawa and interested in Smart.

2. In 1936, in Cornwall, textile workers were organizing unions, some strikes were called during which occurred some mildly violent clashes, and arrests were made.

3. Dr Irene Bliss married Graham Spry in 1938.

4. Franklin Carmichael (1890–1945), a Canadian painter and founding member of the Group of Seven. George Douglas Pepper (1903–1962), a Canadian painter and founding member of the Canadian Group of Painters.

5. Lord Pentland's sister, Peggy Sinclair.

6. Kathlyn Hinton, niece of Mrs Smart.

7. Terry McDermott, university professor, diplomat, and author of numerous articles on education.

8. Phonetic for *Jag tycker om dig* which means 'I like you.'

9. Sam Dickson, an acquaintance she has met in Vancouver.

10. Ella McLean, a close friend of Mrs Smart but no relation to the family.

11. Aunt Lilian, married to Alan Parr, Mrs Smart's brother.

12. Frederick H. Varley (1881–1969), Canadian painter associated with the Group of Seven.

13. Michael Adeane and John Boyle, ADC's of Governor-General Bessborough. Adeane became equerry and assistant private secretary to George VI, 1937–52, and to Queen Elizabeth, 1952–53.

14. Frank Scott (1899–1985), well-known Canadian poet, international law professor, and social philosopher.

15. Oxford Group, the name given to an international religious movement founded by Dr Frank Buckman in Oxford in 1921. The movement was criticized for its use of emotional tactics in making its members confess their sins.

16. *Middletown, A Study in American Culture* (1929) by Robert Lynd and Helen Merrell Lynd.

17. *Inside Europe*, a travel book by John Gunther. He also wrote *Inside Asia; Inside Russia;* and *Inside South America.*

18. Despite a twenty-year difference in their ages, Smart had been attracted to Meredith Frampton when she was twenty. The 'reality of the Frampton situation' had been occasional meetings and a sporadic correspondence.

Part Two/II

1. A young man she has met.

2. Hall, the 'dark boy,' also 'Velvet Eyes.'

3. She is reading Hemingway's *The Sun Also Rises* (1926).

4. ACWW (The Associated Country Women of the World). The organization published a periodical, begun in March, 1934, called *The Countrywoman*. London, Associated Country Women of the World.

5. Jean Batten, (1909–   ), a famous New Zealand pilot who made a solo flight from England to Australia in May, 1934, a return flight in April, 1935, and a solo flight from England to Argentina in 1935.

6. A line from DH Lawrence's poem 'The Triumph of the Machine.'

7. New Zealand artist, Sydney Lough Thompson, born in Oxford (1877), studied in Canterbury, NZ, and Paris, president of Canterbury Society of Arts, 1935–37, and awarded OBE in 1937.

8. In December, 1936, Edward VIII abdicated the throne of England following his decision to marry Mrs Simpson, a commoner, who was American and divorced.

9. The previous year, Lord Pentland had given Smart a Maltese diamond cross as a Christmas gift.

10. An oblique reference to Helen Smart's interest in Charles Ritchie.

Part Two/III

1. Sir Edward William Spencer Ford (1910–   ), Assistant Private Secretary to King George VI, 1946–52, and to Queen Elizabeth II, 1952–66. He was also a private tutor of King Farouk I of Egypt (1920–1965). Farouk was king from 1936–52; he was educated first in Cairo and at the Royal Military Academy at Woolwich in England. When Farouk returned to Egypt in 1936, after his father's death, Ford went to Egypt to act as his private tutor. Ford also accompanied Farouk on a tour of Upper Egypt and to Europe for the coronation of George VI in May, 1937, but his tutorials were reduced to a minimum because Farouk was not interested in serious study. (See Peter Mansfield, *The British in Egypt* [1972].) Smart meets Ford in Cairo.

2. She is referring to poets.

3. Samuel Johnson's *Lives of the Poets*.

4. Emily is a euphemism for menstruation picked up at Hatfield Hall School for Girls.

5. Dragomen, interpreters or guides for travellers.

6. She is probably thinking of GK Chesterton's poem, 'The Donkey.'

7. Lines from Keats' 'Ode to a Nightingale.'

8. The last lines from Keats' 'Ode on a Grecian Urn.'

Part Three/I

1. Victor Cochrane-Baillie, later Lord Lamington and brother of Elizabeth's friend Grisell Hastings, who is married to Eddie Hastings, a naval intelligence officer.

2. 'Details,' the name of the account she is writing of her trip around the world.

3. Diana Battye, known as Didy, will become one of Elizabeth's close friends.

4. She has been sick with a cold and is also suffering from low spirits because of Lord Pentland.

5. Michael Foot, prominent left-wing British writer and member of Parliament, who during the 80s was leader of the Labour Party.

6. Mussolini, the Italian fascist dictator.

7. A line in one of the popular songs of the time, about rearmament and gas masks, went: 'Sir Stafford Cripps should get one and wear it all the time. Ain't nature grand.'

8. The Parrs, Elizabeth's mother's family. She is referring to 'Details.'

Part Three/II

1. Jean Varda (also known as Yanko), has accused her of being a 'vamp.' Varda, a flamboyant and innovative painter and collagist, had settled in the south of France in Cassis. His home was always open to artists (and such notable artists as Picasso, Braque, and Miro stayed there). Varda eventually settled in California and became a close friend of Henry Miller and Anaïs Nin. He died in Mexico in 1971. 'Varda' is a character in Anaïs Nin's fictional work *Collages* (1964). He also did the original covers for some of her books. Henry Miller has written an essay on Varda, 'Varda: The Master Builder,' in *Remember to Remember* (1947).

2. Wolfgang Paalen (1907–1959), a painter associated with the surrealist movement in Paris in the late 1920s and 30s. His wife Alice was a poet. They emigrated to Mexico in 1939. In 1959 Wolfgang Paalen committed suicide. Smart will visit the Paalens in Mexico.

3. Elgin Street, a street in Ottawa.

4. The Roxborough, a residential hotel and apartment in Ottawa. It was the Ottawa residence of many high-ranking officials, including prime ministers.

5. LTS, London Transport System.

6. Michael Wickham, one of the group of friends in Cassis.

Part Three/III

1. England and France declared war on Germany in September, 1939.

2. Although Smart had gone to New York to begin her 'independent life' and to write, she was encouraged because of her looks to do some modelling as a means of making some money. She had not made much money at *The Ottawa Journal* (they had paid her $2.50 a week) and, because of the war, there was a foreign exchange control, which meant she could not get any money from her family.

3. D John MacGillivray (1905–?), a Canadian artist and an Ottawa friend. MacGillivray studied at the Nova Scotia College of Art, Halifax (1921–23); the Ontario College of Art, Toronto (1924); and at the Arts Students' League, NY (1924–27). He returned to Halifax, where he was appointed visiting master at the Nova Scotia College of Art. In 1930 he travelled in the UK and Europe and carried out portrait commissions. He did portraits of Dr Murdock Chisholm, Dr Archibald MacMechan, Caron Vroom, and Dr John Stewart. There is no information for him after 1933. He was sick at this time when Smart saw him in New York. She later received one hundred dollars from him anonymously when she was in California in 1940. He is thought to have died sometime

thereafter. He painted the portrait of Elizabeth Smart sometime in the mid-thirties.

4. Averill Stowell, a brain surgeon, and future second husband of Helen Smart.

5. Pegi Nichol McLeod is living in New York. Miriam Scott (née Dale), artist and wife of poet FR Scott.

Part Three/IV

1. The story of Varda and Smart, based on journal entries from that time. There is a definite stylistic shift in this section; the language strains in its use of image and metaphor.

2. Ruth Beresford and Roland Pym, friends from London who went to Cassis.

3. Julian Trevelyan, a friend from London and a painter, and his wife, Ursula, a potter.

4. Michael and Tanya Wickham, London friends.

5. Simonette, Varda's girlfriend.

Part Four/I

1. Lynn, a woman from New York.

2. This section will become part of 'Let Us Dig a Grave and Bury Our Mother.'

3. Philoctetes, legendary Greek character who on his way to the Trojan War, was bitten by a snake, and left by his companions on the island of Lemnos. But when the oracle said the war could not be won without him, he was brought to Troy and healed. He helped conquer Troy by killing Paris.

4. Lawrence Durrell's *The Black Book* (1938).

5. She is at 'Los Cedros y Begonias' with the Paalens.

6. Wolfgang Paalen.

7. The Chaudière Falls are in Ottawa and will appear in *By Grand Central Station I Sat Down and Wept* as 'frozen and stock-still.'

8. Anaïs Nin's *The House of Incest* (nd).

9. William Hudson's *Green Mansions* (1904).

10. During this time she is translating Alice Paalen's poems from French to English.

11. Diego Rivera (1886–1957), Mexican painter and mural maker and author of *Portrait of America* (1934).

12. Sappho refers to the poet/priestess Sappho of Lesbos, the 'isle of women,' dedicated to the worship of the Goddess, a cosmic parent figure who created the universe and its laws. Smart is infatuated with Alice Paalen.

13. The Paalens' Swiss friend, Eva Sulger. They live in a *ménage à trois*.

14. Smart had bought a manuscript from George Barker. During her stay in London, she had bought two of his early books: *Poems* (1935) and *Janus* (1935). She had been so struck with the poetry that she began to ask people if they knew Barker, and then would inform them that she wanted to meet him because she wanted to marry him. Barker heard that a rich American woman was looking for him. By the time she wrote to him asking him if he had a manuscript to sell, he assumed she was the rich American.

Part Four/II

1. Her plans are to write what she calls 'the Mother Book' and what she now titles 'Dig A Grave and Let Us Bury our Mother.' However, the story will change radically from a rather bitter portrait of her mother (and recollected incidents from the past) to the story of a relationship between two women which acts as the means of confronting and breaking away from the mother/womb.

2. César Moro (1903–1959), Peruvian painter and poet. In 1940, Moro and Paalen organized an international exhibition of surrealism in Mexico City.

3. Statements about George Barker or by him: 'A very honest and

painful fellow' is from a Durrell letter written to Elizabeth; 'My tired lips received their first kiss' is from Barker's poem, 'Narcissus I,' in *Poems* (1935).

4. From Barker's poem, 'The Constellation,' in *Poems*.

5. From Barker's poem, 'Daedalus,' in *Poems*.

6. Frida Kahlo; she is a friend of the Riveras.

7. Undine and Rima are legendary water nymphs.

8. *Undine,* the story of the water nymph, Undine.

9. Catharine, an old girlfriend of Varda's.

10. Teotihucán, a mountain and a town in central Mexico noted for its Toltec ruins and temples.

11. Popocatèpetl, another mountain in central Mexico.

12. Quetzalcoatl, a Mexican god.

13. She is probably thinking of George Barker's poem, 'Daedalus.'

14. Jane Smart married D'Arcy Marsh in Ottawa on January 5 at the Chateau Laurier.

15. Peter Neagroe's books of stories include *Faster Sun* (1934), *Winning a Wife and Other Stories* (1935), and *There Is My Heart* (1936).

Part Four/III

1. From George Barker's 'Daedalus,' *Poems*.

2. The exhibition Paalen and Moro have organized in Mexico City.

3. Varda has left for an exhibition of his own work.

4. She is sitting in on philosophy classes on Bertrand Russell at UCLA.

5. Smart is trying to raise money from people she knew who professed to like poetry, in order to bring Barker and his wife back from Japan.

6. Varda is back but the growing tension between them is obvious.

7. She is working as a maid for a Mrs Kennedy to help raise the money for Barker.

8. Having become impatient trying to raise money for the Barkers, Smart had asked her employer, Mrs Kennedy, to lend it to her. Mrs Kennedy fired her. She was able to raise only a third of the amount needed. She got the rest of the money from Christopher Isherwood, who was in Hollywood working as a scriptwriter.

9. Barker's new poems, possibly *Lament and Triumph* (1940).

10. On May 20, Smart and Varda moved with some friends to Anderson Creek on the Big Sur. She is presumably referring to friends at Anderson Creek.

11. An image that will appear in *By Grand Central Station I Sat Down and Wept*, at the end of Part One.

Part Four/IV

1. The oblique reference to the title of Thomas Wolfe's novel *Look Homeward Angel* (1929) and the biblical allusion to Ruth are rich in association. They both suggest the plight of the prodigal son/daughter who cannot go home. The reference illuminates the use of the 'Song of Songs' in *By Grand Central Station I Sat Down and Wept*. The story of the bride who has not kept her own vineyard because she is searching for her beloved connects with the biblical Ruth, a bride who must forsake her homeland for her husband. The three prodigal daughters are, of course, Helen, Jane, and Elizabeth Smart; they have each left Ottawa to live in foreign lands.

2. Gene Derwood, poet and painter, married to Oscar Williams, compiler of several poetry anthologies. Barker's friends, with whom Smart and Barker stay in New York.

3. At one point Barker, driving Jane's husband, D'Arcy Marsh, to Montreal, had been stopped by the Mounties. It was wartime, George was British, and he had forgotten to take his papers; he was put in jail in Montreal.

4. Thomas Chatterton (1752–1770), died by taking arsenic. He was glorified by the English Romantic poets. He fabricated poems by Thomas Rowley, an imaginary figure from the fifteenth century. Only one of the poems was published within his lifetime and the controversy began only shortly after his death.

5. The allusion is to a WH Auden poem, untitled and not included in his *Collected Poems:*

> In my spine there was a base,
> And I knew the general's face:
> But they've severed all the wires
> And I can't tell what the general desires
> Here am I, Here are you
> But what does it mean? What are we going to do?

An allusion to the line, 'they've severed all the wires,' also appears in the September 21, 1940, entry.

6. Barker has left Smart in a hotel in Vancouver to travel with a friend, John Fitch, through the United States.

7. Smart is now living in Pender Harbour in an old schoolhouse she has rented for five dollars a month. She has had word that George will return.